Creativity and Discovery in the University Writing Class

Frameworks for Writing
Series Editor: Martha C. Pennington, School for Oriental and African Studies
and Birkbeck College, University of London

The *Frameworks for Writing* series offers books focused on writing and the
teaching and learning of writing in educational and real-life contexts. The
hallmark of the series is the application of approaches and techniques to writing
and the teaching of writing that go beyond those of English literature to draw on
and integrate writing with other disciplines, areas of knowledge, and contexts
of everyday life. The series entertains proposals for textbooks as well as books
for teachers, teacher educators, parents, and the general public. The list includes
teacher reference books and student textbooks focused on innovative pedagogy
aiming to prepare teachers and students for the challenges of the 21st century.

Published:

The College Writing Toolkit
Tried and Tested Ideas for Teaching College Writing
Edited by Martha C. Pennington and Pauline Burton

The "Backwards" Research Guide for Writers
Using your Life for Reflection, Connection, and Inspiration
Sonya Huber

Exploring College Writing
Reading, Writing, and Researching across the Curriculum
Dan Melzer

Tend your Garden
Nurturing Motivation in Young Adolescent Writers
Mary Anna Kruch

Writing Poetry through the Eyes of Science
A Teacher's Guide to Scientific Literacy and Poetic Response
Nancy Gorrell, with Erin Colfax

Reflective Writing for Language Teachers
Thomas S. C. Farrell

Creativity and Writing Pedagogy
Linking Creative Writers, Researchers, and Teachers
Edited by Harriet Levin Millan and Martha C. Pennington

Academic Writing Step by Step
A Research-based Approach
Christopher N. Candlin, Peter Crompton, and Basil Hatim

Creativity and Discovery in the University Writing Class

A Teacher's Guide

Edited by
Alice Chik, Tracey Costley, and
Martha C. Pennington

SHEFFIELD UK   BRISTOL CT

Published by Equinox Publishing Ltd.

UK: Office 415, The Workstation, 15 Paternoster Row, Sheffield, South Yorkshire S1 2BX
USA: ISD, 70 Enterprise Drive, Bristol, CT 06010

www.equinoxpub.com

First published 2015

British Library Cataloguing-in-Publication Data

A catalogue record for this book is available from the British Library.

ISBN   978 1 78179 105 9 (hardback)
         978 1 78179 106 6 (paperback)

Library of Congress Cataloging-in-Publication Data

Creativity and Discovery in the University writing class : a teacher's guide /
Edited by Alice Chik, Tracey Costley and Martha C. Pennington.
     pages cm. – (Frameworks for writing)
 Includes bibliographical references and index.
 ISBN 978-1-78179-105-9 (hb) – ISBN 978-1-78179-106-6 (pb)
 1. English language–Rhetoric–Studying and teaching. 2. Creative
writing–Studying and teaching. 3. Report writing–Studying and teaching.
I. Chik, Alice editor. II. Costley, Tracey, editor. III. Pennington, Martha
Carswell, editor.
 PE1404.C734 2015
 808'.0420711–dc23
                        2014044618

Typeset by S.J.I. Services, New Delhi
Printed and bound by Lightning Source Inc. (La Vergne, TN), Lightning Source UK Ltd.
(Milton Keynes), Lightning Source AU Pty. (Scoresby, Victoria).

Contents

Dedication

We dedicate this book to all those who took part in the 2013 Summer Institute on Creativity and Discovery in University Writing, hosted by the English Department at the City University of Hong Kong, and to writing teachers everywhere.

Editor's Preface

This collection was inspired by The Summer Institute on Creativity and Discovery in University Writing organized by the editors of this volume along with colleagues David Gruber and Y-Dang Troeung in the English Department of the City University of Hong Kong. The concept of the Institute was to bring together a group of experienced writing teachers who had expertise in academic and creative writing with the aim of developing synergy and proposing new directions for the teaching of writing in universities in Hong Kong, Asia, and the wider world. The focus of the institute on the dual themes of creativity and discovery would, it was hoped, help to connect writing to these overarching goals of the larger academic curriculum.

Given the centrality of writing to higher education and the increasing numbers of students, both first- and second-language writers, who do not have a good command of written English, the teaching of writing holds an important place in university study. Discovery is a natural focus for university writing instruction, which typically aims to have each student produce a referenced argument or research paper. The writing of these kinds of papers centrally involves discovery processes of investigating a topic and researching sources. In the best case, the process also leads student writers to discover new knowledge within themselves. Yet the focus on discovery is not usually an explicit one, and so there is scope for increasing the awareness of discovery-oriented pedagogy in university writing teachers. This was one of the goals of the Summer Institute and so is one of the intentions of this book.

Creativity has also become an important theme in higher education worldwide; yet it does not usually figure in university writing curricula, which are largely focused on the formal features of language, rhetoric, and genre in argumentative essays and research papers. Although this seems a natural orientation for university writing instruction, there is value as well in incorporating a creative emphasis, as a way to broaden the scope of what students are able to do in their writing, increase their motivation and engagement, and improve the quality of the writing produced. In offering students more choices and options for their writing, creative topics and approaches give students opportunities to develop a unique and authentic writer voice and to incorporate their own identities and experiences into their writing. In these senses, creative opportunities can be empowering to students, giving them greater agency in their writing and in the different kinds of learning connected to their writing activity. Creativity also meshes with discovery, as a creative emphasis enlarges the space for discovery. A combined creativity and discovery orientation to university writing thus has the power to exponentiate the potentials of writing for learning, exploration, and expression of knowledge.

This book can help deepen readers' appreciation of the available options for creativity and discovery learning through writing, and its practical emphasis offers teachers of writing a wide variety of discovery-based and creative options for the classroom. I hope that readers will try out some of the teaching ideas included in the chapters, thereby expanding their own students' ability to use writing to widen their access to the world of ideas and increase their involvement and investment in their own learning, as they both discover and create new knowledge.

– Martha C. Pennington
Series Editor
Frameworks for Writing

Contributors

Dr. Olivia Archibald (Ph.D. University of Iowa) is Professor of English at Saint Martin's University, a liberal arts university near Seattle, Washington. Her academic interests include creative nonfiction, essay theory, composition theory, early medieval literature, and literary criticism. Much of Archibald's current research and writing focuses on reflective practice and creative forms of the essay in higher education, and she is currently working on a book about the essay genre while co-authoring *Writing from the Inside: The Power of Reflective Writing in the Classroom* (coauthor M. P. Hall). Alongside her teaching and research, Archibald directs faculty development activities at her university.

Professor Charles Bazerman – Professor of Education at the University of California Santa Barbara, Steering Committee Chair of the International Society for the Advancement of Writing Research, and recent chair of the Conference on College Composition and Communication – is interested in the social dynamics of writing, rhetorical theory, and the rhetoric of knowledge production and use. His books include *The Languages of Edison's Light*, *Constructing Experience*, *Shaping Written Knowledge*, and *The Informed Writer: Using Sources in the Disciplines*. He has edited the *Handbook of Research on Writing*, *Traditions of Writing Research*, *International Advances in Writing Research*, *Genre in a Changing World*, *What Writing Does and How It Does It*, and many other volumes. He has published over a hundred chapters and articles.

Dr. Pauline Burton is Senior Lecturer in the Division of Languages and Communication at the Community College of City University, Hong Kong, teaching English and intercultural communication. She holds degrees from Oxford University in both English (B.A.)

and Social Anthropology (M.Litt.), an M.A. in Applied English Linguistics from Birmingham University, and a Ph.D. from the University of Bedfordshire. Her main interest is in creativity in education and its development in Hong Kong classrooms through the use of imaginative texts, creative writing and ethnographic exploration of local communities. She has recently published a paper in *World Englishes* on creativity in the Hong Kong English language classroom, and is co-editor of *The College Writing Toolkit* (Pennington and Burton, 2011).

Dr. Alice Chik is Assistant Professor in the Department of English, City University of Hong Kong. She holds a Ph.D. in Philosophy of Education from The University of Hong Kong. Her publications and research interests include the life-long experience of learning a second/foreign language, particularly in the area of identity construction and out-of-class learning, and the ways young people use digital practices and online communities and resources to develop their literacy skills. She has published in *Modern Language Journal*, *TESOL Quarterly*, *World Englishes*, and *Pedagogies: An International Journal* and is the co-author (with Gary Barkhuizen and Phil Benson) of *Narrative Inquiry in Language Teacher and Learning Research* (Routledge, 2013) and co-editor (with Phil Benson) of *Popular Culture, Pedagogy and Teacher Education: International Perspectives* (Routledge, 2014).

Dr. Tracey Costley is Visiting Assistant Professor in the Department of English, City University of Hong Kong. She holds a Ph.D. in Philosophy of Education from King's College London with a focus on English as an Additional Language and a Master's degree in Language, Ethnicity and Education from King's. She is a DELTA TESOL qualified teacher who has taught in London, China, Thailand, Turkey, and Taiwan and also has experience in development of curriculum and teaching materials. Her publications and research interests explore the interface between education policy and curriculum practice in relation to ethnolinguistic minority students in mainstream schooling contexts. She is also interested in academic literacies and genres as well as in processes of academic socialization and student identity in writing at university.

Dr. Fiona English is a Visiting Fellow at Institute of Education, University of London, where she obtained her Ph.D. She has been working in the field of language, communication and linguistics for many years in both research and teaching. She has worked across all educational sectors, including the U.K. National Foundation for Educational Research, but has spent most of her career working in higher education. Her recent book, *Student Writing and Genre*: *Reconfiguring Academic Knowledge* (Bloomsbury, 2011), offers a new approach to genre in university learning and teaching, and she is now co-writing another book for the same publisher to be called *Why Do Linguistics? Reflective Linguistics and the Study of Language*, on the relevance of linguistics in everyday life.

Dr. David R. Gruber is an Assistant Professor in the English Department at City University of Hong Kong. He earned his Master of Professional Writing from the University of Southern California and his Ph.D. from the interdisciplinary program in Communication, Rhetoric and Digital Media at North Carolina State University. His interests bridge the rhetoric of science, new media studies and writing studies. He has published in *Media History*, *Visual Communication Quarterly* and *Public Understanding of Science* as well as in the new media journal, *HyperRhiz*. He is currently investigating how, where, and why neuroscience findings are incorporated into the humanities and social sciences. He also writes poetry and makes digital artworks to explore and visualize his scholarly interests.

Professor Robin Hemley is author of ten books of nonfiction and fiction and winner of many awards including a Guggenheim Fellowship, The Nelson Algren Award for Fiction, The Story Magazine Humor Prize, an Independent Press Book Award, and three Pushcart Prizes for fiction and nonfiction. He recently published his third collection of short stories, *Reply All*, and *A Field Guide for Immersion Writing: Memoir, Journalism, and Travel*. He is a Senior Editor of *The Iowa Review* and editor of the online journal, *Defunct* (Defunctmag.com), featuring short essays on everything that's had its day, and founder of NonfictioNow, a biennial conference. He teaches in the Nonfiction Writing Program at The University of Iowa and in the low-residency M.F.A. Program at City University of Hong Kong.

Sonya Huber is an Associate Professor at Fairfield University in Fairfield, Connecticut, where she teaches composition and creative writing. She is the author of two books of creative nonfiction, *Opa Nobody* and *Cover Me: A Health Insurance Memoir*, and a textbook, *The Backwards Research Guide for Writers: Using Your Life for Reflection, Connection, and Inspiration*. Her work has been published in literary journals and magazines including *Creative Nonfiction, Brevity, Fourth Genre, Crab Orchard Review, Hotel Amerika, The Chronicle of Higher Education*, and the *Washington Post Magazine*. She received the 2013 Creative Nonfiction Award from *Terrain*, and her work will appear in *The Best of Creative Nonfiction*.

Professor Rodney H. Jones is Acting Head of the Department of English, City University of Hong Kong. He holds an M.A. in Teaching English as a Second Language from City University of Hong Kong, an M.F.A. in Creative Writing from University of Arkansas, and a Ph.D. in Applied Linguistics from Macquarie University. His research interests include intercultural communication, discourse analysis, digital literacies, and the teaching of writing. He has won a Pushcart Prize for fiction and is author of *Discourse Analysis: A Resource Book for Students* (Routledge, 2012), co-author (with Christoph Hafner) of *Understanding Digital Literacies: A Practical Introduction* (Routledge, 2012), and editor of the forthcoming *Routledge Handbook of Language and Creativity*. He is Associate Editor and soon to be Editor-in-Chief of *Writing & Pedagogy*.

Dr. Brian W. King (Ph.D. Victoria University of Wellington) arrived at City University in 2012, his teaching career having previously spanned more than 15 years across three continents, with time spent teaching in New Zealand, Canada, and Korea. Focusing primarily on language, his work is located within sociolinguistics and discourse analysis. Methodologically he draws on a number of traditions, including interactional sociolinguistics, corpus linguistics, and linguistic ethnography. Brian's research considers computer-mediated communication, the discursive performance of gender and sexuality, and the social construction of space/place. He has published in international journals such as *Journal of Language Identity and Education*, *Gender and Language*, *Journal of Language and Sexuality*, and *Discourse & Society*.

Professor Shirley Geok-lin Lim (Ph.D. Brandeis University) has published seven poetry collections; short story collections; novels (*Joss and Gold* and *Sister Swing*); a children's novel, *Princess Shawl*, translated into Chinese; *The Shirley Lim Collection*; two critical studies; and edited/co-edited scholarly books and journals. *Crossing the Peninsula* received the Commonwealth Poetry Prize; and her memoir, *Among the White Moon Faces*, and *The Forbidden Stitch: An Asian American Women's Anthology* each won the American Book Award. She received the Multiethnic Literatures of the United States Lifetime Achievement Award and is co-founding editor of *Journal of Transnational American Studies*. Formerly Chair Professor of English at Hong Kong University, she is Research Professor at University of California, Santa Barbara, and has also been Distinguished Visiting Professor at City University of Hong Kong.

Dr. Jeffrey Mather is an Assistant Professor in the Department of English at City University of Hong Kong. Originally from Canada, Dr. Mather completed his Ph.D. in English at the University of Kent at Canterbury, where he examined the intersections between natural scientific writing, China, and imaginative literature during the late nineteenth and early twentieth centuries. His current research and teaching interests are in English literary studies and travel writing. He is currently working on a number of projects, including an examination of contemporary graphic travelogues and works by the American graphic novelist Joe Sacco. Before coming to Hong Kong, Dr. Mather taught English language and literature in Canada, Britain, Taiwan, and Mainland China.

Professor Martha C. Pennington (Ph.D. University of Pennsylvania) is Distinguished Visiting Professor of English, City University of Hong Kong, Professorial Research Associate at the School for Oriental and African Studies, and Research Fellow in Applied Linguistics and Communication at Birkbeck College of the University of London. Professor Pennington is Editor-in-Chief of *Writing & Pedagogy* and served on the editorial boards of *Journal of Second Language Writing* and *TESOL Journal*. Her academic publications range across writing, applied linguistics, and bilingualism, and include *The College Writing Toolkit: Tried and Tested Ideas for Teaching College Writing* (Equinox, coeditor P. Burton), *Language Program Leadership in a Changing World: An Ecological Model* (Emerald, coauthor B. Hoekje), and the forthcoming *Welcome to My World: A Writing Course* (Equinox, coauthor T. M. Welford).

Professor Jack C. Richards (Ph.D. Laval University) is a well-known author and specialist in English language teaching. He has published numerous classroom texts as well as books and articles on language teaching methodology, teacher education, and applied linguistics, including his recent *Cambridge Guide to*

Pedagogy and Practice in Language Teaching (edited with Anne Burns). Professor Richards has had an active career in the Asia Pacific region and is currently Adjunct Professor at the Regional Language Centre, Singapore; Honorary Professor in the Faculty of Education, University of Sydney, Australia; and Distinguished Visiting Professor at the City University of Hong Kong. In 2011 he was awarded an honorary doctorate of literature by Victoria University, Wellington, for service to education and the arts (www. professorjackrichards.com).

Mark Spitzer, Associate Professor of Writing at the University of Central Arkansas, is the author of 18 books (novels, nonfiction, poetry, translation) and the Editor of the award-winning literary journal, *Toad Suck Review*. He has taught composition, world and American literature, and almost all genres of creative writing. His articles on writing pedagogy and theory occur regularly in *The Chronicle of Higher Education*. Other publications appeared in *Studies in the Novel, Review of Contemporary Fiction, Ecotone, Black Warrior Review, Cimarron Review, New Delta Review*, and hundreds of other magazines, anthologies, and journals. A leading researcher of the notorious gar fish, he can be seen on the "Alligator Gar" episode of the Animal Planet series *River Monsters*. See www. sptzr.net for more information.

Dr. Theresa Malphrus Welford, who teaches first-year writing and creative writing, earned a Master's degree from the University of Georgia and a Ph.D. from the University of Essex. Dr. Welford, twice nominated for a Pushcart Prize, has published two collections of poetry (*The Paradelle: An Anthology* and *The Cento: A Collection of Collage Poems*, both with Red Hen Press), along with essays, book chapters, critical articles, and individual poems. Her *Trans-Atlantic Connections: The Movement and New Formalism* is forthcoming from Story Line Press. She is currently working on several creative projects, including books for young readers, and is co-authoring (with M. C. Pennington) two writing texts for college students, *Welcome to My World: A Writing Course* and *Creative Approaches to Essay Writing*.

Xu Xi 許素細 (www.xuxiwriter.com) is author of nine books of fiction and essays, most recently *Access Thirteen Tales* (2011); the novel *Habit of a Foreign Sky* (2010), which was a finalist for the inaugural Man Asian Literary Prize; and *Evanescent Isles* (2008), an essay collection. She is also editor or co-editor of four anthologies of Hong Kong writing in English, most recently *The Queen of Statue Square: New Hong Kong Short Fiction,* to be published in 2014 by CCC Press, Nottingham, U.K. In 2010, she joined City University of Hong Kong as the Writer-in-Residence in the Department of English, where she helped to establish and now directs Asia's first low-residency MFA (Masters of Fine Arts) in Creative Writing (www.english.cityu.edu.hk/mfa). The author holds an M.F.A. in Fiction from the University of Massachusetts at Amherst.

1 Towards a Creativity and Discovery-based University Writing Curriculum

Tracey Costley, Alice Chik, and Martha C. Pennington

> *For learners, creative teaching helps them develop their capacities for original ideas and for creative thinking. It also improves the quality of the experiences learners receive and can help learners develop increased levels of motivation and even self-esteem.*
>
> – Jack C. Richards

Introduction

This book is about the teaching of writing in university classrooms. It poses questions such as:

- What should we be teaching today's university students about writing?
- How should we be teaching writing to university students?
- What does today's university writing teacher need to know?

University writing is an increasingly important and complex area of study. A key characteristic of the teaching of university writing is that it takes place in a broad range of contexts. It can be a supplementary or a required course offered to all students, taught in an English department, an English language center, or a private language school. Writing is also often a basis of assessment in many university courses and thus part of their curriculum, though not always through explicit instruction. This range of contexts reflects the critical role writing plays in the successes and challenges of students' academic studies. While good writing within the university is highly valued and rewarded, approaches to the teaching of writing might not always benefit from the same level of status. In many cases, the teaching of writing is assigned to teachers, lecturers, and indeed professors whose educational background may not have specifically prepared them for teaching writing at an advanced, university level nor especially for teaching writing to students whose major subject is not English.

While we know there is substantial good practice, it is often the case that the approaches to teaching writing at university level are based on traditional pedagogical practices and views of academic writing. These may not be reflective of current thinking about the nature of writing and the advances that have been made in the writing field. These traditional approaches to the teaching of writing at university level tend to focus on grammar and language proficiency as the main route into writing, rather than creativity and the role of discovery in teaching, learning, and the development of good writing of all kinds. In addition, such traditional approaches fail to recognize the need in the current world to be continually innovating in response to rapidly changing student populations and conditions, including advances in media and writing technologies. The editors of this collected volume therefore strongly believe that university writing curricula need to be rethought and reformed to:

- Make creativity and discovery central themes of the university writing course;

- Broaden the notion of the essay and incorporate non-essay and multimodal writing; and
- Center writing on students' personal, academic, and future professional/career identities.

In the summer of 2013, the English Department at City University of Hong Kong hosted a Summer Institute on Creativity and Discovery in University Writing aimed for teachers of English. The Institute featured lectures and workshops that discussed the nature of writing and that illustrated creative and discovery-based pedagogy and practices. A key aim of the Summer Institute was to engage participants in sharing ideas for practice and exploring the ways in which creativity and discovery can be realized in teaching. More importantly, a shared goal of the sessions was to highlight the impact creative and discovery-based approaches can have on learning and on student writing in particular.

This volume collects together the work presented and discussed at the Summer Institute. It is designed to offer those with an interest in writing and the teaching of writing examples of effective and practical ways of introducing a wide range of creative approaches into their classrooms and instructional practice. Broad themes of the volume include:

- creative teaching;
- approaches to the teaching of writing;
- teacher learning;
- creative writing;
- creativity in academic writing;
- discovery-oriented teaching, learning, and writing;
- the nature of academic writing;
- the essay genre;
- alternative genres for research-based writing;
- multimodal writing; and
- digital writing.

The book is divided into four thematic parts, with three to five chapters each. Part 1 ("Framing Creativity and Discovery in the Teaching and Learning of Writing") presents three chapters that have been developed out of the focal lectures given at the Summer Institute. These serve as framing chapters which highlight issues and raise questions that are taken up and discussed in different ways throughout the volume. The chapters in Parts 2–4 are based on the Summer Institute workshops and are organized to provide issues-centered discussions and illustrations of practices. Part 2 ("Enlarging the View of Genre and Community in Academic Writing") contains five chapters, Part 3 ("Applying Techniques from Creative Writing and Literature to University Writing") contains four chapters, and Part 4 ("Supporting Creativity and Discovery in Composing Multimedia Texts") also contains four chapters. In each chapter the authors provide a short theoretical discussion to frame the work before moving on to offer practical ideas and suggestions for pedagogy.

Overview of Contents

Part 1. Framing Creativity and Discovery in the Teaching and Learning of Writing brings together three broad views of the context of creativity and discovery in university writing offered by leaders in the fields of language teaching and composition pedagogy. These three chapters explore the themes of creative teaching, creating a writerly identity, and defining creativity and discovery in writing.

In the first chapter of Part 1, Jack C. Richards explores the broad topic of "Creativity in Language Teaching." Richards is interested in identifying the shared ways in which creative teachers understand and approach practice. Drawing from interviews with teachers in wide-ranging contexts, Richards examines creativity from three perspectives: (1) the qualities creative teachers possess; (2) how teachers apply creativity in their teaching; and (3) how creativity can be supported at institutional and departmental levels. Through the examples provided and the narrative accounts that accompany them, Richards reviews how creative teachers conceptualize their approaches to teaching, and the impact these approaches can have on the teaching and learning of English writing.

In the second chapter of Part 1, "Creating Identities in an Intertextual World," Charles Bazerman begins with the idea that "every act of writing is an act of creating." Bazerman considers how the genres students encounter at university (and indeed beyond) pose not only challenges in terms of developing knowledge and understanding, but also opportunities in terms of negotiating their identities in relation to these texts and the wider communties to which they belong. The chapter points to the different kinds of cognitive work demanded by genres across and within disciplines, and the ways in which different genres may afford and/or constrain opportunities for such creative and generative acts.

The final chapter in Part 1, Martha C. Pennington's "Writing Creativity and Discovery: Process and Pedagogy," anchors the discussion of Part I, building on the premises that creativity and discovery: (1) can be enhanced through teaching; (2) are central to writing; and so (3) should be central to writing pedagogy. Pennington suggests that by centering instruction on motivating and enhancing students' creative and discovery-oriented expression and behaviors as writers, teachers can not only raise the bar for the writing which students produce but also reduce the potential for plagiarism. The final section of the paper presents learnable strategies for enhancing the student writer's creative and discovery-oriented thinking and writing, as well as strategies to enhance self-discovery and originality of expression that draw on those used by creative and scholarly writers.

Part 2. Enlarging the View of Genre and Community in Academic Writing presents new orientations to what we might call "traditional" academic genres, as different ways in which student writing tasks, and students' engagement with the writing process, can be enhanced through reconsideration and expansion of traditional boundaries. Approaches include creative genres for research and argumentation, personal and impersonal modes of essay writing, and nonfiction genres beyond the standard academic essay. Each chapter of Part 2 offers practical and engaging examples of how teachers can ensure that students' papers are not only creative, but also well-developed and substantive pieces of work.

The first chapter of Part 2 is Fiona English's "Writing Differently: Creating Different Spaces for Student Learning." English draws on her work on the affordances of different genres to explore the role in academic writing of alternative genres such as plays, newspaper articles, and radio interviews in enabling students to develop new insights into disciplinary concepts and practices. A key point is how these genres allow student writers to approach and to represent their disciplinary knowledge in ways which conventional genres such as traditional academic essays do not necessarily allow or encourage.

An orientation complementary to that of English is Theresa Malphrus Welford's "Creative Approaches to Research-based Essays." Welford presents a number of creative ways to develop a research-based paper using sample texts produced by her students. The various approaches include drama, multigenre papers, "on-fire" essays, and a 20–25 random things essay. Welford shows how each of these creative approaches can be combined with research to engage students in the writing process.

A different, anthropologically inspired orientation to university writing is that of Pauline Burton, described in "Local Voices, Global Imagination: Using Ethnography as a Creative Approach to Student Research and Academic Writing." Based on a description of the nature of ethnography, Burton shows how ethnography can provide an inspiring, discovery-based introduction to student research and academic writing. She proposes a staged process developing a creative task as a framework for student ethnography, including background reading and discussion; formulating goals and research questions; accessing informants; planning and conducting interviews; and sharing findings with peers and outside audiences.

A key question driving Olivia Archibald's chapter, "Reconsidering the Essay's Definition in the University Classroom: Writing, Disjunction, and the Active Nature of Thought," is why "the typically dry, objective-sounding, thesis-driven essay [is] privileged in educational contexts over more creative, reflective, personal-voiced writing forms?" Contrasting the very different writing styles of Francis Bacon and Michel Montaigne, Archibald argues that the "objective" essay style of Bacon has come to dominate academic writing over the more subjective essay style of Montaigne. She advocates a reconsideration of academic writing to allow forms that offer writers rich possibilities for expressing critical inquiry, discovery, and creativity other than the thesis-driven essay. In particular, she presents the disjunctive essay as a form that can be beneficially modeled and taught as an alternative academic genre.

"The Wide World of Nonfiction: Breaking Barriers of Form to Empower and Improve Student Writing" is the final chapter of Part 2. Sonya Huber looks at the ways in which approaches to non-fiction writing often focus on the end product as the goal for students rather than writing itself as the goal. Huber highlights how those approaches not only impose unnecessary constraints on writers but also stifle the creative and multimodal processes involved in the conceptualization and production of texts. Drawing from her own classroom practices, Huber shows how approaching writing from multiple modes, including journalism and creative writing, can help students develop highly readable prose that uses multiple rhetorical strategies to connect with a reader.

Four creative writers bring techniques used in the teaching of creative writing into university writing classrooms in **Part 3. Applying Techniques from Creative Writing and Literature to University Writing.** Some techniques are familiar to creative writing students, such as workshopping and freewriting. There are also some innovative techniques such as using puppetry to cultivate critical thinking and using the metaphor of travel to cultivate a fresh eye for descriptive writing.

In the first chapter of Part 3, Xu Xi advocates a workshop approach to expose the narratives in all of us by exploiting our instinctive need to tell a story and so give voice to writing. In "The Creative 'I' Workshop," Xu Xi walks readers through techniques to bring out the voices and story forms in both fiction and non-fiction writing. She introduces an innovative way to raise writers' consciousness of their options, showing how different types of writing might be conceptualized in a story form with very different beginnings, and so might give writers a way to get started and to bring their voices forward in any kind of writing.

While Xu Xi wants readers to awaken their inner narrative urges, Robin Hemley, in "Travel Writing without Leaving Home," takes readers on metaphorical trips. One pitfall for first-year students is the lapse into cliché when doing writing so that in the end their writing resembles that of the most jaded travelers. Hemley provides exercises to make the metaphorical trips, and to use those experiences and techniques to polish jaded descriptive writing into sparkling gems.

Puppetry is not only for young children, as Mark Spitzer proposes in "May the Farce Be with You: Reflections on 'Extreme Puppet Theater' as a Vehicle toward Something Else." As he has developed it, puppetry is an avenue for students to speak freely as children, to engage in playful activity leading to writing. Spitzer uses puppetry to link two seemingly unrelated genres, poetry and argumentative writing, to help students test out emerging arguments through ludic play. His chapter guides teachers in the use of Extreme Puppet Theater as a form of pedagogy to lay the groundwork for logical and rehearsed arguments that become the basis for both performance and writing.

To conclude Part 3, Shirley Geok-lin Lim offers a range of creative writing practices and teaching strategies in "Highways and Sinkholes: Incorporating Creativity Strategies in the Writing Classroom." A brief introduction on the history of creativity connects creative writing to composition teaching, which is followed by Lim's banks of creative strategies. The value in these strategies lies not only in generating creative sparks among students, but also in the holistic approach of creating psychological and physical spaces to nurture creativity in composition classrooms. This holistic approach embraces the essence of the four chapters in this section: creativity is enhanced when both teachers and students find security and support in a learning community.

In the 21st century, writing is no longer restricted to print, and many more teachers are experimenting with multimodal writing in their composition classrooms. In **Part 4. Supporting Creativity and Discovery in Composing Multimedia Texts**, four university teachers introduce effective approaches for bringing multimodal texts into the composition curriculum. The multimodal texts range from graphic novels, to digital infographics and timelines, to collaborative wiki writing, and on to other kinds of texts that utilize new Web 2.0 practices. These four chapters are not "old wine in new bottles" but are rather genuine exploratory steps to help teachers and students alike to employ multimodal and digital texts for discovery in writing.

Although some graphic novels may still be received as "superhero" tales, Jeffrey Mather demonstrates in "Watching/ Reading: Graphic Narratives and University Writing" that graphic narratives are inspiring and provocative tools to enhance creativity and critical thinking. Mather introduces contemporary graphic novels which discuss cross-cultural and social issues, pointing to the tension between visual and verbal expression in these texts. The discussion and pedagogical suggestions provide a practical ground to integrate graphic novels into a discovery-based writing curriculum.

David R. Gruber, in "Re-Presenting Academic Writing to Popular Audiences Using Digital Infographics and Timelines," takes the old and familiar graphic presentation and timelines into the digital age. Contrary to the usual perception of the complementary or supplementary nature of graphic presentation and timelines, Gruber introduces technology-friendly approaches to using infographics and timelines for understanding, refining, and presenting research in the classroom and beyond.

Collaborative writing can be done in new ways in the digital age with Web 2.0 tools. In "Online Writing as a Discovery Process: Synchronous Collaboration," Brian W. King reviews different possible online platforms for collaborative work and gives detailed suggestions for collaborative written work carried out through Web-based interaction. In an online environment, King suggests, students can gain benefits and be inspired by peer work through the affordances of synchronous writing.

In the final chapter, "Mashing, Modding, and Memeing," Rodney H. Jones asks students to take a step back to think critically about their digital practices. A critical attitude is essential in exploring knowledge and discovery, rhetoric and persuasion, creativity and voice, and plagiarism and the ownership of texts. The concepts of mashing, modding, and memeing are not unknown to many of our millennial students in their informal digital practices, but Jones provides avenues for teachers to appropriate students' informal experiences for academic writing. The issues raised in Jones' chapter, as across the other chapters of Part 4, remind us of the importance of helping students to adopt and adapt essential new digital and multimodal practices to academic writing in the 21st century.

Concluding Comments

> *Writing is a manifestation of the human drive to learn and to explore, to discover things through personal experience.*
> – Martha C. Pennington

A hope of the Summer Institute and of this volume has been to provide suggestions for a move away from traditional models of academic writing and writing pedagogy towards models that recognize the essentially creative and discovery-oriented nature of writing. Such a move requires teachers and the institutions in which they are based to continually innovate in teaching practices to meet the changing needs and conditions of society. The ideas in this volume therefore seek to break new ground in teaching university writing in ways that go beyond or even challenge standard English as a Second Language (ESL), English as a Foreign Language (EFL), English for Academic Purposes (EAP), and English for Specific Purposes (ESP) models to give a more prominent place to creative and discovery-oriented approaches.

As this volume highlights, we university teachers do not have to look too hard to find creative ways with which to engage the students in our classes. In most cases, we do not need to look much further than ourselves as our most creative sources. We hope that readers of this volume will find the ideas and suggestions in this book as engaging and motivating as we do, and we wish to thank all of the contributors for their inspiring work and ideas.

Part 1
Framing Creativity and Discovery in the Teaching and Learning of Writing

2 Creativity in Language Teaching

Jack C. Richards

Introduction

One of the consequences of the spread of English as an international language is a growing demand at all levels in both the public and private education sectors for good English language teachers. Schools want teachers who are dedicated, well-qualified, have a good command of English, who work well with their colleagues, who can engage and motivate their students and who are committed to helping their learners succeed. But above all they want individuals who are good teachers. The notion of what it means to be a good teacher is a complex one, since good teaching draws on many different qualities that teachers bring to their classes – reflecting the knowledge, skills and understanding they have built up from their professional education and from their experience of teaching. In this paper I want to explore one quality among the many that characterize effective teachers – the ability to bring a creative disposition to teaching.

In recent years research and theorizing on the nature and impact of creativity has been a focus in almost every discipline and domain, from those where it has traditionally been central such as fashion design and literature, to areas where it is perhaps less familiar such as business or management. Talk about creativity is everywhere today, driven by the need for companies and organizations to be more competitive and by the movement towards learned-centered rather than test-driven teaching in schools. Ministries of education in different parts of the world have encouraged schools to focus more on creativity in the curriculum across all subject areas – something that is believed to have widespread consequences. Creative teaching is said to increase levels of motivation and self-esteem on the part of learners and to prepare them with the flexible skills they need for the future. Developing the capacity to be creative is believed to have the potential to enrich lives and help contribute to a better society. However not all students have the opportunity to experience creative teaching.

In education creativity is important because it can improve academic attainment. Robert Fisher reports:

> Research...shows that when students are assessed in ways that recognize and value their creative abilities, their academic performance improves. Creative activity can rekindle the interest of students who have been turned off by school, and teachers who may be turned off by teaching in a culture of control and compliance. (Fisher, 2004: 11)

In language teaching, Alan Maley's (Maley, 1997) work has emphasized a focus on creativity through the use of texts drawn from a variety of different literary and non-literary sources that can be used to elicit creative thinking and foster the ability to make creative connections. Creativity has also been linked to levels of attainment in second language learning. Many of the language tasks favored by contemporary language teaching methods are believed to release creativity in learners – particularly those involving student-centered, interaction-based, and open-ended elements, and are therefore in principle ideally suited to fostering creative thinking and behavior on the part of learners. Creative intelligence seems to be a factor that can facilitate language learning because it helps learners cope with novel and unpredictable experiences. Communicative teaching methods have a role to play here since they emphasize functional and situational language use and employ activities such as role-play and simulations that require students to use their imaginations and think creatively. So what does creativity look like in a language classroom?

Here is an example of a creative teacher at work. She was confronted with the following situation:

> *A teacher has just called in sick. You are going to teach her 50-minute spoken English class, lower-intermediate level, in five minutes. Your only teaching aid is an empty glass.*

The teacher thought about it for less than a minute and then elaborated her idea for the lesson.

1. *I would start by showing the glass and asking students to form groups and brainstorm for five minutes, to come up with the names of as many different kinds of containers as possible. They would then group them, according to their functions. For example, things that contain food, things that are used to carry things, things that are used to store things in and so on. I would model how they should do this and suggest the kind of language they could use. (10 minutes)*
2. *Students would present their findings to the class to see who had come up with the longest list. (10 minutes)*
3. *For a change of pace, and to practice functional language, I would do some dialogue work, practicing asking to borrow a container from a neighbor. First, I would model the kind of exchange I want them to practice. Then students would plan their dialogue following this outline:*
   (a) Apologize for bothering your neighbor.
   (b) Explain what you want and why you need it.
   (c) Your neighbor offers to lend you what you want.
   (d) Thank your neighbor and promise to return it on the weekend.
4. Students would then perform their dialogues.

But how do teachers arrive at creative solutions to problems like this and what exactly does creativity consist of? There are many different ways of defining creativity depending on whether we see it "as a property of *people* (who we are), *processes* (what we do) or *products* (what we make)" (Fisher, 2004: 8). Hence creativity is usually described as having a number of different dimensions:

- the ability to solve problems in original and valuable ways that are relevant to goals;
- seeing new meanings and relationships in things and making connections;
- having original and imaginative thoughts and ideas about something;
- using the imagination and past experience to create new learning possibilities.

When creativity is viewed as a *product* the focus might be on a particular lesson, a task or activity in a book, or a piece of student writing. What are the specific features of the lesson that enables us to say that is creative? When viewed as a *process* the focus is on the thinking processes and decisions that a person makes use of in producing something that we would describe as creative (Jones, 2012). It is these two dimensions to creativity that I want to illustrate in here by focusing on both the special attributes and qualities of a group of creative teachers of English – this is the product dimension if you like – and then to consider how these attributes lead to particular classroom processes in language teaching. I will also consider how schools can foster a culture of creativity and the benefits it can bring for the school as well as for teachers and students. But first let me say something about my data sources.

My most recent interest in creativity in teaching was prompted by reading a report of a UK research project that was carried out in Kent by a team from Canterbury Christ Church University (Cremin, Barnes, and Scoffham, 2009). This involved an initial survey of 20 schools followed by a more detailed study undertaken in four of the schools – two primary and two secondary – in which the quality of creative teaching was acknowledged to be outstanding. The teachers in these schools were not TESOL teachers but the research identified three interrelated dimensions of creative teaching that are both product and process related and which also emphasized the school context as a crucial factor in facilitating creative teaching. The findings in the Kent study highlighted three factors:

> (a) the personal qualities of the teacher
> (b) the pedagogy the teacher adopts; and
> (c) the ethos of the class and school

I decided to look further into these dimensions of creative teaching in relation to the thinking and practices of teachers of English, by first asking a group of English teachers to write about their philosophies of teaching. I then selected from the teacher's stories those that appeared to reflect a creative disposition. Following this I conducted follow-up interviews – both spoken and written - to probe further into the teachers' thinking and to find examples from their classroom practice that illustrated creative approaches to teaching. In order to summarize the results of these conversations and interviews and following on from the Kent research I will discuss three different dimensions of creative teaching:

1. The qualities creative teachers possess
2. How teachers apply creativity in their teaching
3. How creativity can be supported in the school

The Qualities Creative Teachers Possess

We can probably all recall teachers we know who were very creative in their approach to teaching. Of course we have all encountered teachers who make use of carefully developed lesson plans, who keep their lessons focused on accurate performance of tasks, who are strict about getting homework in on time and returning it with detailed corrections and suggestions. Hopefully however we also have powerful and fond memories of a teacher who sparked our imagination, who inspired us by their individual and personal teaching style, who motivated us to want to continue learning and perhaps to eventually decide to become an English teacher? What makes teachers like this different?

Creativity depends upon the ability to analyze and evaluate situations and to identify novel ways of responding to them. This in turn depends upon a number of different abilities and levels of thinking. Let me now try to describe eight aspects of teacher ability and cognition that characterize some of the qualities of creative teachers.

Creative Teachers are Knowledgeable

Creative teachers have a solid knowledge base. They know their subject – English, teaching English, and learning English – and they draw on their subject matter knowledge in building creative lessons. A knowledge base is important because without knowledge, imagination cannot be productive. Creativity doesn't mean making unfocussed and unprincipled actions. It doesn't mean making it up as you go.

Let me first give an example of creativity *without* a solid knowledge base – which I characterize as misplaced creativity. I once worked with a native-speaker teacher who had no formal education in TESOL but had taught for 8 years in an EFL context by virtue of the fact that he was a native speaker. He had developed a technique he called "sponting," which he used as a feature of every class he taught. For example, he might take a word to begin a lesson: "English". He would ask students to come up with words that started with E-N-G-L-I-S-H. Then he would take the ending *-ish* and ask for nationalities that ended in *-ish*. Suddenly he was comparing "Finnish" – the nationality, with "to finish." Next, he was asking students if they knew what a finishing school was. And so it went on. When I asked him to explain the theoretical rationale for this activity and what it was supped to achieve, he could not come up with a convincing response.

This is what I mean by creativity not linked to a solid knowledge base. It leads to activities that have no legitimate goals or purpose. Compare that approach to creativity with this teacher's account of a lesson:

Drawing on Knowledge of Texts

When I teach I may not have a detailed lesson plan but I keep my goals firmly in mind and I know what I am trying to teach, whether it is a reading lesson, a speaking lesson and so on. And if I decide to do something that I hadn't planned it's because I suddenly thought of a more interesting and engaging way of practicing something. For example the other day we were studying narratives and were looking at a text in the book when it occurred to me that it would be fun if students created a jigsaw narrative in groups. Each group would prepare the opening section of a narrative, and then pass them around so that each group added the next section to the story. It turned out to be a good way of reinforcing what we had been studying, about the features of narrative texts – you know about setting, characters, events, problem, and resolution. – Carolina, Mexico

In the next example, the teacher refers to differences in the use of formal and casual speech:

Making Use of Sociolinguistic Knowledge

One of the things that my students seem to find interesting and even amusing is when I present a different point of view from an idea presented in one of the texts we are using. I guess this is just a matter of confidence but I feel it is good for learners to see that ideas in print can be challenged. The most obvious example of this is when texts we are reading have been written by someone writing in a different cultural context. For instance, the other day we were reading a text, written in the USA, about taking part in a job interview. The text said very clearly that the interviewee should call any male interviewers "Sir" and any females "Ma'am". So I explained that in the country I come from, that would be completely inappropriate because those terms of address are not familiar. This opened up a very interesting discussion about terms of address, formality and respect. My intention was to highlight for the learners that such matters are defined very differently in different cultural contexts and it is important to be sensitive to the context. The same issues of formality and informality occur in writing of course, so I was able to refer to this conversation later when we started working on letter writing. – Sara, UAE

Having a solid knowledge base means that the teacher has a rationale and purpose for the creative activities he or she uses. They have not been chosen merely for their novelty value but because they reflect the teachers' knowledge and understanding of teaching and learning.

Creative Teaching Requires Confidence

This attribute partly follows on from the preceding one, since knowledge of subject matter can provide a sense of confidence that enables the teacher to be original and creative. One feature of confidence is that it gives teachers a sense that they are in control of their classroom and that is the teacher – not the book or the curriculum- that can make a difference. Creative teachers see their input to the lesson as being decisive and so they have a sense of personal responsibility for how well learners learn.

Following One's Intuitions

At first I used to worry about what my students thought about me – did I know my subject, did I know how to introduce the material, was I in control of the class and so on. Now that I am much more confident as a teacher I am more willing to follow my intuitions, to try out new approaches and strategies, to take risks and experiment. It makes teaching more enjoyable for me. – Manuel, Peru

Creative Teachers are Committed to Helping Learners Succeed

Conversations with creative teachers confirm that they are very committed to their learners' success. The fact that they are creative means they are constantly adjusting their teaching in order to better facilitate learning. They want their learners to succeed and they try to find out as much as they can about their learners to enable them to best cater to their needs. They also seek to develop their learners' self-confidence.

Developing Self-confidence in Learners

The more I know about my leaners, the better I can help them learn.

Self-assurance can inspire second language learners to pass through the door of the world of English especially those who do not believe in themselves. Why is it important for a student to believe in one self? I have to deal with this question when working with students. Learners who boost self-confidence, boost success in acquiring the knowledge of a foreign language. In other words, they awake their credence in learning English. – Rosalyn, Mexico

Creative Teachers are Non-Conformists

Conformity is the enemy of creativity. It reduces the likelihood of creating fresh points of view and new insights. Jerome Bruner defined creativity as "an act that produces *effective surprise*" (Bruner, 1962: 3). Fisher (2004: 9) comments:

> It is originality that provides effective surprise. To do the same things in the same way is not to be creative, to do things differently adds variation to mere habit, but when we do or think things we have not done before, and they are effective, we are being original and fully creative.

The creative teacher does not simply present lessons from the book. He or she looks for original ways of creating lessons and using the textbook and teaching materials and seeks to create lessons that reflect his or her individual teaching style. This is another way of saying that being creative means seeking to adapt and modify lessons to better match the learners' needs. For this reason creative teachers are generally very different from each other. Learning to be a creative teacher does not mean modeling or copying the practices of other creative teachers, but rather it means understanding the principles that underlie creative teaching. Individual teachers will realize these principles in different ways. We see this approach reflected in principles articulated by creative teachers:

Creating Effective Surprises

I like my students to feel that when they come to my class they will always experience something a little different and unexpected. Not novelty for its own sake but a different way of doing things. For example, in addition to teaching how to write I make a point of teaching students how not to write. I try to find the worst possible examples and ask students to mark these as if they were the teacher. I then reveal to them who the texts were written by. Students love finding out that some of the texts came from Ministry of Education documents and websites! I try to add new techniques to my repertoire every year. – Leon, Mexico

Avoiding Repetition

I have been using the same textbook for over five years, along with lots of other teachers in my school. Each time I teach from it I try to do different things with it, to use it ways that are a little bit different from the ways my colleagues use it. They tend to stick to the book a lot of the time. I find it much more interesting to try to find different ways of teaching it, sometimes reversing the order of exercises in a unit, having students rewrite some of the reading texts, sometimes having the students teach the book themselves, taking turns. It becomes more interesting for me as well as more fun for the learners too. I try to challenge myself by not repeating things too many times. – Rosalyn, Mexico

Creative Teachers are Familiar with a Wide Range of Strategies and Techniques

Creativity in teaching means having a wide repertoire of routines and strategies which teachers can call upon, as well as being ready to depart from established procedures and to use one's own solutions. In general I find that novice teachers are much less likely to be creative than experienced teachers simply because they are familiar with fewer strategies and techniques. The danger is that once a teacher becomes comfortable in using a core set of techniques and strategies these become fixed.

Varying Tasks and Activities

I have a repertoire of at least 20 different ways of dealing with a writing task depending on which stage of the process we are working on. Sometimes we work with brainstorming techniques like listing, cubing or mindmapping. Sometimes we do continuous writing on topics they generate, just to focus on fluency. Other times we work with the organization of texts, identifying the best sequence in which to present elements of the text and allocating different learners to generate the ideas and language for different parts. This way we come up with a collaborative text. I also use reformulation in class a lot – this involves presenting two versions of a completed text: the learner's original text and then a version of it that I have reworked to make it communicate more effectively. The positive thing about reformulation is that it involves no "correction" of the learner's text but invites students to identify the changes that have been made and to discuss why they have been made. In this way it is developing their critical skills and helping them find ways of evaluating and improving their own texts. The key is to keep the activities fresh and to encourage learners to contribute the content. – Sara, UAE

Creative Teachers are Risk-takers

The creative teacher is willing to experiment, to innovate, and to take risks. Risk-taking reflects the flexible mindset of creative teachers as well as their self-confidence. They are willing to try things out, even if at times they may not work quite the way they are intended.

Pausing to Rethink

Last year I got students to keep a writing portfolio. The idea was to get them to reflect on their progress and motivate them by getting them to see evidence of their work. They hated it! They just thought it was more work and didn't help them with their exams. I will really need to rethink this one. – Effron, Mexico

So the teacher is willing to rethink or revise, or if necessary abandon her original plan and try something else. But this is seen as a learning moment and not an indication of failure.

Trying Something New

Recently in my writing class I asked learners to find any website or a blog that interested them and submit a question to that blog and see if they got an answer. I was a bit nervous that learners might choose unsuitable sites but thought I'd give it a go anyway. As it happened only a few students completed the assignment but one of them who did reported on a Tandem Language Learning website she had found that welcomed learners to join for free. She had been paired up with an Australian girl who was learning Spanish and they had already exchanged a number of emails and were planning to have a Skype meeting. Her report was completely unexpected but ended up motivating a number of other students to visit the same site and find their own partners. Whereas at first I thought the activity had been unsuccessful because not everyone did it, in fact this one student's enthusiasm ended up influencing several others to follow her lead, which eventually provided lots of additional written communication practice in English. – Sara, UAE

Creative Teachers Seek to Achieve Learner-Centered Lessons

A trait that is reflected in several of the comments above is that of learner-centeredness. This is seen in teachers who listen to their learners and who seek opportunities for learners to take responsibility and control of their learning. An important feature of learner-centered lessons is the extent to which the lesson connects with the learners' life experiences.

Personalizing Lesson Content

As far as I can I try to involve my students in developing the content of lessons. For example if I am teaching students to write narratives, while the textbook provides examples of what narratives are and what their features are, as soon as possible to shift the lesson focus to sharing personal stories. When students share accounts of their childhoods and write about important events or experiences in their lives they become much more involved in their writing. – Soo Lian, Singapore

Another teacher describes how he develops students' awareness of texts through focusing on texts they bring to class:

Using Student-Selected Content

I ask my students to collect examples of interesting texts they encounter out of class and bring these to class. I use these as the basis for teaching them about different text types and styles. The texts they bring to class are often more interesting than the ones in the book because these are the texts THEY are interested in. – Jose, Ecuador

Creative Teachers are Reflective

Lastly, a quality that creative teachers seem to possess is what we can call critical reflectivity. They review and reflect on their own practice, seek to expand their knowledge and try to find new ideas and practices that they can apply in their own classrooms. They ask questions like these:

- Do I vary the way I teach my lessons?
- Do I try out new activities and assess their role in my classes?

- Do I compare my teaching with the teaching of other teachers to find out creative solutions that they may have developed?
- Can I find ways of making my tasks more creative and hence more engaging for learners? (For example by presenting a reading text as a jigsaw reading).
- Can I adapt the activities I use so that they increase the personal value of my lesson to my learners? (For example by adapting an activity so that it centers on the students' lives rather than on characters in a textbook?)

Here is how two teachers engage in this process of critical reflection:

Reflecting through Journal-Writing

I keep a teaching journal in which I jot down thoughts and reflections on my teaching. I try to take 30 minutes or so, once week, to look back at my teaching and reflect on things of interest, or issues that arose that I need to think more about. If I have tried out a new activity and it worked particularly well I may make a note of it for future reference. I find journal-writing to be a useful consciousness-raising tool. It helps me focus on things that I may otherwise forget and helps me make better decisions about my future teaching. It's interesting to read things I wrote at different times to get a sense of my understanding of myself as a teacher. – Effron, Mexico

Getting Feedback from Learners

One way that I help myself remain reflective on my teaching is to regularly ask my learners to scribble on a piece of paper at the end of a morning's teaching what they remember about the class. This can be very telling. Sometimes the learners refer to something that I didn't pay much attention to, and that makes me wonder why it was so salient for them and not for me. Sometimes I realize that they are more focused on the content of what we are writing about than the strategies and skills and elements that contribute to effective written texts. This information is extremely valuable as it gives me an inkling of how the learners perceive what goes on in class and gives me the opportunity to make adjustments to my practice where I think this is needed. – Sara, UAE

How Teachers Apply Creativity in Their Classrooms

How does having some of the traits I have described so far influence the way a creative teacher teaches his or class? We see a creative disposition reflected in several different dimensions of creative teachers' lessons.

Creative Teachers Make Use of an Eclectic Choice of Methods

Typically rather than being bound to a particular method, creative teachers often adopt an approach that might be called *principled eclecticism*. In other words they don't choose methods and procedures at random but according to the needs of their class. They use a wide variety of teaching approaches and a wide range of resources and activities. Instead of depending on a single method, creativity is promoted by a mixture and combination of styles.

Using a Blend of Methods

I teach at a private language school where learners from all over the world come to study five days a week for anything from two weeks to two years. In order to keep learners engaged for that many hours, one methodology simply doesn't cut the mustard. I've lived through quite a few briefly fashionable movements and gleefully looted whatever I could from each. With more experience, one blends them all and develops a best practice which utilises anything that works with one's own particular learners.
– Peter, New Zealand

Creative Teachers Use Activities Which Have Creative Dimensions

Teaching creatively means assessing activities and materials for their potential to support creative teaching. Researchers have identified a number of dimensions of creative tasks: they are said to involve open-ended problem solving, to be adapted to the abilities of the participants, and to be carried out under constraints (Burton 2010). Some of the features that Zoltan Dörnyei identifies as productive language learning tasks can also be seen to promote creative responses:

> **Challenge**: tasks in which learners solve problems, discover something, overcome obstacles, or find information;

> **Interesting content**: topics that students already find interesting and that they would want to read about outside of class, such as stories we find about sports and entertainment personalities we find on YouTube and the internet;

> **The personal element**: activities that make connections to the learners' lives and concerns;

> **The novelty element**: aspects of an activity that are new or different or totally unexpected;

> **The intriguing element**: tasks that concern ambiguous, problematic, paradoxical, controversial, contradictory or incongruous material stimulate curiosity;

> **Individual choice:** tasks which give students a personal choice – for example, students can choose their own topics to write about in an essay or choose their own topics and group members in a discussion activity;

> **Tasks that encourage risk-taking:** they don't want their students to be so worried about making mistakes that they feel reluctant to take part in activities, so they reward them for effort and not only for success;

Tasks that encourage original thought: activities that require an original response, so instead of comprehension questions after a reading passage that test recall, they seek to use tasks that encourage a personal and individual response to what the student has read;

The fantasy element: activities that engage the learners' fantasy and that invite the learners to use their imagination for creating make-believe stories, identifying with fictional characters or acting out imaginary situations.

(Dörnyei, 2001)

Here are examples of creative tasks that reflect some of these characteristics:

Making Use of a Personal Element

Even though my students don't seem to like writing in class, I realised that they do quite a bit of writing in their daily lives, in the form of tweets and Facebook updates for example. I created a twitter account and a Google+ page for our class and got students to start writing short messages in response to each other. Gradually I assigned them different roles and had everyone contribute different parts to a short story we wrote collaboratively. The students loved it as it made the activity more familiar to their out-of-class experiences. – Caroline, Colombia

Encouraging Original Thought

In my Business writing course we have to work with lots of very routine texts such as email messages, blogposts and business letters. To make it more interesting I ask students at the start of the semester to invent their own company, logo, staff list and products so that they can use this material when they are developing their own scenarios and situations throughout the semester rather than having to stick rigidly to examples in the textbook. In this way, they create a kind of personal narrative throughout the semester, telling different stories about what has happened in the company and what they need to communicate about. – Manuel, Peru

Here Sara describes the use of an activity with a fantasy element:

Making Use of Fantasy

One of my learners popped into my office the other day and asked me if I had a minute to read something written on his telephone. I was intrigued. When I read it, I saw that it was the opening lines of a thriller, rich with description of place and person. Because he's in my Research Writing course, I had no idea he had such a lively imagination and an ability to write such creative text, so I asked him how we could find a way of seeing more of his talent for words in his research writing. He took a risk in showing me that writing but I figure that he did so because he wanted me to know what he is capable of. Since that day I've encouraged him to be as creative as possible during our free writing sessions and to focus on personal links to the rather academic and serious topic that he is exploring in his research paper. – Sara, UAE

Creative Teachers Teach in a Flexible Way and Often Adjust Their Teaching during Lessons

Flexibility is another feature we often observe in the lessons of creative teachers. Flexibility in teaching means being able to switch between different styles and modes of teaching during the lesson, for example if necessary changing the pace of the lesson and, giving more space and time to learners. The teacher may not need to refer to a lesson plan because he or she is able to create effective lessons through monitoring the learners' response to teaching activities and creating learning opportunities around important teaching moments. This kind of teaching can be viewed as a kind of skilled improvisation. Here a teacher describes how he makes use of "teachable moments."

Making the Most of Teachable Moments

The longer I teach the more often "teachable moments" emerge in my teaching. It might be a topic, it might be a type of text, it might be a situation – many prompts can invite me to share a story

or an experience with my learners which relates to the lesson goals. Usually I find these diversions are helpful; sometimes they relieve tension when we have been working hard on something. For instance, one day I was working through some examples with my EAP class of how to integrate another writer's ideas into my own text. In the example I was using, one of the learners suddenly stopped me to ask about the name of one of the authors in the in-text citation. Since I had noticed that my leaners frequently confused the first name with the family name of Western authors, this gave me a perfect opportunity to draw attention to the names of the authors in the text and to ask them to suggest what the citation would be if each of them had written the original text. Personalizing the example in this way, and being willing to be diverted from the focus of the activity at hand is sometimes necessary. It's important to be ready to let the learners' agenda take over at times. – Peter, New Zealand

Creative teachers often improvise around their teaching materials, moving back and forth between book-based input and teacher-initiated input. Hence even though a teacher may teach the same lesson from a textbook many times, each time he or she teaches it becomes a different lesson due to the improvisations the teacher initiates during teaching.

Creative Teachers Look for New Ways of Doing Things

Learning to teach means mastering the formats of different kinds of lessons – reading lessons, conversation lessons, listening lessons, and so on. Lessons are structured in different ways depending on their content but typically consist of openings, tasks, and closings. Delivering lessons over time, teachers develop routines and procedures that enable these dimensions of lessons to be carried out efficiently and effortlessly. But there is a tendency for teaching to become increasingly standardized – the "one size fits all" approach – particularly when teachers are working within a prescribed curriculum and teaching towards tests. This often results in a teacher working from pre-packed materials such as a textbook and "transmitting" it efficiently. This is perhaps appropriate at the beginning stages of a teacher's career but should not characterize the lessons of experienced teachers. Here are some comments by a teacher on how she seeks to introduce variety into familiar activities:

Giving Learners Choices

I find that the easiest way to do something new in the lesson is to invite the learners to make the decisions about different aspects of the activities. There is no reason why the teacher has to decide which activities to focus on or in which order to complete them. There are also many possibilities for arranging the grouping of learners as they work on tasks, from individual to pairs to small groups. I try and work through different aspects of lesson organization and systematically vary the following: text type, audience, purpose, skill focus, learning configuration (individuals, pairs, groups, whole class). I also routinely ask the learners to tell me how long they believe they will need in order to complete a particular activity. They have a much better idea than me and I always make sure I write some kind of "extension task" on the board while they are working, so that anyone who finishes early has something else to do. – Carmen, Mexico

Creative Teachers Customize Their Lessons

Creative teachers develop custom-made lessons that match their students' needs and interests or adapt and customize the book to match their students' interests. While in many cases a book may work perfectly well without the need for much adaptation, in some cases different levels of adaptation may be needed. Through the process of adaptation the creative teacher personalizes the text, making it a better teaching resource, and individualizes it for a particular group of learners. Here are two examples.

Adapting the Textbook

In using international textbooks, some of the topics included can be problematic for both students and teachers. For example, when asked who John Lennon or Nelson Mandela were, my Cambodian students had absolutely no idea, let alone how to the use the information about these people in the book to practice specific rules of grammar and discourse.. For various reasons, Cambodian students have very limited knowledge of famous people and places outside of their country. Therefore, trying to introduce new language and unfamiliar content at the same time creates an unnecessary learning burden for my students. To help connect learning English to their own lives I generally localize the content of the lesson by using names of people and other information that my students are familiar with, which helps them connect learning of English with their own knowledge and interests. – Therea, Cambodia

Encouraging Students to Question the Textbook

I have to work with a writing textbook which is rather prescriptive. It lays down a lot of rules about how things should be done in different types of texts and leaves very little to the imagination. At first I found this rather limiting but now I use it as a talking point at the start of each lesson. I actively encourage the students to comment on the extent to which they believe the approach recommended by the textbook would work in every context and whether it is possible to generalize about how to produce a particular kind of text in every situation. Of course the learners realize that the textbook writer cannot anticipate every situation and they are very creative in these discussions, often mentioning aspects of their culture which would oblige writers to do something differently. In this way I believe that questioning the textbook "rules" ends up teaching them more about writing and gives them a more sophisticated understanding of the way that context affects writing. – Jose, Ecuador

Creative Teachers Make Use of Technology

Creative use of technology in the classroom can support the development of imagination, problem-solving, risk-taking, and divergent thinking on the part of teachers and students.

Using Blogging as a Resource

A productive way of engaging my students and helping them to improve their writing skills is through Creative nonfiction (CNF). CNF involves using creative literary techniques and devices when writing about non-fiction events, e.g, diaries, memoirs, autobiographies, essays, obituaries, journalism, travel writing. I have incorporated a CNF strand into my writing course – blogging.

I begin by showcasing blogs to the class as a whole using the classroom computer and screen, e.g. a leading newspaper, The Guardian, ran a blogging competition and I bring up the winning sites, e.g. 'Scaryduck. Not scary. Not a duck.' This blog is full of short, often witty pieces, about whatever interests the blogger. The blogs express a particular point of view, are funny and aimed at a younger adult audience, which reflects the age range and interests of my students. The blog is reader-friendly consisting of short, lively texts liberally punctuated with photographs. I find that my students engage very quickly. I look in more detail at one of the blogs eliciting ways that the writing is creative, e.g., use of adjectives, irony, voice, register, metaphor. My students bring their tablets, laptops, smartphones to class and after the showcase I give them the web address for three other suitable blogs and ask the students to browse them and be prepared to comment.

I then set up their blogging task. Each student has to set up an online blog and then blog on five separate subject areas from a choice of eight subject areas: food, music, transport, sport, media, politics, religion, fashion. Students are encouraged to read and interact with their fellow students' blogs. After each set of blogs I give a whole class commentary on selected student blogs highlighting areas of successful creative writing, e.g. alliteration, original use of adjectives, realization of a distinctive voice. I also give personal, online feedback to my students about their blogs through one to one emails. The intrinsic interest of their chosen material and freedom to express their own point of view has a highly motivating effect on my students and there is a crossover into their academic writing, which I foster in class and through individual feedback to their academic writing tasks. – Dino, United Kingdom

Creative Teachers Seek Creative Ways to Motivate Students

Creative teachers express a desire to motivate students, to challenge them, to engage their curiosity, to encourage deep learning rather than surface learning. They try to develop a classroom atmosphere that encourages and motivates students in their learning.

There are of course many ways in which motivation can be addressed in a lesson. For example:

Using Activities that Showcase Students' Talent

One fun way in which I introduce motivation into writing classes is to ask students who have written a narrative which includes a lot of interaction, to turn it into a movie script. This provides really excellent language practice with a strong focus on interaction. The work can also be shared by two students so that they have fun improvising the dialogue and then writing it down. – Sara, UAE

Using Activities from the Learners' World

My students all play video games so I have found this a good way to motivate them. This year I introduced digital games in class for the teaching of writing. It sure raised some eyebrows among my colleagues at first! I linked it to our writing curriculum as closely as I could – for example, when discussing different ways to organise a piece of writing, I asked students to describe their favourite games and the way the stories within them are built up. I also found some games that involve a great deal of language use. Ace Attorney is one in which players take the role of an attorney and have to develop a strong case, present it convincingly and so on. Students created their own cases as practice in argument writing and had

to respond to each other's writing to practice writing rebuttals. –
Soo Lian, Singapore

When less creative students are linked with more creative and imaginative ones, they can benefit from seeing the techniques, strategies and approaches that others use in the creative process.

How Can Creative Teaching be Supported in the School?

One way of considering creativity is to take a *laissez-faire* approach and assume that it is over to the individual teacher. Schools have other concerns and are judged by how well their students perform on national exams, on how much use the school makes of technology, or on the quality of the students the school is able to attract. But a commitment to creative teaching requires a change in mind set within a school. As Fisher (2004: 17) comments:

> Success in any grand project needs help from other, means making alliances, means benefiting from the distributed intelligence of others – developing the "info-structure" – interconnectivity through learning conversations with others.

There are a number of ways in which schools can *discourage* creative teaching:

- When the curriculum, tests, and constant monitoring drives teaching and teachers cannot depart from established or approved practices. There is too much of an emphasis on book learning, rote learning and test scores.
- When teachers are not given time to be creative.
- When teachers are not encouraged to be creative and innovate or to develop an individual and personal teaching style.
- When teachers are stuck with fixed routines and procedures.

Here is a good example of how a school can *discourage* creative teaching rather than encourage it:

Discouraging Creativity

Sometimes, the institution may not allow teachers to adapt their coursebooks, and this can become a problem for the teacher, especially for someone who is trying to meet learners' needs and teach creatively. Once I was teaching in a school and I was given a coursebook to use with a particular group of students. When I said 'Thanks, I'll see what activities I can add to it' I was told in no uncertain terms that I was not to do this. The students, I was told, measure their progress in terms of how far they have got through the coursebook and the company that was funding the classes did the same thing. If I added anything to my lessons, I was told, the students weren't going to progress and the Director wouldn't be able to show the company how far they had progressed. – Brian, Australia

By contrast a school that believes in the value of creative teaching expresses confidence in teachers and encourages adaptation and innovation, that is open to new ideas and innovation and that supports, encourages and rewards creative teaching. Fisher (2004: 17) characterizes a creative school as follows:

The creative school is a place where individuals, pupils and teachers are:

Motivated
- focused on purpose, ultimate goals, and shared destiny;
- open to new ideas, innovation, and enquiry;
- have passion to succeed, are willing to take risks, and accept difference and diversity.

Given time and responsibility for creative activity
- involving all in the search for creative solutions;
- being tolerant of mistakes in the search for better solutions;
- avoiding impulsivity, allowing time for practice and for ideas to come.

Able to collaborate with partners to share creativity and ideas

- learning with partners to generate, extend, and provide feedback on ideas;
- collaborating as part of a team on creative projects and productions;
- developing creative connections and links beyond the organization.

So let's look at some ways in which a school can *encourage* rather than *discourage* creative teaching.

The School Helps Teachers Recognize and Share What is Creative in Their Own Practice

There are usually creative and innovative teachers in every school, but often their teaching skills are not necessarily recognized or familiar to others in the school. Here are some examples of how schools provide opportunities for teachers to share creative approaches to teaching:

In our school we are encouraged to post notes about innovative techniques we use on a noticeboard in the teachers' room. – Jose, English teacher, Ecuador

We have our own website where we exchange ideas and resources we have developed. – Effron, Mexico

We have regular brown-bag lunches where we share accounts of new things and innovations we have tried out in our classes. – Caroline, Columbia

The School Encourages Creative Partnership

We are often most creative when we get the support and encouragement of others. There are several ways in which this can be achieved.

- Through team teaching
- Through peer observation
- Through shared lesson planning

Using Shared Lesson-Planning

We have been implementing the process of shared lesson-planning. How it works is we work in groups of three or four and take a unit from our textbook or some other materials that we might use as the basis for a class, and brainstorm different ways in which the material could be taught. We try to be as creative as possible and it's amazing how many different ideas people can come up with. Then we teach the lesson to our own class and the other group members observe the lesson. Later we meet again to discuss and review how the lesson went. – Manuel, Peru

The School Provides Resources to Support Creative Teaching

If teachers want to develop creative teaching resources to support their teaching they need access to a good resource centre with up-to-date books, magazines, realia, projectors, technology, whiteboards, etc. that teachers can make use of to complement their lessons. An environment and culture that encourages creativity and provides the resources teachers need in order to realize their creative potential is a key component of the creative capital needed to support creative teaching.

The School Rewards Creative Teachers

A school can acknowledge the value of creative teachers be recognizing their contributions in different ways. For example:

- by acknowledging them when appropriate
- by giving them opportunities to mentor novice teachers
- by encouraging them to share their ideas with others through brown-bag lunch sessions, participation in seminars and workshops

Summary Points

The Qualities of Creative Teachers

To summarize, here are some aspects of creativity we find in creative teachers:

1. Creative teachers are knowledgeable.
2. Creative teaching requires confidence.
3. Creative teachers are committed to helping learners succeed.
4. Creative teachers are non-conformists.
5. Creative teachers are familiar with a wide range of strategies and techniques.
6. Creative teachers are risk-takers.
7. Creative teachers seek to achieve learner-centered lessons.
8. Creative teachers are reflective.

How Creative Teachers Apply Creativity in Classes

We can summarize some ways in which creative teachers approach their lessons:

1. Creative teachers make use of an eclectic choice of methods.
2. Creative teachers use activities which have creative dimensions.
3. Creative teachers teach in a flexible way and often adjust their teaching during lessons.
4. Creative teachers look for new ways of doing things.
5. Creative teachers customize their lessons.
6. Creative teachers make use of technology.
7. Creative teachers seek creative ways to motivate students.

How a School Fosters and Supports Creativity

The following points summarize the school's role in fostering and supporting creative teaching:

- The school helps teachers recognize and share what is creative in their own practice.
- The school encourages creative partnership.
- The school provides resources to support creative teaching.
- The school rewards creative teachers.

Conclusion

I have focused here on just one aspect of teaching. There are many other important dimensions to effective teaching. But adding the concept of creative teaching to our understanding of what it means to be an effective language teacher has benefits for teachers, for learners, as well as for schools. For learners, creative teaching helps them develop their capacities for original ideas and for creative thinking. It also improves the quality of the experiences learners receive and can help learners develop increased levels of motivation and even self-esteem. For the teacher it provides a source of ongoing professional renewal and satisfaction – since when learners are engaged, motivated, and successful, teaching it motivating for the teacher. For the institution it can lead to increased levels of satisfaction for both teachers and students as well as contribute to the quality, effectiveness, and reputation of the school. To summarize, creative learners need creative teachers and teachers need to work in schools where creativity is valued and shared.

References

Bruner, Jerome (1962) *On Knowing: Essays for the Left Hand*. Cambridge: Belknap Press of Harvard University Press.
Burton, Pauline (2010). Creativity in Hong Kong schools. *World Englishes* 29(4): 493–507. http://dx.doi.org /10.1111/j.1467-971X.2010.01677.x.

Cremin, Teresa, Barnes, Jonathan and Scoffham, Stephen (2009) *Creative Teaching for Tomorrow: Fostering a Creative State of Mind*. Kent: Future Creative CIC.

Fisher, Robert (2004) What is creativity? In Robert Fisher and Mary Williams (eds.) *Unlocking Creativity: Teaching Across the Curriculum* 6–20. New York: Routledge.

Dörnyei, Zoltan (2001) *Motivational Strategies in the Language Classroom*. Cambridge, U. K.: Cambridge University Press.

Jones, Rodney (ed.) (2012) Introduction: Discourse and creativity 1–13. *Discourse and Creativity*. Harlow: Pearson.

Maley, Alan (1997) Creativity with a small 'c'. *The Journal of the Imagination in Language Learning and Teaching* IV. Retrieved on 15 April 2013 from http://www.njcu.edu/cill/journal-index.html.

3 Creating Identities in an Intertextual World

Charles Bazerman

Introduction

For students, universities open new worlds of knowledge and culture. Universities open new identities as professionals, citizens, and members of society – local and global. The worlds opened are richly and deeply saturated with texts of all sorts. To take action and form identities within these intertextual worlds, students need to learn to draw on and address relevant texts at the same time as they stake out their own positions in writing. The *intertext* (that web of texts that surround, are invoked by, give meaning to, or are otherwise relevant to any new text) establishes a virtual world of meaning upon which writers create and innovate to make their contribution. This is as true for the emerging multi-media designer as the emerging scientist, as true for the emerging journalistic blogger as the emerging business executive. Such is the nature of the modern world where writing has become the communicative infrastructure of major social institutions, transforming purely local lives into ones played out on worldwide stages mediated by texts.

While high school has prepared students within a contained literacy world, the university transitions students into the powerful knowledge, financial, and professional systems within which they will carry out the work of societies, cultures, and economies. In a high school class, a single textbook may have defined all relevant knowledge and established all relevant perspectives; the student in writing needs only to follow the path prescribed by the textbook and reinforced by the instructor. Academic writing at the university, however, challenges students to innovate meanings and plans, to begin to form the identities upon which to build careers. Students need to encounter and evaluate multiple conflicting texts with disparate knowledge in order to come to their own conclusions that carry discussions and projects forward. Teaching reading and writing at the university is more than teaching a contained set of skills; it is teaching students how to claim their place and accomplish meaningful actions in the worlds they are growing into. Teachers need to invent the environments and tasks that will nurture the students' invention of themselves as powerful academic writers.

The Creativity and Challenges of Writing

Every act of writing is an act of creating – bringing a new artifact into the world, even if it is only a Facebook post. Writing creates new meanings through cobbling together pieces of language, familiar to the reader from other texts, other utterances. The new act of writing draws on and evokes, either explicitly or implicity, the wealth of prior texts. These texts can be drawn on simply for their language, but the ideas or descriptions or moods of those prior texts may also be reprised. More explicitly, the new text may rely on claims made previously or answer directly to the arguments proposed in related texts, sometimes called the literature on the subject. A Facebook post helps create an identity, a presence, a set of relations, and a set of facts about us. Each post asserts a place among the many prior posts of the author and posts in the circle of friends. The posts may not claim to be fictional (though they might) and may not draw on the literary canon for allusions, genres, or models (though they might, but they could equally draw on current music lyrics or news headlines or YouTube links). But the lack of literary aspirations does not make them any less meaningful accomplishments of the language arts, asserting the writer's presence, meaning, value, and actions in a social world of importance to the writer. In fact, representing the world as it is, drawing on the actual material of the world with accuracy, responsibility, and purpose draws on arts of language distinct from the ones that make for successful fabulation. Further, finding how one wants to represent oneself to the people with whom one maintains real and concrete relations calls on arts of language different from those of the literary performer.

So what does Facebook have to do with university writing? One doesn't need a university education to create an effective presence on Facebook (though we should remember that Facebook grew out of a closed university social communication application.) Simply put, when students enter the university they step into expanded worlds of knowledge that are closely attached to the professional worlds of practice they desire to contribute to, and to create careers and identities within. The worlds of knowledge of their high schools were smaller, contained by the narrow selectivity of curriculum and exams, and embodied in a small number of textbooks. The knowledges of the university are open-ended, extended into all the domains of the world, and ever changing with access through the full resources of the library and internet.

It is easy for the new university students to lose their way in the ever-expanding universe of print and digital texts. Perhaps even more challenging, the identities and roles of students to be expressed through writing change (or at least should change) radically in the shift from high school to the university (see Sullivan and Tinberg, 2006; Sullivan, Tinberg, and Blau, 2010). Secondary students as writers are largely test takers, reproducing received knowledge from textbooks, with little expectation of originality or fresh thought, though if they are lucky high school may offer a few beginning opportunities for personal expression, critical reasoning, and social engagement. Over the years of a university education students increasingly need to become familiar with and draw on extensive bodies of knowledge to carry out new tasks, complete protoprofessional projects, and build identities as creative, intelligent, analytical, knowledgable professionals – sharing all the competencies expected of practitioners but also asserting unique perspectives and ideas, based on deepening understanding of knowledge of their chosen fields (for examples of studies of writing at the university, see Carroll, 2002; Herrington and Curtis, 2000; Thaiss and Zawacki, 2006).

Learning Academic Writing

Much of the student writer's growth is tied to changing knowledge of the literature of the field, then purposeful synthesis and criticism of that knowledge to come to fresh conclusions (for practical curriculum to achieve this, see Bazerman, 1995). The maturing student's presence or identity in the field then depends on how well s/he asserts her/his views with force and clarity, in ways convincing to knowledgable practitioners. This assertion embodies representation of data and evidence, which need to be collected and reported in credible ways, consistent with other representations in the professional literature. The assertion may also involve plans and designs, again intelligible, credible, and valuable according to the standards already expressed in the field. Any variation from the standards and knowledge already in the field needs vigorous and credible argument for how and why one varies. These disciplinary standards are typically first made visible to students through the assessments and comments of instructors in class dialog, in giving assignments and criteria, and in assesssments and comments in response to student writing. Typically these comments become more disciplinarily focused as students move towards the upper years of their undergraduate program. In postgraduate years the advisor may ventriloquate the critiques that may be made of students' claims by others in the field (Paré, Starke-Meyerring, and McAlpine, 2009), but also students may face disciplinary standards directly as they begin to attend departmental colloquia and major conferences and as they attempt to publish in disciplinary and professional venues.

Students typically are introduced to the texts, ideas, theories, and methods of representing data of a field in their coursework in the various subject areas, and then in their writing, they learn to reason and make arguments on the bases of these resources. These are highly creative acts for them, but highly focused and constrained by the materials they are working with, the genres they express themselves through, and the criteria of evaluation they need to meet. Yet in those respects it is hardly different than the young poet writing love sonnets or the painter doing large landscapes in oils. Each field of creation has criteria of truth and insight as well as of compositional coherence. Although emotional resonance in lyric poetry or naturalistic grandeur in landscape painting are different from fresh observation based on precision and accuracy of measurement in geology, they each have their discipline and creativity. Similarly, stanzaic unity or compositional focus and coherence are no doubt different from logical relations among theory, method, findings, and results, but they each establish expectations of larger organization.

Also, we need to remember that students are novices in these genres, so that acts of great creativity and imagination for them may seem familiar and pedestrian to our jaded eyes, but so might most youthful attempts at poetry or high school art exercises. Although genres may be defined in a number of ways (see Bawarshi and Reiff, 2010, for a discussion of the varieties of approaches to understanding genre), I here adopt an approach to genre that sees them as attributions by readers that allow them to make sense of utterances as typified within typified situations; this view recognizes the constant evolution and fluidity of genres and the way genres facilitate the creation of locally meaningful and novel utterances. Thus, the genres students encounter in school are not only regulated forms to be fulfilled, but opportunities to develop ideas, meaning, and styles of thinking.

Writing with Data and Concepts in an Oceanography Course

So let's see what this intellectual development within school-assigned genres looks like in actuality. A number of years ago I participated in a series of investigations of writing in a general education oceanography course. The professor of the course wanted the students to come to understand that science was based on arguments drawing on theory and using disciplinary evidence. In one major assignment, after students read the textbook presentation of plate tectonic theory, listened to several lectures on the topic, and engaged in related class discussions and laboratory exercises, they were asked to use the standard database of geologic events in order to identify features and argue how the data supported plate tectonic theory. As part of the assigment they had to select three profiles (or point-to-point slices) of sea floor depth that would isolate and define features in a small geographic area. It is like trying to see an object in a room from the outside if you can only view it through three narrow slit windows. This is not a trivial task, as strategically locating the profiles (that is, where do you put the "windows" to get a good view of the object?) was important to identifying the features with clarity and finding features that could be argumentatively linked with the theory. Looking at examples from the literature as well as examples discussed in the lab manual and classes would help the students identify strategies for locating profile cuts. Then there were a number of interpretive creative acts involved in seeing the profiles as actual features, and then locating the features as part of processes that would best be understood by the dominant plate-tectonic theory, presented in their textbooks, handouts, and other class assigned readings.

The first time my colleagues collected data from the students' written assignments and analyzed it, the difference between the successful papers and the less successful were obvious. Successful papers created a tight and dense network of statements that went from detailed concrete observations, through identification of features, processes, and theories,while the less successful papers were missing claims at different levels and had few identifiable semantic connections among the claims. As a result, writers of the less successful papers were unable to develop and support ideas, and were more closely tied to textbook statements randomly inserted into their papers. To analyze the kinds of claims and their connections, we identified task- and subject-specific categories of epistemic levels of each claim. These epistemic levels (or levels of abstraction from the data, based on the theoretical constructs of the field of oceanography) were defined in consultation with the instructor and through examination of the student scripts, as evaluated by the instructor and the teaching assistants. These reflected the specific intellectual goals of the task, embedded within the course and the discipline (see Kelly and Takao, 2002, for further details). Specifically the epistemic levels consisted of:

I. data charts, and other representations of untransformed data
II. topographical features
III. relative geographical relations
IV. geological theoretical claims
V. propositions in the form of general theoretical claims
VI. general propositions describing geological processes and referencing definitions, experts, and textbooks (Kelly and Takao, 2002: 322)

The lowest level claims were based on concrete observations and measurements recorded in professional databases. Each level required some further abstraction or inference. That is, features were identified by the relation of data points (level II), and then features would be placed in relation to each other (III). Then, the relation of features would provide the basis of making theoretical claims about the research site (IV), and representing these theoretical claims as more general propositions (V), and then relating claims to processes explained by plate-tectonic theory (VI). The next time the course was taught, students were introduced to this framework showing how to make concrete and abstract statements at different epistemic levels so as to tie claims at different levels together. That time, the student papers were more uniformly successful, but now difficulties arose in some students making their claims in random places throughout their papers, so they were unable to develop their arguments cleary and fully, as the reasoning was being presented in disrupted ways, not in a coherent order. So our research team performed a move analysis on a selection of the student papers to confirm how the more coherent papers differed from the less coherent ones. Move analysis (first developed by John Swales) is a method of identifying standard rhetorical moves made within a genre (for further details, see Swales, 1990).

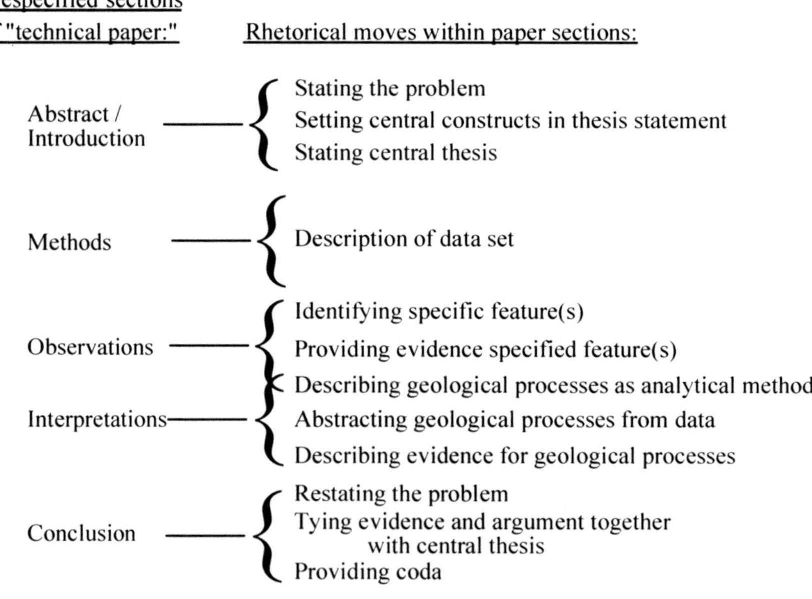

(from Kelly and Bazerman, 2003: 41)

The next time the course was taught we introduced the students to the above model, and students' writing again improved. By this point most students had a full range of epistemic levels of claims and were able to make coherent arguments that made theoretical sense of the data (Kelly, Bazerman, Skukauskaite and Prothero, 2010). Then, in our next investigation, we found that each section of the paper had characteristic patterns of epistemic levels. That is, the introduction and discussion sections tended to have statements of higher abstraction and theoretical representation (epistemic level V or VI) while the methods section tended to have concrete statements of level I. Observation and interpretation sections were in the middle with level III and IV statements, with interpretations tending to be at a slightly higher overall level than observations. To fulfill the assignment students had to think through and make claims at all these levels in the appropriate sections of the paper and make reasoned connections among them, dictated by the expectations of the genre and structured by the organization of the genre. In a further study we examined lexical cohesion, and this further clarified the pattern by which theoretical and more concrete terms were distributed throughout the papers in order to build elements of the argument and tie them together (Kelly and Bazerman, 2003; Kelly, Bazerman, Skukauskaite, and Prothero, 2010). In so doing they would be seeing how concrete observable data could be made sense of through tying data to the theoretical terms developed in the disciplinary literature. Thus, they saw how experience becomes inscribed in the world of disciplinary meanings.

Growth in Thinking through Writing in a Teacher Education Program

Learning these disciplinary forms of representing data, ideas, and their relationships, including the typical phrasing as well as organizing arguments, not only taught students how to meet disciplinary expectations; these forms of expression also expanded the student's expressive power, as they were in a position to make more powerful and effective original arguments. The more the students understood the constraints of the genre, the more they could use those constraints to develop their own thinking and assert their own identities, as I explored with some associate researchers in another set of studies based on our teacher education program. This program had its primary goal to develop reflective understanding of classroom events, student learning and actions, and teacher choices, so that the teacher candidates would continually examine their own practices and develop reflective habits to help them continue developing across their careers, long after they had completed the program.

The teacher education program has a series of assignments that direct the teacher candidates' attention to details of students and classroom events. The major assignment of the fall term was a detailed examination of students who seem to be avoiding reading. During the winter teacher candidates needed to assemble a teaching portfolio, with commentary and reflections on a video of their teaching a lesson. Finally, in the spring, teacher candidates had to complete an action research thesis, based on data collection throughout the year and constant rethinking of fundamental questions about teaching in light of the evidence from their classes. These three major assignments (case study of low-reading students, teaching portfolio, and action research thesis) each asked teacher candidates to make observations and reason about them in order to increase their understanding of teaching and learning in concrete classroom situations. We found that the genres they wrote in and each of the sections of each of the genres evoked specific kinds of thinking, posing specific intellectual problems for students to solve, which then advanced their own thinking and emerging identities as teachers. That is, even within a single genre, each of the typified parts of the genre had its own cognitive work: in order to complete the total intellectual work of the genre, the students had to complete many reasoning sub-tasks within the separate sections of the assignment. Further, as teacher candidates gained practice in these forms of writing requiring reflection on the classroom, their ability to make sophisticated judgments improved.

Through a combination of ethnographic observation, interviewing, and grounded analysis of texts, we developed a subject- and program-specific set of codes to identify the kind of thinking evoked by each assignment and each section, in support of the developmental expectations of the program. The codes reflecting the least developed thinking according to program goals attributed student and teacher behavior as based on fixed or prior characteristics (e.g. "[I hoped] he would be encouraged to make mistakes, but this seems to be an unlikely outcome in light of his insecurity.") and moral obligations (e.g. "I was disappointed with his apathetic response to reading."), while mid-level codes identified statements recognizing that classroom behavior reflected many influences, reactiveness to immediate events, and complexities of situation. The codes reflecting the most developed thinking according to program goals identified statements recognizing learning came in the students' response to dynamic situations and that both students and teachers were attempting to make sense of the unfolding situation to make choices about actions (Bazerman, Simon, Ewing, and Pieng, forthcoming).

We also discovered that discussing and citing their disciplinary reading had a strong effect on these future teachers' thinking. We found that when teacher candidates cited the professional literature on teaching and literacy, they overwhelmingly used the sources to identify concepts that helped them make sense of their experience, and were thus creating their perspective on what happens in a classroom through the lenses provided by the concepts in their readings. We also found that the thinking expressed in the sentences which included citations (or which continued discussion of a text cited in a neighboring sentence) was at a higher level than thinking in sentences not connected to references. And over the sequence of assignments, the teacher candidates became better able to engage in extended discussions of their readings and to maintain continuous passages of higher order reasoning (Bazerman, Simon, and Pieng, 2014).

Use of reading, just as defining generic expectations, did not serve to homogenize teacher candidates, but rather provided them advanced tools to create their own thinking and develop their own teaching identities. Academic writing provided the space in which to forge their teaching identities and ways of approaching professional problems and choices. The theses they produced were more thoughtful, individual, and distinctive than their work when they first arrived. One developed a complex view of the relationship of responsibility and motivation, while another developed a finely tuned understanding of student difficulties and challenges. They each became their own kind of teacher in this process, finding their own ways of thinking through the problems of creating a successful classroom.

Implications for Teaching

So what does this mean for where and how we teach writing and what kinds of programs we develop?

First, we can see all forms of writing as potentially creative, developing new meanings for students. Even as we introduce them to and give them practice in standardized forms, students need to see these as tools to express ideas they want to express, to explore new thoughts, to develop unique perspectives and messages. We should treat genre as an opportunity space for expression. The genres we assign provide invitations to express new contents, represented in new ways, and pieced together in new kinds of coherence – all to foster new thought and cognitive development. So in assigning students to write in various genres we should be mindful of which ones might produce the most appropriate challenges to advance student thinking in our courses. Also, in assisting students to write in each genre we should not only help them to adhere to the proper form but to build those thoughts that will accept the invitation of the genre and take advantage of the opportunity the genre provides to grow intellectually and expressively.

By providing pathways through disciplinary-influenced but developmentally appropriate genres, we can help students see that their unique thoughts and identities can be developed within rich and complex communities with already substantial knowledge. Of course, we must be careful not to overwhelm them with too difficult and extensive readings and knowledge, but we should not constrain their intellectual worlds. Rather, we should bring students from the very beginning of their higher education experience into dialog with the resources of those domains of knowledge that excite and engage them, with the engagement growing in depth and complexity as students progress in their studies, coming to understand and participate more fully in the worlds of their chosen disciplines. The intensity of engagement with literate communities of thought and knowledge is as important as the details of the area they engage in.

We should also provide tools for them to express deeper understanding of what they are reading, so that they can evaluate and discuss their responses, and can transform what they have read for their own purposes. These tools of intertextuality go from the simple textual practices of quotation, citation, and commenting structures to purposeful paraphrase, directed synthesis, and strategic rhetorical deployment within larger arguments. Typically, when students first are asked to make reference to other texts, they are likely only to use extensive quotations with cursory introductions and little discussion afterwards. In short, they hand the voice of their text over to the person they are quoting. As students learn the tools of integrating reference to others' ideas within the body of their own texts (by well-introduced paraphrase, summary, or simply by naming an idea, followed by a discussion of the importance of the referenced material for their own argument or analysis) students retain control of what the text is stating. Similarly, when students start needing to reference multiple texts, at first they may create disjunct pastiches jumping from the voice and argument of one author to those of another. Students need to learn the skills of showing the relationship of one author's ideas to another's, and then placing both authors' ideas within the students' own purposes and argument. Even if a text requires extensive quotations from multiple authors, the quotations should be selective and purposeful, and framed within a discussion showing why the readers need to pay attention to the quotations and what they have to do with each other and the larger purposes of the text. The writer then still remains in charge as the orchestrator of multiple voices.

Of course, as students advance from first-year general education to advanced studies in their chosen disciplines, the problem of which area of engagement to work with is solved, in a way. But students still need further development of their literacy skills to bring them into deeper engagement with their professional tasks and roles while working within the constraints of their disciplines: addressing more difficult readings, synthesizing larger amounts of information and varieties of texts, developing critical stances, deploying the resources of the fields for their own ends, and developing their own statements incorporating evidence they have gathered and resolving problems and projects of their choosing. These daunting tasks suggest that literacy support does not end with first year courses, and students would benefit from a continuous plan of literacy support from first year through graduation, and even in post graduate studies, as students must produce their dissertations, theses, and publishable research and other articles (for examples of how this has been pursued in various regions, see Bazerman, Little, Chavkin, Fouquette, Bethel, and Garufis, 2005; Castello and Donahue, 2012; Natale, 2012; Thaiss, Bräuer, Carlino, Ganobcsik-Williams, and Sinha, 2012).

For us as scholars the role of language in engaging with others, with the world, and with the world of knowledge is a theoretical research issue. For students it is the practical path they will follow as professionals and citizens in a knowledge, information society. Their life trajectories will enter ever more deeply into existing richly built symbolic environments which they need to learn to navigate, engage in, and help build further. Our role as teachers is to give them the tools and encourage the dispositions to head out on that exciting, creative journey.

References

Bawarshi, Anis and Reiff, Mary Jo (2010) *Genre: An Introduction to History, Theory, Research, and Pedagogy*. Fort Collins, Colorado: Parlor Press and WAC Clearinghouse. Available at http://wac.colostate.edu/books/bawarshi_reiff/.

Bazerman, Charles (1995) *Informed Writer* (5th edition). Boston: Houghton Mifflin. Available at http://wac.colostate.edu/books/informedwriter/.

Bazerman, Charles, Little, Joseph, Chavkin, Teri, Fouquette, Danielle, Bethel, Lisa and Garufis, Janet (2005) *Writing across the Curriculum*. Fort Collins, Colorado: Parlor Press and WAC Clearinghouse. 2005. Available at http://wac.colostate.edu/books/bazerman_wac/.

Bazerman, Charles, Simon, Kelly, Ewing, Patrick and Pieng, Patrick (forthcoming). Domain-specific cognitive development through writing tasks in a teacher education program. *Pragmatics and Cognition*.

Bazerman, Charles, Simon, Kelly and Pieng, Patrick (2014) Writing about reading to advance thinking: A study in situated cognitive development. In Pietro Boscolo and Perry Klein (eds.) *Writing as a Learning Activity* 249–276. Leiden: Brill.

Carroll, Lee Ann (2002) *Rehearsing New Roles: How College Students Develop as Writers*. Carbondale: Southern Illinois University Press. Available at http://wac.colostate.edu/books/rehearsing/.

Castelló, Montserrat and Donahue, Christiane (eds.) (2012) *University Writing: Selves and Texts in Academic Societies*. Bradford, U. K.: Emerald.

Herrington, Anne and Curtis, Marsha (2000) *Persons in Process: Four Stories of Writing and Personal Development in College*. Urbana, Illinois: National Council of Teachers of English.

Kelly, Greg and Bazerman, Charles (2003) How students argue scientific claims: A rhetorical-semantic analysis. *Applied Linguistics* 24(1): 28–55. http://dx.doi.org/qo.1093/applin/24.1.28.

Kelly, Greg, Bazerman, Charles, Skukauskaite, Audra and Prothero, William (2010) Rhetorical features of student science writing in intro-ductory university oceanography. In Charles Bazerman, Bob Krut, Karen

Lunsford, Susan McLeod, Suzie Null, Paul Rogers, and Amanda Stansell (eds.) *Traditions of Writing Research* 265–282. New York: Routledge.

Kelly, Greg and Takao, Allison (2002) Epistemic levels in argument: An analysis of university oceanography students' use of evidence in writing. *Science Education* 86: 314–342. http://dx.doi.org/10.1002/sce.10024.

Natale, Lucía (ed.) (2012) *En Carrera: Escritura y Lectura de Textos Académicos y Profesionales*. Los Polvorines, Buenos Aires: Universidad Nacional de General Sarmiento. Available at http://www.ungs.edu.ar/prodeac.

Paré, Anthony, Starke-Meyerring, Doreen and McAlpine, Linda (2009) The dissertation as multi-genre: Many readers, many readings. In Charles Bazerman, Adair Bonini and Débora Figueiredo (eds.) *Genre in a Changing World* 179–194. Fort Collins, Colorado: WAC Clearinghouse and Parlor Press. Available at http://wac.colostate.edu/books/genre/.

Sullivan, Patrick and Tinberg, Howard (eds.) (2006) *What is "College-Level" Writing?* Urbana, Illinois: National Council of Teachers of English. Available at http://wac.colostate.edu/books/collegelevel/.

Sullivan, Patrick, Tinberg, Howard and Blau, Sheridan (eds.) (2010) *What is "College-level" Writing?* Vol. 2. Urbana, Illinois: National Council of Teachers of English.

Swales, John (1990) *Genre Analysis: English in Academic and Research Settings*. Cambridge: Cambridge University Press.

Thaiss, Chris, Bräuer, Gerd, Carlino, Paula, Ganobcsik-Williams, Lisa and Sinha, Aparna (eds.) (2012) *Writing Programs Worldwide: Profiles of Academic Writing in Many Places*. Fort Collins, Colorado: WAC Clearinghouse and Parlor Press. Available at http://wac.colostate.edu/books/wpww.

Thaiss, Chris and Zawacki, Teresa (2006) *Engaged Writers and Dynamic Disciplines: Research on the Academic Writing Life*. Portsmouth, New Hampshire: Heinemann.

4   Writing Creativity and Discovery

Process and Pedagogy

Martha C. Pennington

Introduction

In this chapter, I explore commonalities as well as differences between creative writing and the kind of writing we think of as non-creative, and then draw implications for pedagogy related to writing of the second kind. I will especially have in mind the kind of writing taught in university classes – typically, academic essays or research papers. A central point is that creativity and discovery are at the heart of writing and, moreover, that discovery is part of the creative process. Other key points are that creativity and discovery are forces in all human beings and can be enhanced through teaching. These are important notions for education and specifically for writing pedagogy.

The discussion is divided into four parts: First, I briefly describe creativity in written language starting from a framework developed by Sky Marsen (Marsen, 2012). Then, I present some creative content in the form of a one-paragraph example of scholarly essay-type (expository or analytical) writing and describe some of the different kinds of creativity it exhibits. On the basis of this examination, I make some reflections on the nature of writing and compare literary writing that is normally classified as creative with academic writing. In the final section, I make observations and then suggestions regarding the teaching of writing that emerge from the earlier parts of the discussion.

Creativity in Writing

Every instance of language use draws on a speaker's or writer's resources for conventional and creative expression. Even highly conventionalized forms of linguistic expression, such as greetings and leave-takings, weather reports, resumes, and tallies of items bought from a store or restaurant, allow for novelty and choice in expression. At the same time, no form of writing is 100% creative, as the requirements of comprehension put limits on how original expression can be and still be understood by others. Creativity in writing is therefore not an all-or-nothing thing.

In the view of Sky Marsen:

> Creativity in written discourse can be traced when a text challenges genre conventions, and/or when it includes juxtapositions or contrasts between two different contexts or patterns, thereby producing surprising or unpredictable forms. Creativity can be viewed as a continuum, rather than as one side of a dichotomy, with more original combinations on one end (*high-level creativity*), and more conventional combinations on the other (*low-level creativity*). (Marsen, 2012: 210)

The contrast of creative and non-creative writing can thus be recognized as a false dichotomy, and creativity can be more properly represented by a cline, as shown in Figure 1. In considering creativity in writing within a university context, it is therefore instructive to take a broad view that looks beyond creative writing of a literary kind to include creative writing of an academic kind. Creativity is

Figure 1. Cline of Creativity in Writing

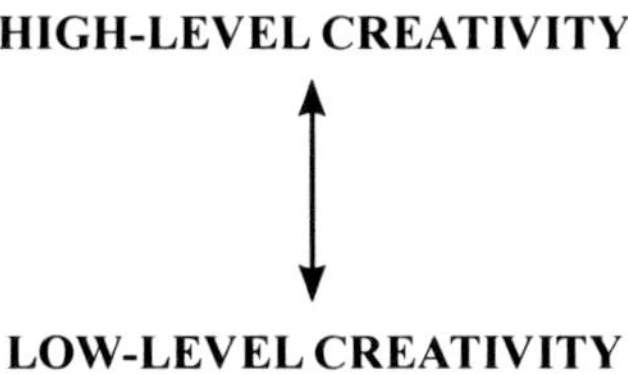

in fact a feature that can be found in academic writing of all types: while certain conventions must normally be obeyed, there is a margin – often considerable – for creative expression of ideas.

In writing, creativity is achieved in a number of ways. Both scholarly and other so-called "non-creative" writers make use of linguistic techniques which creative writers also apply. Marsen (2012) discovered four main strategies of creativity used by both creative writers and other writers. I summarize these as follows under my own headings:

> **Contextual Creativity:** *Associations between different domains*, through metaphor and analogy used for purposes of clarification and dramatization or highlighting, and through the juxtaposition of different registers for purposes of metalinguistic commentary;

> **Lexico-Semantic Creativity:** *Semantic deviations and surprising lexical choice* that point up contradictions between a word and its context, thus creating new meanings, in addition to neologisms, the creation of new words;

> **Syntactic Creativity:** *Syntactic deviations and unconventional sentence structures*; and

> **Narrative Creativity:** *Narrativization of agents and actions*, that is the casting of agents and actions in the frame of a story as a way to gain the reader's empathy and emotional investment and also to give abstract concepts "a concrete form and agency" (Marsen, 2012: 226).

A Text Illustrating Creativity in an Essay

A text which Marsen (2012: 225) uses to illustrate syntactic strategies of creativity, given below, can illustrate all four of these types of creativity. It is a paragraph taken from Donna Haraway's "Cyborg Manifesto" (Haraway, 1991), a nonfictional, scholarly feminist essay which uses the concept of the *cyborg*, "a hybrid of machine and organism" (Haraway, 1991: 149) to describe contemporary women's experience.[1]

> By the late twentieth century, our time, a mythic time, we are all chimeras, theorized and fabricated hybrids of machine and organism; in short, we are cyborgs. This cyborg is our ontology; it gives us our politics. The cyborg is a condensed image of both imagination and material reality, the two joined centers structuring any possibility of historical transformation. In the traditions of "Western" science and politics – the tradition of racist, male-dominant capitalism; the tradition of progress; the tradition of the appropriation of nature as resource for the productions of culture; the tradition of reproduction of the self from the reflections of the other – the relation between organism and machine has been a border war. (Haraway, 1991: 150)

Marsen characterizes syntactic deviation and unconventionality in this passage as consisting of a number of features, in particular, the fact that the information is not presented in a conventional structure of main and subordinate clauses. Instead, the author uses the devices of:

- Long, one-clause sentences of simple structure
- Repetitive parallelism
- Multiple semicolons
- Multiple phrases that carry much of the propositional content

My own analyses of the Haraway text complement these points about the syntactic deviations from the norm and unconventionality of the text noted by Marsen and make a number of additional points about the process of discovering and creating a new construction of ideas in language through writing.

Analysis 1 of Haraway Text: Phrase Structure

Although the sentence structure of the passage is simple in the sense that there are no subordinate clauses, the passage is highly complex in the structure of the noun phrases, which contain a large amount of information and abstract content. These can be seen as creative choices made by the author which introduce grammatical complexity at the phrase level. As has been discussed by Jay Lemke, Jim Martin, and Michael Halliday (e.g., Halliday, 1993; Halliday and Martin, 1993; Lemke, 1995), the packaging of information content in complex noun phrases is characteristic of the technologized and compacted discourse of the modern era, especially in academic writing.

A notable feature of the passage is that there are a number of multiple-component noun phrases (underlined below) that incorporate appositives (italicized) linked by commas to an initial noun phrase. The appositives add to or elaborate on the meaning of the initial noun phrase, as in the first instance, where the time referred to is first stated as "By the late twentieth century" and then the phrases "our time" and "a mythic time" expand the initial prepositional phrase. This use of complex noun phrases with appositives is a main strategy which the author uses to build up the meaning of the passage cumulatively, step by step.

> <u>By the late twentieth century, *our time, a mythic time,*</u> we are all <u>chimeras, *theorized and fabricated hybrids of machine and organism*</u>; in short, we are cyborgs. This cyborg is our ontology; it gives us our politics. The cyborg is a condensed image of <u>both imagination and material reality, *the two joined centers structuring any possibility of historical transformation*</u>. <u>In the traditions of "Western" science and politics – *the tradition of racist, male-dominant capitalism; the tradition of progress; the tradition of the appropriation of nature as resource for the productions of culture;*</u>

the tradition of reproduction of the self from the reflections of the other – the relation between organism and machine has been a border war.

The last instance is an especially complex noun phrase that is constructed as a series of noun phrase appositives attached to an initial noun phrase, "In the traditions of 'Western' science and politics." The four noun phrases which follow this initial one continue building the meaning of the passage by expanding on the traditions the author has in mind. The complex appositive made of these four phrases interrupts the main sentence structure, as shown by the dashes, and delays the main clause till the very end. In placing such a complex prepositional phrase before the main clause, the author creates an unconventional sentence structure in the service of evolving the meaning of the passage in a piece-by-piece, cumulative way.

Analysis 2 of Haraway Text: Verbs and Nouns

Also notable in this text is that the only verb that occurs in the entire passage, other than one instance of "gives" (boldface) is the verb "to be" (underlined), as shown below, where verbal elements not functioning as verbs are italicized.

By the late twentieth century, our time, a mythic time, we <u>are</u> all chimeras, *theorized* and *fabricated* hybrids of machine and organism; in short, we <u>are</u> cyborgs. This cyborg <u>is</u> our ontology; it **gives** us our politics. The cyborg <u>is</u> a *condensed* image of both imagination and material reality, the two *joined* centers *structuring* any possibility of historical transformation. In the traditions of "Western" science and politics – the tradition of racist, male-dominant capitalism; the tradition of progress; the tradition of the appropriation of nature as resource for the productions of culture; the tradition of reproduction of the self from the reflections of the other – the relation between organism and machine <u>has been</u> a border war.

This heavy use of the verb "to be" is consistent with the definitional purpose of the passage, which is to introduce and begin to explain the author's conception of the human cyborg. Also notable is the fact that all of the language not underlined or in boldface in the above analysis of the verbs in the text – which is most of the passage – falls into the category of noun phrases, meaning that the proportion of nominal to verbal units is extremely high. This *nominalized* form of text is suitable in a passage like this one, which is not about actions or events, but is rather about ideas – concepts and information – as is typical for much academic writing. An accepted norm for academic writing is very reduced originality and information in verbs, with the simple present tense of the verb "to be" dominating, matched with high information-content and complexity in nouns, with noun phrases dominating (Halliday, 1993; Halliday and Martin, 1993; Lemke, 1995). Other verbal elements of the sentence (italicized) function not as verbs but as adjectives within the dominant grammatical structure of complex noun phrases.

Analysis 3 of Haraway Text: Repetition

The cumulative force of repetition is a linguistic device used by Haraway to gradually build up and link different parts of her idea:

...our time, a mythic time,

we are all chimeras...; in short, we are cyborgs....

...cyborgs. This cyborg is our ontology; it gives us our politics. The cyborg is a condensed image...

In the traditions of... – the tradition of racist, male-dominant capitalism; the tradition of progress; the tradition of the appropriation of nature...; the tradition of reproduction of the self...

The repeated words help to link new information to old, or *given*, information. Thus, the concept of "our time" is introduced and then expanded by the new notion that the "time" is "mythic"; the idea that "we are all chimeras" is introduced and then revised to a new idea of what "we are": "in short, we are cyborgs." The now given notion of "cyborg" is further developed in the equative sentences that follow with the repeated phrase "cyborg is." The new notion of "the traditions of 'Western' science and politics" is introduced and then elaborated in a series of phrases which repeat the given noun "tradition" to list the traditions the author includes as those of "'Western' science and politics." In this way, the different parts of the author's idea are laid out for the reader in an evolving structure of meaning, via a syntactic construction that makes heavy use of noun phrases and repetition to help the reader gradually discover that idea as the author unfolds it in language – in words and sentences.

Analysis 4 of Haraway Text: Other Forms of Creativity

Beyond its syntactic features (which are the only type of unconventional or creative element discussed by Marsen), the Haraway text illustrates an academic application of *contextual creativity*. This can be seen in Haraway's placement of the cyborg, equated to us, within a historical, philosophical, cultural, and ideological discussion about technology, capitalism, race, gender, "Western" science, and politics. The author's grand creative construction is capped by the metaphor of the "border war between organism and machine" at the end of the passage, an example of *lexico-semantic creativity*, a strategy which is also evident in the text in the description of all of us as "chimeras, theorized and fabricated hybrids of machine and organism" – a surprising and original application of the word, "chimera." This phrase exemplifies contextual creativity as well, in the dramatization and highlighting of our late twentieth century condition through the metaphorical comparison or reconceptualization, and the implied reduction, of human beings (and specifically, women) to chimeras.

Using the word "cyborg" to apply to human beings is thus both lexically creative and dramatic in all of the meaning potential – through both popular and technical usage and associations – that comes with using this word; and it is part of Haraway's creativity that the reader is not quite sure whether it is meant as a metaphor or rather meant to capture a more literal or essential sense in which humans (and specifically, women) have become cyborgian. Whichever way it is taken to apply, Haraway has in effect *made it so* by *stating it to be so*, creating a discourse context in which it is true, one in which this new cyborg exists: By creating and explaining it, she presents her discovery to others and brings them into the process of learning about it and evaluating it.

There is *narrative creativity* here too, in the casting of the discussion in a story frame, set in a specific time, the late twentieth century, and also "a mythic time," casting the cyborg as a character that has entered the human story and become us. In this way, Haraway has made the cyborg relatable and has stimulated readers' story schema, thus engaging anticipatory schemas for interpretation and increasing their investment in the reading comprehension process. The author has created a discourse context which pulls the reader into her world – both the imaginary, intellectual world of this written text and the world behind that world, which is that of the author's *mind*.

Lessons from Haraway Text

This one illustrative essay text gives a sense of how creativity in academic writing can be achieved, using linguistic techniques that overlap those used in what normally goes by the name of *creative writing*. The Haraway text is a good example of the different kinds of creativity, in the four types described above, that occur in academic writing, as the writer stretches imaginatively and rhetorically to represent a new insight – that is, a *discovery* which she has made – in a novel and insightful way. A high degree of originality in ideas compels a writer to use a range of linguistic resources to express those ideas in a way that a reader can understand, including creation of novel linguistic modes of expression built on conventional ones.

To make this passage work, that is, to make it understandable and also acceptable within the scholarly essay genre, the author has to start from a base of conventionality that she then embellishes in novel ways. Some of her creativity is in fact her specific interplay of original or novel expression and nonoriginal or ordinary expression – such as her lexically and contextually creative uses of "chimera," "cyborg," and "border war" defined by means of the entirely ordinary and lexically simple verb "to be" – and of complexity and simplicity – such as her use of complex noun phrases within grammatically simple equative constructions. Creation of a simple grammatical structure of sentences within which to present novel ideas takes considerable linguistic skill. In many forms of writing, simple sentence structures can be quite elegant and difficult to produce, as in the novels of Ernest Hemingway and in much poetry. As Steve Jobs once remarked in an interview:

> Simple can be harder than complex: You have to work hard to get your thinking clean to make it simple. But it's worth it in the end because once you get there, you can move mountains. (Back to the future at Apple, 1998)

My analyses show how Haraway, using various forms of syntactic, lexico-semantic, contextual, and narrative creativity, is able to bring her insight about our late twentieth century selves *into being*, that is, *to discover it* (conceptually)*and create it* (semantically and syntactically) *in words*. It also shows how, through these uses of language, she is able to *bring her discovery of this insight to others* in a way that will help them understand it and see it as she does. Thus, both the writer and the reader of the text participate in discovery of meaning and ideas.

A point to emphasize is that the author's degree of creative, discovery-oriented expression through skilled use of language is an essential part of the process of this new idea being born and taking shape. While Haraway may have had her idea of the cyborg before writing about it, the detail of the idea is embodied in the semantic and syntactic construction which she built in the specific words selected and sentences made from these. It can therefore be said that while the conceptual foundation of the idea may be independent of language, the details of its construction are built through language. And, as often as not, the actual idea for a text does not exist prior to writing about it. This is because the building of the conceptual structure is facilitated by the building of the linguistic structure. Many ideas do not exist until they are constructed linguistically, as semantic structure bridges between conceptual and syntactic structure. Thus, ideas and language are to a greater or lesser extent co-constructed through the writing process, so that the creativity and discovery of the *idea* is bound up with its creative and discovery-oriented expression *in words*. This is a two-way street:

Figure 2. The Process of Creation and Discovery in Writing: A 2-Way Street

CREATING + DISCOVERING ⟷ **CREATIVE + DISCOVERY-ORIENTED**
AN IDEA **EXPRESSION OF THE IDEA IN WORDS**

It is also a two-way street in another sense. Because of its realization in language, in *words*, this is a creation-and-discovery process in which not just the writer but also others who read the author's words participate. The language in which this insight about cyborgs is written requires active participation by a reader to unpack and comprehend all of the different aspects of the meaning. The way the passage is written – using a narrative structure at the beginning; introducing new ideas dramatically through surprising use of words; connecting to other known areas of content; and building meaning cumulatively through apposition, repetition, and linkage of given and new information – draws the reader into an interpretational process of re-experiencing the writer's own creation-and-discovery process of her original idea and the language in which that idea, in all its complexity, could be expressed. When an author writes on this level, the reader can experience some of the thrill which the author must have experienced in first discovering/ creating this idea and expressing it precisely as intended.

I now move to some reflections about creativity in writing that build on this illustrative example.

Reflections on Creativity in Nominally Creative and Non-Creative Writing

Creativity in Writing Reflection 1: Balance of Novelty and Convention

We can first reflect that skilled writers know how to create a linguistic construction of ideas that creatively diverges from the norm, while still linking to linguistic and genre conventions to a greater or lesser extent. In so doing, they highlight their own skill and uniqueness as thinkers and writers. Humans need to operate within conventional categories and structures in their behavior. That is our common culture. At the same time, humans are a creative species. As I have pointed out elsewhere (Pennington, 2001a: 13), our primate cousins, the apes and monkeys, can imitate very well. Unlike, for instance, chimps or orangutans, humans have a certain drive to make changes when imitating – to embellish, to modify, to personalize – in other words, not merely to imitate or copy, but to show our individuality.

Creativity in Writing Reflection 2: Creativity to Differing Degrees

A second reflection is that the difference between creative writing and so-called non-creative writing is generally one of degree, the degree of stretch in use of creative means of language and other media. The degree of stretch, the novelty or unconventionality, of a text is influenced by the writer's intention and purpose, including the genre which the writer is aiming the work for. While some writers (e.g. those writing instruction manuals or lab reports) must follow genre conventions closely, "creative writers [are able to] stretch structure and language to maximize originality and to remake the genres in which they work" (Pennington, 2012: 152). Such "creative stretching" and remaking of genres can be noted especially nowadays in hypermedia and computer-animated works which juxtapose not only many different types of writing, but also many different types of media and media contexts (for examples, see Bolden, 2012; Strickland and Coverley, 2012). An especially novel element of many digital texts is their interactive nature, which allows and indeed encourages readers to rework them as new texts, producing new types of collaborative authorship.

With this range of adherence to specific genre conventions in mind, we can posit, alongside a continuum of creativity, a continuum of genre requirements or conventionality for different kinds of writing (Figure 3). At one end of this generic continuum are types of writing such as instruction manuals, which, because of their strong utilitarian purpose of presenting a procedure which can be easily understood and followed, must adhere to genre conventions in structure and language. In contrast, many kinds of academic and essay writing, in addition to forms of creative writing, have allowable leeway in terms of straying from standard generic structures and language in order to achieve uniqueness within convention.

Figure 3. Cline of Genre Requirements for Writing

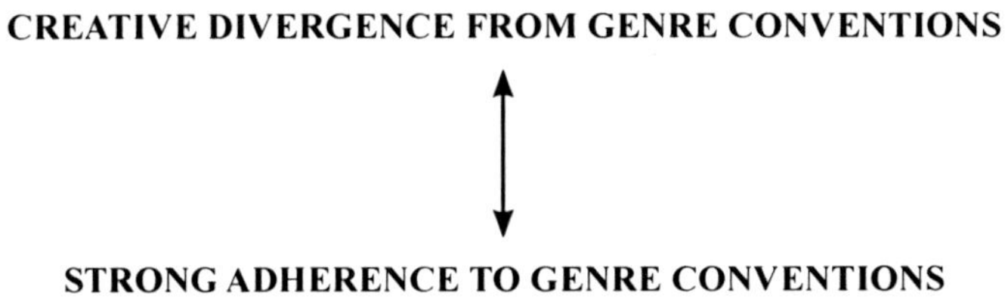

Creativity in Writing Reflection 3: Specific Types of Creativity

What is considered creative and what is acceptably creative in terms of degree and type of creativity varies by field and genre. For example, poetry typically does not make use of highly complex grammar or lexis (e.g. clause structures with multiple levels or types of subordination or embedding, nominalizations made up of a long series of nouns[2]) but otherwise encourages high creativity (in the sense of novelty) in grammar and lexis. As noted by Lillis (2013: 65), literary writing aims "to use and craft language in interesting and novel ('deviant') ways." Academic writing, on the other hand, allows high complexity in sentence structure and lexis but has a lower tolerance for high creativity or novelty in grammar (e.g. incomplete or unconventionally ordered sentences) and lexis (e.g. undefined new words). Creativity in academic writing, although it may employ the same range of techniques, puts stricter limits than creative writing on use of those techniques – limits which vary from discipline to discipline.

Creativity in academic writing, like poetry and fiction, commonly involves contextual creativity. Often, what makes a poem interpretable is the context that is attached to, or instantiated, by it. Similarly, in academic writing the assumed and/or instantiated context is often crucial to its interpretation. Fiction can have highly conventionalized sentence structure and language; the creativity in fiction often comes not from unusual sentence structure or lexis but from the creation of unusual narrative structure, characters, and/ or the imaginative context, as a type of contextual creativity. Note that the feature of contextual creativity aligns academic writing in terms of one of its characteristic creative strategies with fiction and poetry – though, again, there is likely to be a difference in degree if not in kind between contextual creativity in academic writing versus what is normally termed creative writing.

Creativity in Writing Reflection 4: The Thrill of Creativity and Discovery

A fourth reflection is that skilled writers use writing as a thinking and languaging process to discover new ideas (thinking) and to create them in words (languaging). Writing is a manifestation of the human drive to learn and to explore, to discover things through personal experience. This drive to learn and explore is the whole basis for building our brain structure, our intelligence, and, as part of that, our language structure.[3] All writers know the thrill of discovery when an idea comes together as something created through the writer's mind and fingertips (Pennington, 2001b) in the writing process. Of course, the ideas do not just come together out of nowhere, nor does their expression emerge from just thinking hard or thinking hard with a pen in hand or a keyboard at the fingertips.

All writing is first, a search or research process, to differing degrees *external* – what we would normally think of as research – and *internal* – searching through the writer's own store of experiences and the language connected to those experiences in memory. Writing is then the representation of that search or research process on the page – or, perhaps more likely these days, on the screen. All writing is furthermore an expression of the author's identity (Ivanič, 1998), a "performance of the self on the page" or screen (Pennington, 2012: 155). It is the presentation of the writer's vision, the writer's perception or way of seeing things, and the writer's way of saying things. Writing draws on all of the experiences and pieces of language stored in the writer's long-term memory banks and mixes and matches those in working memory, often remixing and realigning those pieces of memory as new thoughts and language, during the writing process. Without time to collect and process thoughts and language, students cannot learn to write and will never "know the sheer joy of writing for discovery and self-expression" (Pennington, 2012: 155). The process of inquiry that leads to new discoveries and understandings fuels the writing process, creating a desire to put those new discoveries and understandings into words – the writer's own unique expression. As Crank (2014) observes, the process of inquiry is as much a driving force in writing as it is in science.

Part of what it means to think like a writer is to sustain an *inquiry* mindset: to understand a situation or problem from many angles, to pose responses and solutions, and to test those solutions by writing about them; in other words, to use writing to explore *answers*, *insights*, *solutions*, and/or *reflections*. The problem may look different in an English class than in a science class, but the process of inquiry is as crucial to the epistemology of writing as to the sciences.

Pedagogical Reflections and Suggestions

Now I move to the pedagogical discussion, first making some reflections on students as writers and how they are being taught to write.

Pedagogical Reflection 1: Good Ideas – More Than Half the Battle

Teachers often say that when students do not write well, the reason is that they do not have sufficient knowledge of vocabulary, grammar, and written genres. In other words, it is commonly said that without a good store of language experiences, of words and expressions in memory, students have reduced resources for the creative discovery process that is writing. While this is no doubt true, I remind you that Hemingway wrote in simple sentences, and Haraway used no subordinate clauses and hardly any verbs other than "to be" in the illustrative passage. In fact, much of what makes her writing special is the novelty of the cyborgian idea and her connection of this idea to other ideas and areas of knowledge. Getting a *good idea* is more than half of the battle of what students need as a basis for good writing. If they have a good idea, one that they really want to express, they will stretch for the language in which to express it. However, if they have no good idea, their writing will be dull and lifeless as a reflection of the fact that they have nothing worthwhile to say.

Writing pedagogy does not always help student writers find a good idea, that is, something original and interesting to write about. Rather than focusing on ideas, writing pedagogy often focuses on written structure, such as in many genre-based or ESP-oriented writing texts or courses. Materials and courses which focus students' attention on structure limits their writing process and options and may discourage them from creatively adapting or diverging from the generic structures which are taught. In a pedagogical focus on the structure of texts, students can easily get the idea that academic writing is essentially about building textual structures of a relatively simple kind rather than about building a complex construction of ideas. In a pedagogy that privileges structure over content, students can be misled into believing that following the generic structures they are taught will result in good writing.[4] However, writing to genre templates results in formulaic writing which, in being low in creativity, is at best conventional or standard – and therefore mediocre – writing.

Although academic writing is very essentially a process of discovery (Richardson, 1997: 93) and invention, as David Bartholomae warned about learning, student writing in the university often "becomes more a matter of imitation or parody than a matter of invention and discovery" (Bartholomae, 2005: 67). Instruction which encourages imitation and reproduction rather than creativity and discovery teaches far less than it might otherwise. We who are writing pedagogues and writers ourselves need to guard against students' writing being a mere shadow of the writing which we ourselves engage in and produce – or worse, a kind of false *writing product*, in the sense of not being anything the student has personally experienced or discovered and wants to express, or a false *writing process*, in the sense of just going through the motions to complete an assignment for a grade.

Pedagogical Reflection 2: Student Writers' Non-Engagement

Students who write in the false way described above are simply not involved enough, not self-invested or engaged enough, in the *thinking-and-languaging* writing process that produces the authentic insights of creative discovery and expression seen in Haraway's piece. What I would call *real writing* – meaning writing in which the writer has personal involvement and investment in ideas and expression – is distant from them. Their own writing in contrast is nothing joyful or exhilarating, nothing through which they can express their skill and uniqueness as thinkers, as writers, as human beings.

Pedagogical Reflection 3: Students as Pseudo-Writers

As they write in an inauthentic and detached manner, student writers become like stick-figure puppet writers engaged in a shadow play, rather than real, flesh-and-blood writers sweating the writing process, digging into their deepest thoughts and pushing themselves to the limits of what they can know, understand, and express. They are pseudo-writers engaged in pseudo-writing, that is, seemingly writing but actually just compiling and then piecing together scraps of text from here and there. Or these student shadow-writers, rather than making a cut-and-paste whole from their compiled scrapheap of ideas, take out a ready-meal of an essay, more or less what everyone else is eating and has eaten before, or a desiccated version of this ready-meal – just add water – and present it as if it were a home-cooked meal created from their own recipe. They are, in truth, as much non-writers as writers, as they perform this sort of shadow-puppet writing which locates them forever outside the real community of writers and which banishes them to stay forever at best in the shallows of literacy. They will therefore never swim in what might be called – by analogy to Sven Birkert's notion, in The *Gutenberg Elegies: The Fate of Reading in an Electronic Age* (Birkerts, 1994), of "deep reading" – *deep writing*, the companion piece making up what could be termed *deep literacy*.

Pedagogical Reflection 4: Negative Effects of Writing Instruction

Standard genre or ESP approaches to writing pedagogy are often counterproductive, producing humdrum, shallow, highly derivative writing, and having other long-term seriously negative effects, as students approach writing with dread and fear, as they feel detached from the world of writing and from their own writing. While there are some very good writing courses and teachers, students commonly say that the way they are taught writing makes them hate writing,[5] and also makes them ready to take any kind of shortcut that is on offer – cutting and pasting from Wikipedia and other websites, plagiarizing entire papers available on the Internet, and motivating themselves by the nervous energy gained from waiting till the very last minute to write a paper or by taking artificial stimulants to push through in an all-nighter.

Pedagogical Reflection 5: Lack of Attention to Creativity and Discovery- Enhancing Behaviors

It is known (see e.g. Reisman, 2012) that flexible endpoints and open-endedness, not set assignments, foster creativity and discovery, as do relaxed and tolerant environments, not test-driven ones. These offer mental space for creative play and "flow" experiences (Csikszentmihalyi, 1990, 1996) – when a person is highly engaged cognitively and loses track of time and place – that help to develop a creative and discovery-oriented writing mindset. This is a mindset which "seeks out novelty and enjoys playing with language and ideas" (Pennington, 2012: 155), "which resists premature closure [in seeking shortcuts and quick solutions to problems] and is comfortable remaining in an indeterminate and fluid state for long periods of time" (pp. 154–155), and "which has a high tolerance for ambiguity and risk" (p. 154). Yet how often is teaching done with such creativity- and discovery-enhancing goals in mind? Most of the writing we assign our students is done outside of class and for graded set assignments that do not necessarily encourage them to write with any sense of pleasure, flow, relaxation, or play.

The current creative education movement offers learnable strategies that can be taught for enhancing the student writer's creative and discovery-oriented mindset (see Reisman, 2012, for a review of creativity education and testing, along with a range of suggested creativity-enhancing techniques) at both initial and middle stages of writing, along with other learnable strategies to enhance self-discovery and originality of expression that draw on those used by creative and scholarly writers. By centering instruction on motivating and enhancing students' creative and discovery-oriented expression and behaviors as writers, teachers can not only raise the bar for the writing students produce but also tackle such perennial problems as student motivation and plagiarism as a form of non-invested, false or pseudo-writing.

Pedagogical Recommendations

If students dread, fear, hate, feel detached from, and shortcut writing, writing pedagogy needs to tackle these problems head-on, by making them feel excitement, joy, love, and engagement with writing so they would not want to shortcut the process, so they feel possessive and proud of their own work and would never give it up for other people's words. Let's look at some pedagogical recommendations for making this happen.

Pedagogical Recommendation 1: Research Internally before Externally

An important first step involves motivating the writing process and getting sufficient buy-in and attachment to a topic to drive the whole process from beginning to end, and to make it truly a process of discovery. To help make this happen, instead of sending students out to do research on a topic as the first step, if they have a certain writing assignment or topic they will have to write on, the teacher can help start the students' writing process by having them reflect, especially in written form, on what they already know or don't know about the topic. If they start every writing assignment by writing down their own starting thoughts on a topic, they develop a commitment to those thoughts and are much less likely to write a paper that is made up of other people's thoughts, such as available in Wikipedia or any other sources they consult before thinking about their own ideas and experiences connected to the topic. If students start with Wikipedia or the Internet, their strong tendency is just to use what they find there to "patch-write" (Howard, 1993) a paper, following nothing like any kind of real research and writing process.

Of everything I have ever tried to help students really commit to and engage in their own writing, this one simple step of having them do *internal research* before *external research* seems to be the most important one. This means exploring in class, through discussion with other students and especially through a quick-write of 25–30 minutes, their own thoughts on a topic before they do any external research on it. In the best case, students turn in these initial reflections for comments and suggestions from the teacher that pick up on whatever they have written about their interests, personal experiences, or questions related to the topic before they do any external research.[6] It is simply astonishing how big a difference it makes to the writing process and the final outcome if students start a topic through internal research, by clarifying, especially in written form, their own connections to the topic *before* going to outside sources. If students have to write a final essay for any course, I have them do an in-class quick-write on the essay topic at the end of the very first lecture and then give them feedback on those quick-writes. I spend time in class later for them to review these when they are getting ready to do the final essay.

Pedagogical Recommendation 2: Make Creativity a Priority in Grading

A second thing I have done that has produced real effects in students' writing is to make creativity and personal discovery a priority in writing. This means talking about it, stressing it, and modeling it. To make creativity tangible for the students, they should be given a higher grade on a paper if they show creativity – especially in the overall idea of the paper but also in use of language – or if they show that they have discovered something original through their process of writing, searching, and researching. The teacher can stress to students that writing should be a discovery process, that is, a process of discovering something original which is worth sharing with others. The teacher can then talk about the writing of a paper as taking the reader on a journey of discovery, too, by giving necessary background, definitions, and examples that lead the reader step by step to a full understanding of the writer's idea. Such a concept can motivate the structure of a paper, as the student considers the reader's starting point and what s/he needs to do to (1) attract the reader, (2) provide necessary background, and (3) lead the reader step by step into and through all of the different facets of the writer's ideas.

Pedagogical Recommendation 3: Set up Facilitating Conditions for Creativity and Discovery

As a general point about the writing class, the teacher needs to set up conditions for creativity and discovery to occur, such as by:

- encouraging flow experiences, giving students time to let their minds wander and wonder by writing in class;

- showing flexibility and open-endedness in writing assignments, such as not having to turn in or get a grade on every assignment;
- taking a writing workshop approach in which students help each other with finding and narrowing topics, read each other's work, and offer feedback;
- encouraging and modeling reflection, such as on a reading or an issue considered outside of class, or after discussion of a reading or an issue in class.

Pedagogical Recommendation 4: Use Activities that Encourage a Creativity and Discovery-Oriented Mindset

The teacher can use class time to help students develop a creative and discovery-oriented writing mindset. Other than in-class brainstorming on a topic, helpful activities for this purpose are contests in which students working in small groups try to create/discover:

- *The most different ideas on a topic* in terms of quantity and quality (the highest number of different ideas, the highest quality of ideas, the most creative or unusual ideas);
- *The most original connection to a topic from some other context*;
- *The most different pro and con ideas* (two lists) *on an issue* in terms of quantity and quality and then a further contest to come up with as many possible compromise positions as they can, also judged in terms of both the quality and quantity of ideas as above;
- *The most creative elaborations or developments* (in terms of quantity and quality) *of a simple statement or paragraph.*

These kinds of activities encourage students to seek out novel ideas and language, to go for unusual ("risky") rather than ordinary ("safe") options, and to be creative in connecting ideas from different domains and in putting their own personal stamp on a topic. In encouraging them to stretch in these ways and to make continuing efforts to build up their lists and responses rather than closing off options early on, such activities around topic selection help to engender a creative, discovery-oriented mindset while also modeling how one topic can be approached from a great variety of angles.

Pedagogical Recommendation 5: Teach Specific Strategies for Thinking Creatively and Discovering New Insights

There is much that can be taught which is helpful for being able to think creatively and discover new insights. A variety of suggested activities that can be done by students working alone or in pairs or groups are given below.

(1) *Comparison/contrast:* make two separate lists, one of comparisons and one of contrasts, between two very similar or very different things, people, or places;
(2) *Argue the counterposition:* argue the opposite of what you or most people think;
(3) *Extremes:* argue extreme positions on an issue;
(4) *Connect to personal experience:* make a connection of personal experience, values, and beliefs to a topic;
(5) *Connect to a different domain:* use analogy and metaphor to link to a different domain of knowledge or reference;
(6) *Hypothetical:* use *if*-statements to stimulate creative thinking and discovery of new ideas;
(7) *Fantasy* – create *what-if* scenarios as a way to exercise imagination.

Pedagogical Recommendation 6: Teach Specific Strategies for Writing Creatively and Expressing New Insights

There is much that can be taught which is helpful for being able to write creatively and express new insights. A variety of suggested activities that can be done by students working alone or in pairs or groups are given below.

- Use *personal knowledge/experience/viewpoint* to introduce or conclude an essay, or as an example within the body of an essay;
- *Word associations:* synonyms, antonyms, associated adjectives, contextual associations, etc.;
- *Adaptation:* Start from a writing model and change aspects of it;
- *Expansion (Focus on structure of sentences, paragraphs, genres):*
  Expand headlines to sentences, then to whole stories;
  Expand a word or phrase to a sentence.
- *Condensation (Focus on lexical expression – words and phrases):*
  Condense a story or essay to a paragraph or a sentence;
  Condense a sentence to a word or phrase.
- *Creative Expression*
  Recreate a sentence as a line of poetry or a metaphor;
  Recreate a paragraph as a stanza of poetry.
- *Academic Expression*
  Recreate a line or stanza of poetry as a sentence;
  Recreate a line or stanza of poetry as a paragraph.
- *Different genres*
  Write about academic topics in creative genres, such as humor, poetry, a story, or a play.
- *Give examples and practice on creative writing techniques described by Marsen or others*; Marsen's (2012) article and her book, *Seriously Creative Writing* (Marsen, forthcoming) provide many examples of creative strategies used in academic or essay writing.

All of these are likely to be new and challenging for student writers, and may be especially so for second-language writers. They are however equally valuable for all novice writers, not only for getting students to stretch beyond the confining requirements of the writing tasks they are usually assigned but also for allowing them to do creative and unusual types of tasks that can increase their interest in writing as well as English language.

Pedagogical Recommendation 7: Help Students Analyze Difficult Texts

Finally, I think we have to face up to the fact that all university students – and secondary students as well – need to grapple with difficult texts, as much as they don't want to. I'm talking Plato, Aristotle, Shakespeare, even Joyce and Pound, and the equivalent tough, deeply meaningful texts in their own fields of study. They need to read and unpack texts like the one by Haraway that I partially unpacked for you; they need many more examples and help understanding texts like this and how they are put together linguistically. All students, both first-language and second-language learners, will need considerable help and guidance in doing this – the equivalent stretching in their reading that will ultimately help them to stretch in their writing.

Students are typically amazed at how relevant Plato and Aristotle are still today, and they often love Shakespeare once they are guided to understand his works, and especially if they can see them performed – which they easily can on the Internet and in DVD versions of the plays. Unpacking Joyce and Pound, or a text like Haraway's, while not for most people as affectively engaging as a Shakespeare play, can be an intellectually stimulating exercise. I have also used well-known satires like Jonathan Swift's "A Modest Proposal" (Swift, 1729) and Douglas R. Hofstadter's "A Person Paper on Purity in Language" (Hofstadter, 1985), in addition to Woody Allen stories (e.g. Allen, 2007) – all of which can be very challenging but also stimulating in their lexico-semantic and contextual creativity as well as their humor, and so worth the effort to analyze. As in the case of the other classic works mentioned above, once students "crack the code" of these challenging texts, they feel a great sense of achievement and discovery, as they begin to realize the kind of creative and discovery-oriented processes that underlie good writing.

Conclusion

This discussion has reinforced the notions that (1) creativity is an aspect of academic writing; (2) creativity and discovery are central to an authentic writing process; and (3) both creativity and discovery in writing can be enhanced through teaching. These are important notions for education, and specifically for writing pedagogy. By leading students in a direction that is centered squarely on motivating and enhancing their creative discovery and expression, writing teachers can turn their writing classes around, and help students turn a corner and head down a road of a lifetime of pleasure that can be obtained inside every person, as a writer. What I am advocating is a pedagogy which aims to bring students in from the margins of writing practices to make them more central members of the community of writers, so they might experience first-hand the power of the written language to create and explore ideas. Such a pedagogy can be seen as one which situates writing within a wider view of literacy as a personal journey of discovery through reading and writing (Pennington, forthcoming).

Notes

1   As Haraway (1991: 149) states: "The cyborg is a matter of fiction and lived experience that changes what counts as women's experience in the late 20th century." This quote and the illustrative passage used here are from the revised version of the original 1985 essay later published as a chapter in Haraway's 1991 book, *Simians, Cyborgs and Women: The Reinvention of Nature*.
2   English has an extensive group of compound words made up of two nouns in which the first noun serves an adjectival function of modifying the second one. Examples are *grocery store, computer program, wine*

bottle, paint brush, ice tray. The serial (or "stacked") noun construction with modification of a later noun by an earlier one is in fact a highly productive construction in English that can be used to make a series or stack of up to at least eight nouns in a complex nominalization. The complex is characterized by progressive and cumulative modification such that the first noun modifies the second one and then the combination of the first and second noun modifies the third noun, and so on. An example is:

elevator manufacturing (*elevator* modifies *manufacturing*)

elevator manufacturing convention (*elevator manufacturing* modifies *convention*)

elevator manufacturing convention hotel (*elevator manufacturing convention* modifies *hotel*)

elevator manufacturing convention hotel site (*elevator manufacturing convention hotel* modifies *site*)

elevator manufacturing convention hotel site construction (*elevator manufacturing convention hotel site* modifies *construction*)

elevator manufacturing convention hotel site construction equipment (*elevator manufacturing convention hotel site construction* modifies *equipment*)

elevator manufacturing convention hotel site construction equipment breakdown (*elevator manufacturing convention hotel site construction equipment* modifies *breakdown*)

Such serial nouns are common in academic discourse but rare in poetry other than two- or three-word combinations.

3   This is my own conclusion from years of studying and teaching linguistics and psychology of language. Support for this conclusion can be found in a summative video and links to research reports, working papers, and brief summaries of scientific research on the website for the Center on the Developing Child (2013). For more in-depth discussion, see Ellis (1998; 2011).

4   While I believe that learning about the kinds of generic structures and language that are associated with different purposes and disciplines is valuable and I try to incorporate this kind of knowledge into teaching writing to my students, I maintain that the simplified genres that are usually taught as a genre or ESP approach to composition can do as much harm as good. These approaches tend to define genres in a narrow or circular way so that a text will not be recognized as belonging to a specific genre or will be evaluated negatively, as not a good exemplar

of the genre, unless it has certain accepted characteristics or structure (Lillis, 2013: 163). Conventional genre or ESP models give a false idea of the extent to which specific structures and language apply in specific fields or types of writing and of the allowable flexibility to diverge from those models. In fact, most writing (other than in made-to-order pedagogical readings and writing exercises) is not describable in terms of one type of structure or language but more typically in terms of less easily classifiable hybrid structures or meshed strategies and purposes. The reason is that the driving force of most writing, rather than seeking to insert content into a predetermined structure, is to create a structure in and around the content as that evolves through the writing process. Genre-based approaches to teaching writing can therefore stifle students' initiative to explore and evolve ideas. Turvey (2007) makes a similar point in noting that the focus on form that characterizes a genre approach usually entails a lack of focus on student writers' ideas. It is probably more realistic, given students' stronger conceptual and oral skills than their written skills, to start with ideas developed and expressed in spoken language and then help them to translate (though not literally) those into written form.

5   For several years in which I taught basic writing classes containing few if any students whose major subject was English or writing, I surveyed the students on their attitudes towards writing on the first day of class. The result was always that the majority of students (in every case more than 80%) taking required writing classes had low confidence as writers, very negative attitudes to writing, and low motivation to write going into the course. I did the survey as a jumping-off point for selling the students on my course and the innovative instructional approaches they would experience in it, which were designed to help them find their voice as writers, teach them usable strategies for writing, and so build their confidence and motivation to write. The pedagogical strategies outlined here are ones I used in those classes, and they were effective in changing most students' views of writing and themselves as writers from negative to positive, as judged by their reported end-of-course attitudes. Those interested in knowing more may wish to consult a writing course that I developed with Theresa M. Welford, *Welcome to My World* (Pennington and Welford, forthcoming), which includes examples of students' writing and their reflections on their writing, and a forthcoming paper on creative approaches to the teaching of writing (Pennington, forthcoming).

6   Sonya Huber's university writing course (Huber, 2011) is built around the idea that research and writing should always start from questions arising from the writers' own life and experience.

References

Allen, Woody (2007) *The Insanity Defense: The Complete Prose*. New York: Random House.

Back to the future at Apple (1998) *Businessweek*. Information Technology: Computers. May 24, 1998. Retrieved on 1 June 2013 at http://www.businessweek.com/stories/1998-05-24/back-to-the-future-at-apple.

Bartholomae, David (2005/1985) Inventing the university. *Writing on the Margins: Essays on Composition and Teaching* 60–85. Boston: Bedford/St. Martin's. First appeared in Mike Rose (ed.) *When a Writer Can't Write: Studies in Writer's Block and Other Composing Processes* 134–166. New York: The Guildford Press.

Birkerts, Sven (1994) *The Gutenberg Elegies: The Fate of Reading in an Electronic Age*. Boston: Faber and Faber.

Bolden, Emma (2012) Permanent evolution: E-Literature and (r)evolutions of authorship and readership. *Writing & Pedagogy* 4(2): 345–354. http://dx.doi.org/10.1558/wap.v4i2.337.

Center on the Developing Child (2013) 1. Experiences build brain architecture. Harvard University. Retrieved on 22 August 2013 from http://developingchild.harvard.edu/index.php?cID=428.

Crank, Virginia (2014) Thinking like a writer: Inquiry, genre, and revision. *Writing & Pedagogy* 6(1): 89–105. http://dx.doi.org/10.1558/wap.v6i1.89.

Csikszentmihalyi, Mihalyi (1990) *Flow: The Psychology of Optimal Experience*. New York: Harper and Row.

Csikszentmihalyi, Mihalyi (1996) *Creativity: Flow and the Psychology of Discovery and Invention*. New York: Harper Perennial.

Ellis, Nick C. (1998) Emergentism, connectionism and language learning. *Language Learning* 48: 631–664.

Ellis, Nick C. (2011) The emergence of language as a complex adaptive system. In James Simpson (ed.) *Handbook of Applied Linguistics* 666–679. London: Routledge/Taylor Francis.

Halliday, Michael A. K. (1993) New ways of meaning: A challenge to applied linguistics. In Michael A. K. Halliday *Language in a Changing*

World 1–41. Occasional Paper No. 13, Applied Linguistics Association of Australia. Deakin, Australia: ALAA Publication.

Halliday, Michael A. K. and Martin, James R. (1993) *Writing Science: Literary and Discursive Power*. London: Falmer Press.

Haraway, Donna (1991) A cyborg manifesto: Science, technology, and socialist-feminism in the late twentieth century. In *Simians, Cyborgs and Women: The Reinvention of Nature* 149–181. New York: Routledge. Originally published as "Manifesto for cyborgs: science, technology, and socialist feminism in the 1980s." *Socialist Review* 80 (1985): 65–108.

Hofstadter, Douglas R. (1985) A person paper on purity in language. *Metamagical Themas: Questing for the Essence of Mind and Pattern* 187–196. New York: Basic Books. Retrieved on 23 August 2013 from http://www.cs.virginia.edu/~evans/cs655/readings/purity.html.

Howard, Rebecca (1993) A plagiarism *pentimento*. *Journal of Teaching Writing* 11(3): 233–46.

Huber, Sonya (2011) *The "Backwards" Research Guide for Writers: Using Your Life for Reflection, Connection, and Inspiration*. Sheffield, U.K. and Oakfield, Connecticut: Equinox.

Ivanič, Roz (1998) *Writing and Identity: The Discoursal Construction of Identity in Academic Writing*. Philadelphia: John Benjamins.

Lemke, Jay L. (1995) *Textual Politics: Discourse and Social Dynamics*. London: Taylor and Francis.

Lillis, Theresa (2013) *The Sociolinguistics of Writing*. Edinburgh: Edinburgh University Press.

Marsen, Sky (2012) Detecting the creative in written discourse. *Writing & Pedagogy* 4(2): 209–231. http://dx.doi.org/10.1558/wap.v4i2.209.

Marsen, Sky (forthcoming) *Seriously Creative Writing*. Sheffield, U.K. and Oakville, Connecticut: Equinox.

Pennington, Martha C. (2001a) *Changing Relationships Between Context and Communication From Pre-Language to Post-Language*. Research Report 4(1). Language Research Centre. University of Luton.

Pennington, Martha C. (2001b) Writing minds and talking fingers: Doing literacy in an electronic age. In P. Brett (ed.) *CALL in the 21ˢᵗ Century*. ESADE Institute (Barcelona) and IATEFL (Hove, U.K.).

Pennington, Martha C. (2012) Towards a creative writing pedagogy. *Writing & Pedagogy* 4(2): 151–158. http://dx.doi.org/10.1558/wap.v4i2.151.

Pennington, Martha C. (forthcoming) Creativity in composition: Approaches to pedagogy. In Rodney H. Jones (ed.) *Routledge Handbook of Language and Creativity*. London: Routledge.

Pennington, Martha C. and Welford, Theresa Malphrus (forthcoming). *Welcome to My World: A Writing Course*. Sheffield, U.K. and Oakville, Connecticut: Equinox.

Reisman, Fredricka (2012) Underlying factors of creative thinking as a foundation for creative writing pedagogy. *Writing & Pedagogy* 4(2): 233–262. http://dx.doi.org/10.1558/wap.v4i2.233.

Richardson, Laurel (1997) *Fields of Play: Constructing an Academic Life*. New Brunswick, New Jersey: Rutgers University Press.

Strickland, Stephanie (2009) Born digital. *The Poetry Foundation*. Retrieved on 5 May 2012 from http://www.poetryfoundation.org.

Strickland, Stephanie and Coverley, M. D. (2012) Creativity and writing in digital media: New frontiers and cutting edges. *Writing & Pedagogy* 4(2): 345–354. http://dx.doi.org/10.1558/wap.v4i2.345.

Swift, Jonathan (1729) A modest proposal for presenting the children of poor people in Ireland being a burden on their parents or country, and for making them beneficial to the publick. Retrieved on 23 August 2013 from http://www.gutenberg.org/ebooks/1080.

Turvey, Anne (2007) Writing and teaching writing. *Changing English: Studies in Culture and Education* 14: 145–159. http://dx.doi.org/10.1080/13586840701442950.

Part 2
Enlarging the View of Genre and Community in Academic Writing

5   Writing Differently
Creating Different Spaces for Student Learning

Fiona English

How to start, how to find some sort of context to unload what was in my mind and to put some sort of order on my thoughts.
– Siobhan

Introduction

The above comment came from a mature postgraduate student on a practice-based course in theatre direction at one of the colleges of London University. The student herself (let's call her Siobhan) is a professional actor with no formal academic background beyond her secondary schooling but who had been accepted onto the degree program because of her experience and expertise in theatre and her undoubted knowledge and understanding of theatre literature.

The reason that I have started my discussion with Siobhan's comment is that it expresses a feeling held by most, if not all, of us at the start of a writing project, but one which is particularly acute for those who have little experience of writing for academic purposes. Of course, Siobhan is not unique in this as the extensive literature on the subject confirms. Among these are Ivanič's (1998) discussion around student identity or Jones, Turner, and Street (1999), whose edited collection uses an academic literacies frame (Lea and Street, 1998) in exploring writing issues with both native and non-native speaking students. Others, including Lillis (2001) or Thesen and van Pletzen (2006) have explored the experiences of students from non-traditional backgrounds while Turner (2011), with her focus on international students, examines the challenges of interacting with the literacy norms of university writing. These discussions, with their academic literacies perspective, originate in practice and foreground the student and the student experience of writing at university. As Lillis and Scott (2007: 2) have pointed out "the research methods [of academic literacies] are aimed at getting inside what is said, seen or enacted in specific situations."

The aim of this chapter is, then, to consider writing as a facilitator in the context of university study. More specifically, it foregrounds the role writing has in *developing* learning as opposed to, what is more usually the case, its role in demonstrating learning. It focuses particularly on the use of genre, and, building on my earlier work (English, 2011), it offers an alternative to traditional approaches to genre pedagogy which prioritize genre "forms" and offer exemplary models to be emulated or templates to be filled. Instead, this discussion shows how genre can be used as a dynamic, transformative resource in the development not only of student writing but also student disciplinary learning. In other words, instead of genre being the pedagogical goal, genre becomes a pedagogical resource.

The discussion is organized around the case of the student referred to above who chose a non-conventional genre in producing her final written assignment. Using interview data about her experience of adopting this approach along with examples from her work, I show how the choice of genre offered this student new and different ways of thinking about her discipline and her position within that discipline.

Using Genre as a Pedagogical Resource

My approach to genre, which uses a social semiotic understanding of communication (e.g. Halliday, 1989; Kress, 1994; 2010) alongside my academic literacies philosophy, combines observations from textual analysis with insights provided by interviews. My earlier study (English, 2011) explored the work produced by a group of undergraduate students on a minor, cross-disciplinary module called Language, Power and Ideologies that I offered as part of their first-year studies. The final assignment entailed them reworking an essay they had already written for one of their major course modules such as political theory or African linguistics, only this time using a different genre, a process I now call regenring. I asked them to submit their original essays along with the new versions as a point of reference for my reading of the new versions, even though the focus of my evaluation (these were assessed pieces of work) was intended to be on their genre awareness, their flexibility with different kinds of writing and their understanding of audience. However, what the students actually produced went far beyond these somewhat limited horizons. Whatever genre they used (dramatic, journalistic, oriented to a younger readership, etc.), it quickly became clear that regenring involved far more than simply relocating material from one "frame" into another. It involved a clear shift not only in the "shape" of the work, but in its materiality. For instance, choosing to produce the "body of knowledge" as a play, with its specific speech modes and its characters, props, and other dramatic paraphernalia, requires a very different set of representational resources when compared to an essay.

The fact that I had asked the students to submit both versions of the work turned out to be a fortunate decision as it put me in the position of being able to compare both versions and explore the different ways in which the genres used affected what was essentially the same body of knowledge. As a result of this analysis which was also strongly informed by interviews with the students involved, I used the concept of orientation to help explain the different affordances of genres; that is, the ways in which genres promote (or limit) particular ways of perceiving, experiencing and representing. The framework (Figure 1) uses a social semiotic view of communication (e.g. Kress, 2010) and incorporates tools provided by multimodal analysis (e.g. Kress & Van Leeuwen, 2001).

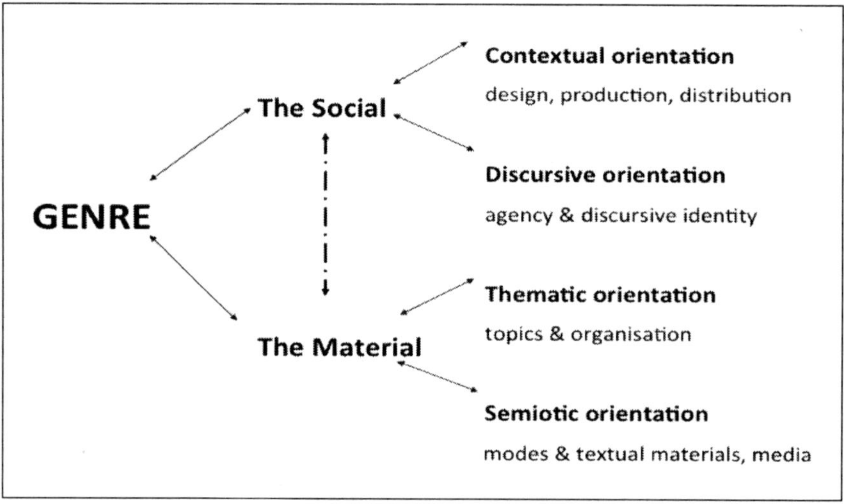

Figure 1. The Orientation of Genres

To illustrate how this works, I use an example from my book. The two extracts below are taken from the work of one student who decided to rework a politics essay on the classification of political systems, using a tabloid newspaper article genre. Extracts 1 and 2 exemplify each version of his work. In each case, the student is drawing on the same information source (Sinclair), but there is clearly a marked difference in how the ideas are articulated. The two genres used offer the student different representational possibilities and in so doing enable a different take on the information itself.

Extract 1. Essay

> ...Aristotle also gives too great a focus on the political elite when analysing the political system. As Sinclair points out in his introduction to The Politics, 'the privileges of citizenship were to him a matter of supreme importance' (Sinclair, 1962) mainly because he was not a 'citizen' himself....

(English, 2011: 98)

Extract 2. Tabloid Newspaper Article

> Malicious rumours have also been spreading about Aristotle that there is a hidden agenda behind his model, which clearly focuses on the political elite rather than the ordinary man in the forum. A senior source from the peripatetic school in Athens (at which Aristotle is a key teacher) has revealed that 'the privileges of citizenship [are] to him a matter of supreme importance'.
>
> The Daily Lie can today reveal that Aristotle is not in fact a citizen of Athens, but an asylum seeker from the Kingdom of Macedon. This being the case, there is only one question that is now on everybody's lips. We demand to know if Aristotle's book, praising as it does his own government, is merely an attempt to curry favour with the Athenian authorities?

(English, 2011: 98)

Although the assignment was submitted in the normal way and graded according to university regulations, the regenred work transgresses the "rules" of this practice because it offers an obviously fictionalized account of the disciplinary material. The tabloid is not a real tabloid nor is the student a real journalist. Nevertheless, by using the tabloid genre the student is enabled to have a very different kind of experience relating to factors such as the purpose, readership and impact (contextual orientation) when compared to these same factors in a student essay. As a student writing an essay, this writer was positioned as a novice "looking to engage in the predominant discourse of the discipline," as one of the lecturers I interviewed put it and as such was working within a highly regulated context. The new genre offered him the chance to adopt a very different kind of identity (discursive orientation) which, in turn, enabled him to handle the disciplinary material in a substantively different way. These differences are evident in the material orientations of the new genre in the ways in which the topic was developed and in the explicitness of the opinion offered. In the tabloid version, for instance, the writer's attitude is undisguised whereas in the essay it is more hedged. This shift is achieved by the inclusion of certain textual materials such as "malicious rumors" or the term "asylum seeker" used as a negative attribute – both of which promote a very different kind of critique compared to the more hedged version in the essay. Furthermore, in contrast to the essay, the tabloid genre allows the student to tap into modern day attitudes towards politics and migration, thereby offering a new thematic dimension. However, perhaps the most important difference is that the student has used irony and humor more generally as the key driver in the new version, which affords him the chance to both reflect and comment on the material that he is working with. Such an inclusion is unlikely in an essay, as it might well be misunderstood although, for an experienced academic, humor may be less of a taboo.

This brief explanation gives an overview impression of the orientation of genres and shows how using different genres can enable students to think differently about their disciplinary knowledge and reach different understandings. In the next part, which examines Siobhan's case, we can see how the different orientations played out in her work and experience following her decision to write using a non-conventional genre. In contrast to the students in my earlier study, Siobhan did not rework an existing essay but wrote in the genre of her choice directly.

How to Start

As already explained, Siobhan was a mature student on a Master's degree in theatre direction which combined apprentice-like practice (assistant directing in a theatre) with university-based theoretical and reflective study. As well as the practice-oriented aspects of the course, students had to produce short written reports associated with the different productions they had been involved in, focusing on issues such as casting or set design to describe what they had done and why. For the final assignment, which replaced the traditional dissertation which typifies U.K. Master's degree programs, the students were asked to select and direct a play that was to be performed in the theatre where they had been apprenticed. This entailed casting, set design, and stage management as well as direction of the play itself. Students were also required to engage in a range of different supporting activities, specifically an oral presentation, an oral examination, or viva voce, and an extended piece of writing which offered a theorized reflection on the play and the production itself.

As Siobhan herself pointed out, unlike the short pieces of writing, this final assignment presented her with a serious challenge, not only in relation to difficulty in starting out, but also in relation to her lack of expertise, as she saw it, in scholarly writing and the need to "intellectualize" her directorial decisions.

> *I definitely felt I had to put it in a more academic way and intellectualize it and that was the real difficulty for me. Because I didn't have a basis for that. You know a lot of people on the course had all come straight out of university and knew how to write an essay. I was flailing around thinking, "What's an essay?"*

While it is certainly true that she had not had the same academic experience that the others had, Siobhan's professional experience far outweighed theirs. Her knowledge of the work of the actor, the experience of performing on stage, and her expertise in reading and interpreting plays should have made her considerably more confident than her fellow students as well as the success of the play she actually directed, which received excellent reviews, including from the Guardian newspaper's leading theatre critic. In fact, she had already written other pieces of work as part of the course requirements and had found these largely unproblematic because, as she says, they were based on her first-hand experience and her practice-based observations.

> *...they were more descriptive, I suppose, about what you would say, how you would order a rehearsal, what you think the relationship is and all of that.... They were more specific and I felt more able and more capable there in that situation.*

This final assignment made a different kind of demand on her. It required her not only to use the discourse associated with disciplinary knowledge but also, and perhaps more scarily, to offer an academically theorized discussion about her own practice and about the production she directed.

> *Here it was more about my ideology, if you like, what was my credo as a director, so I had to fathom that. And I found that very difficult.*

Clearly, for Siobhan, this piece represented a step up from the previous written assignments, and she did not feel fully up to the task. It was not that she didn't know why she had done what she had in the way she did it or that she was unable to explain this. It was that she had to do it in an unfamiliar way. Her own sense of personal identity was not as a scholar, nor as an academic writer, but as someone who was essentially a practitioner – a hands-on actor–director. Adopting a theoretical perspective was, she assumed, outside of her sphere of activity and even ability.

Such feelings are not uncommon among practice-based professionals when they move into the academic domain, as has been discussed by researchers such as Rai (2008), writing about social workers on degree programs or Wood (2000), discussing art and design students. Actors and other performance professionals are no exception to these feelings and, in my personal experience, can sometimes overcompensate for this by making their writing hyper-intellectual to the point of being impenetrable, although they are not alone in this. The perception that writing academically involves using "difficult" words which "sound" academic is widespread among students and the question of what makes writing academic is often raised by both students and writing specialists alike. This is not surprising, given the plethora of coursebooks and courses that promote academic word lists and academic style guides and offer writing frames for producing the genres typically used in higher education.

Perhaps the best answer to the question of what makes writing academic is not the words and sentences but the fact that we are writing about academic things. This is not to say that academic writing is easy. It certainly is not as it entails knowing about, understanding and participating in disciplinary debates and undertaking disciplinary activity all of which requires not only hard intellectual work and engagement with academic writing practices but also the emotional strain associated with putting ourselves out onto the public arena, whether as a student or a professional academic. Added to this are, of course, the innate difficulties associated with writing per se. As Siobhan noted above, and as I myself have argued "Getting thoughts 'down on paper' is not a process of simple transfer but rather one of transformation" (English 2011: 168). Compared to speaking (and thinking), writing requires a very different range of textual resources, such as nominalization and embeddedness, which, in turn, impose different organizational strategies in its expression.

Writing Differently

After worrying about how to proceed, Siobhan eventually contacted me for help. She wanted to know whether she could approach the task from a different perspective but was unsure of how to move forward on that idea. I sent her a copy of a short article, based on my book, about using different genres in academic contexts (English, 2012), in the hope that it might give her some ideas. During a follow-up conversation she told me that she was keen to try out the approach suggested. I advised her to discuss it with her supervisor before embarking on what must surely have been a risky journey to make sure that he would agree to this departure from the norm. Interestingly, he proved open to this plan, albeit with some reservations, and now armed with institutional approval, Siobhan got down to the work (see Appendix A).

The genre she chose was that of an interview for an imagined university radio program that she entitled "Masterstrokes." She was to be the interviewee and would be responding to questions related to the assignment at hand. The reason she decided to represent her work in this way was because she felt much more confident in her ability to talk about ideas rather than write about them. Speaking, she said, was her strong point and responding to questions, as in a viva, was something that she particularly enjoyed.

> *Responding to ideas and ideas coming on top of ideas and answering questions really about my thoughts, so that's why I kind of landed on the notion of doing the transcript of a radio because I could put myself in the position of the interviewer and the interviewee and ask the questions and answer them and expand on them.*

This genre, she realized, would free her up both to articulate and to develop the ideas that she had noted down whilst reading about the issues that she wished to raise in this assignment. She specifically wanted to locate her discussion in the wider context of Irish literary diaspora and identity, and the ownership of Irish literature more generally. She had, as she puts it,

> *lots of these ideas written down but had no idea how to get them shoehorned into an essay. But with this question and answer I did. I felt that I could do that more easily.*

Foregrounding the Personal

I come from a different background!

In the following section, I want to show how the genre Siobhan chose acted as a facilitative resource in enabling her to develop an argument that would value her own lived experience whilst at the same time developing her disciplinary knowledge in a way that could underpin her professional activity. Coming as she did from a non-academic background, it was largely knowledge based on lived experience that shaped her understanding of the issues and only latterly knowledge based on academic resources. This was one of the main difficulties she had in trying to 'shoehorn' her thinking into a conventional essay which would not comfortably accommodate these different sources of knowledge. The 'celebrity' interview, on the other hand, with its interest in the personal alongside whatever its main topic might be, offered Siobhan the chance to integrate these different aspects. In fact, as is clear from the written work itself (Extract 3), it is precisely her lived experience that underpins her professional and academic perspective.

Extract 3. Introduction to Siobhan's Written Work, "Masterstrokes"

Q: [having introduced Siobhan] but let me take you back to when you started and ask you first of all what brought you to Birkbeck?

SIOBHAN: After many years as an actor and after the birth of my children, I became closely involved in my local community, holding drama workshops for teenagers and directing plays at the local school. It was a wonderful experience and triggered in me the urge to learn more about directing and to increase my confidence.... Its appeal for me was the fact that the course was practical, with a placement at a drama school and a theatre where I would be able to learn and observe professional practitioners at work, and also sufficiently academic to get me thinking in a more measured and analytical way especially in terms of examining and interacting

> with text critically and in detail, questioning and looking beyond
> the words on the page, at themes, symbolism, motives, conflict
> and subtext and asking questions about who I am and the plays I
> want to direct.
>
> **Q: And have you found those answers?**
>
> SIOBHAN: Well not really, in fact I have found more questions but
> also lots more possibilities! Particularly about the work I want to
> do. As regards myself, I will stick to the facts for the moment and
> try to see how they fit in with what I want to do. I am a woman,
> a feminist, a political activist, an actor, a director, a mother and
> last but maybe most importantly in terms of my outlook, an Irish
> immigrant to Britain.

Extract 3, which is the introduction to Siobhan's writing, sets out
the themes that are to be discussed later on just as would happen in
a conventional essay. However, unlike an essay, this introduction is
oriented towards Siobhan's life (family, community, professional,
and academic) rather than towards disciplinary issues and debates.
It places her self and her experience at the center of her ideas,
prioritizing these above the disciplinary and, in so doing, helps
her overcome the feeling of academic inadequacy commented on
above. This is something she specifically referred to throughout
my interview with her.

*I think that it's been an absolutely wonderful facilitator for me and
a real confidence builder.*

In the fictional radio program (Masterstrokes), the initial
interview question, "What brought you to Birkbeck?" gives
Siobhan a context in which to foreground the personal. As already
mentioned, there is little space for this, particularly in student
writing, and where there is, it is often in the context of the marginalized "reflective journal" genre. Here, however, the personal is
authorized by the genre, giving her the freedom to prioritize it in
an assignment that was, after all, a key component of her final

dissertation. In this way, she not only asserts her own identity (I am a woman, a feminist, a political activist, an actor, a director, a mother, and last but maybe most importantly in terms of my outlook, an Irish immigrant to Britain.) but she does so in a way that insists on this being taken seriously in an academic context.

Managing the Material

As with students in my earlier study (English, 2011), Siobhan found that the spokenness of the genre helped her to organize her ideas. She had already had a viva, with her lecturers and had found that a highly positive and empowering experience as it gave her the opportunity, as she said, to expand on her ideas. Of course, not all students have the same positive approach to the viva genre but given her reported success in that event, producing her "essay" as an interview makes perfect sense. Of course, not all interviews successfully elicit the information desired. It very much depends on the quality of the questions asked and whether an interviewer is skilled as a conversational facilitator. Any research methods course will teach that a bland question will elicit a bland answer and questions that do not offer an interviewee scope to expand will usually result in superficial responses. Equally, if the interviewee does not have much to say, then no amount of careful questioning will help. In Siobhan's case, the problem was not a lack of things to say, but rather how she could say them. In other words, it was an organizational problem rather than a problem of content.

> *I had so many notes and I had an idea about what I wanted to write about…. So in a way I kind of did know what questions I wanted to ask myself. And that's what kind of facilitated the whole thing for me.*

In Extract 3 above, we can see how the questions helped Siobhan focus on particular themes that would normally be outside the remit of student academic writing, in Extract 4, we see how questions were used to organize the material and drive the discussion forward into either new topics or deeper consideration of existing topics.

We have already seen the first three questions in Extract 3, but below (Extract 4) I annotate the subsequent questions to illustrate how they enabled Siobhan to incorporate the different themes she wanted to include. The full text can be seen in the Appendix.

Extract 4. Interviewer's Questions from "Masterstrokes"

> **Q: *Can you tell us something about that*** [lack of voice, agency, migrant identity]***?***
>
> [detailed response about issues of identity in relation to Irish writers and literature]
>
> **Q: *I can see you feel very strongly about this, but what do you intend to do about it?***
>
> [discussion about the values of fringe theatre and the opportunities it gives to marginalized work]
>
> **Q: *How did you choose which play to direct?***
>
> [practical rationale for directorial choice]
>
> **Q: *I know that as an actor you have been associated with Brian Friel's work and also Edna O'Brien's as well as O'Casey's, Synge's and Yeats'.***
>
> [discussion about identity, gender and stereotypes in familiar Irish literature in contrast to the literary school from which her directorial play emerges.]
>
> **Q: *How did you personally connect to this play?***
>
> [overview of the plot, themes, and issues linked to he own ideological and emotional perspective]
>
> **Q: *How did you approach the production?***
>
> [description and explanation about casting – linked to issues of Irishness]

Q: *What was the set like?*

[explanation used to challenge stereotypic representations of "the Irish" and to comment on audience reception]

Q: *How was the play received?*

[comment on both the critical and the audience reception, linked to sociopolitical context of the play and the Irish experience]

Q: *What is next for you and how do you see yourself in say five years' time?*

[discussion of Irish identity, marginalized literature, and gender]

Q: *Have you enjoyed your time at Birkbeck?*

[link back explicitly to the personal in relation to the academic and professional]

Organization is one of the most difficult aspects of writing. Deciding what story to tell and deciding how it will unfold involves making tough decisions about what to include and, often, what to exclude. Essayist and other academic genres are particularly problematic in this regard as they are usually limited in terms of length and constrained by the field or the topic. This, combined with the insistence (at least in the Anglo-American tradition) on a linear, unfolding structure, offers little opportunity for digression, thereby making the inclusion of what might be considered tangential themes problematic. As Siobhan's analytical thinking involves themes that might well be considered tangential in the academic domain, "shoehorning" those into an academic essay was a serious challenge. However, the affordances of the interview, based around questions in a conversation, albeit a formal conversation, offers an organizational strategy which is more flexible and recursive. It allows for an additive approach rather than the embeddedness that typifies the written academic discussion, allowing for the inclusion of remembered points of personal reflection as well as tangential themes in the flow of conversational exchange. Siobhan used this characteristic of spokenness to ensure that all her themes were included and all her points were made.

> *Well, once I got down to it I found it really did [flow]. I managed to tap into it. I also was referring backwards and forwards in my notes and saying, "Well, did you manage to get that bit in?" and "You'd better ask another question so that you can get that in."*

This strategy enabled Siobhan to profile her central theme, that of the identity of the Irish diaspora, throughout the discussion as the topics provided by her disciplinary knowledge or directorial experience were explored. Moreover, the affordances of the interview enabled Siobhan to position the "everyday" arguments derived from her own lived experience of these issues as a valid resource in academic debate. The result is a discussion that moves backwards and forwards between the different themes, mingling them rather than presenting them, and in so doing enables her own agency to be visible and foregrounded. Agency here is not the "romantic self expression as agency, where students are asked 'to put themselves' in their writing, to establish a sort of identity and selfhood" that Scott (2012: 173) criticizes. It is, rather, an agency that is fundamental to the origin of the issues raised and the ideas developed in the work.

Conclusion

This discussion has proposed an approach to university pedagogy that can have a major impact on student learning. It opens up new possibilities for both writing and disciplinary teaching by encouraging us to think differently about what we ask our students to do.

From the teacher's perspective, working with different genres encourages a revitalizing of writing in the learning and teaching domain. Writing in the university curriculum has become synonymous with assessment, grades, and outcomes, associated with the development of skills rather than the development of learning. Academic writing itself, typified by the essay or term paper, has come to be seen as separate from the production of knowledge, something that is further institutionalized in the typical separation of writing centers from their disciplinary counterparts in academic departments. Teaching students how to write an essay is always going to be a troublesome activity as it is based in the assumption that essays are singular, monolithic entities made up of academic words and formal grammatical structures organized in highly systematized ways. Unfortunately, such assumptions deny the centrality of both disciplinary knowledge and student agency in the process of successful student writing. Working with genres as diverse as plays, interviews, posters, or websites can help remind us that presenting academic work is a dynamic activity of meaning-making and not just a process of putting words and sentences down on a page (or screen).

From the student's perspective, using different genres gives them a different outlook on their disciplinary knowledge, as was shown in my earlier work (English, 2011) with student comments like, "…presenting those theories in that way made them much more concrete" or "I felt a lot more ownership over it." For all of them, the experience of writing differently for an academic purpose was transformative, in terms of how they understood their disciplines; empowering, in how they could position themselves in the disciplinary debates; and challenging in the ways in which they "had to have more of a take" on the disciplinary issues, as one student put it. From the academic's perspective, this approach can reveal levels of student learning and understanding that might never otherwise be recognized. As one of my faculty interviewees said in response to reading the work of one of the students in my earlier study (English, 2012: 134), "…this is a perfect example of a student – incredibly in the first year – who was able to take these ideas and manipulate them in a very creative way – so it was both academically erudite and simply entertaining." This is what we might consider a win-win situation. Not only can the approach encourage erudition and creative use of the disciplinary materials but it is also enjoyable to read. My research certainly had an impact on my own teaching as I began to introduce a much wider range of assignment tasks into the curriculum and found that students, despite some initial reservations, found it interesting, even fun, but also intellectually challenging.

Returning to the study at the heart of the present discussion, using a non-conventional genre undoubtedly had an enabling effect on Siobhan. This was not just in helping her to get started but, more importantly, in giving her the confidence to produce her ideas in a way which encompassed and valued her self. The interview genre oriented her away from being a student demonstrating her learning in the context of assessment and towards being an expert sharing her thoughts and ideas with an interested audience. This, in turn, oriented her towards representing those thoughts and ideas on her own terms. This comment from Siobhan sums up the experience:

> *[I]t opened up the whole process for me of writing and I did really begin to enjoy it and I found I had so much more to say because it led me to think other things so I was able to expand my view…. I found that in the end, you know, I did have lots to say.*

Can her work be considered academic? The response from her examiners, whose comments included "highly creative," "interesting ideas," and "innovative thinking," indicates that it can. Is it academic writing? That can only be answered by deciding whether academic writing needs to be limited to essays and other traditional student writing genres. Perhaps, instead, the more interesting questions to ask could be: What kind of learning is going on? What kind of knowledge is being produced? The answers to such questions might lead us to realize that a wider repertoire of pedagogical tasks might not only help to refresh the essay, as Richard Andrews suggests, but also revitalize learning and teaching for all concerned:

Refreshing a genre like this, or indeed challenging more vigorously its dominance as the default genre is what keeps the most important qualities alive: clear thinking, exchange of views, reasoned commitment and lively expression. (Andrews, 2003: 126)

Of course, the issue of authority and empowerment among teaching staff is highly relevant to this discussion as it is not always within the power of individuals to introduce new approaches. However, if it can be demonstrated that the use of different genres facilitates learning and encourages disciplinary engagement, as I hope my work goes some way to achieving, then it may be possible to shift entrenched positions about learning and assessment at university.

Note

1   Social Semiotics is the approach to language and communication established by Michael Halliday (Halliday, 1978) and developed by Hodge and Kress (1988). It emphasizes both the material (textual resources) and the social (contextual factors) aspects of communication whereby meanings are made and interpreted within a given situation.

References

Andrews, Richard (2003) The end of the essay? *Teaching in Higher Education* 8(1): 117–128. http://dx.doi.org/10.1080/135625103200005 2366.

English, Fiona (2011) *Student Writing and Genre: Reconfiguring Academic Knowledge*. London: Bloomsbury Academic.

English, Fiona (2012) Écrire différemment, apprendre différemment : Repenser le genre. *Pratiques* 153/154: 177–194. http://www.pratiques-cresef.com/cres06e.htm#English.

Halliday, Michael A. K. (1978) *Language as Social Semiotic*. London: Arnold.

Halliday, Michael A. K. (1989) *Spoken and Written Language*. Oxford: Oxford University Press.

Hodge, Robert and Kress, Gunther (1988) *Social Semiotics*. Cambridge: Polity Press.

Ivanič, Roz (1998) *Writing and Identity: The Discoursal Construction of Identity in Academic Writing*. Amsterdam: John Benjamins.

Jones, Carys, Turner, Joan and Street, Brian V. (eds.) (1999) *Students Writing in Higher Education*. Amsterdam: John Benjamins.

Kress, Gunther (1994) *Learning to Write* (2nd edition). London: Routledge.

Kress, Gunther (2010) *Multimodality: A Social Semiotic Approach to Contemporary Communication*. London: Routledge.

Kress, Gunther and van Leeuwen, Theo (2001) *Multimodal Discourse*. London: Edward Arnold.

Lea, Mary R. and Street, Brian V. (1998) Student writing in higher education: An academic literacies approach. *Studies in Higher Education* 23(2): 157–172. http://dx.doi.org/10.1080/03075079812331380364.

Lillis, Theresa M. (2001) *Student Writing: Access, Regulation, Desire*. London: Routledge.

Lillis, Theresa M. and Scott, Mary (2007) Introduction: New directions in academic literacies research. *Journal of Applied Linguistics* 4(1): 5–32. http://dx.doi.org/ 10.1558/japl.v4i1.1.

Rai, Lucy (2008). *Student Writing in Social Work Education*. Unpublished Ph.D. thesis, The Open University.

Scott, Mary (2013) *A Chronicle of Learning: Voicing the Text*. Unpublished Ph.D. thesis, University of Tilburg.

Thesen, Lucia and van Pletzen, Ermien (eds.) (2006) *Academic Literacy and the Languages of Change*. London: Continuum.

Turner, Joan (2011) *Language in the Academy: Cultural Reflexivity and Intercultural Dynamics*. Bristol: Multilingual Matters.

Wood, John (2000) The culture of academic rigour: Does design research really need it? *The Design Journal* 3(1): 44–57. http://dx.doi.org/10.2752/146069200789393599.

6 Creative Approaches to Research-Based Essays

Theresa Malphrus Welford

Introduction

In 2009, Ken Robinson delivered a talk called "How Schools Kill Creativity" (Robinson, 2009). The online video of his talk features no glamorous stars, no rough-and-tumble action scenes, no dazzling graphics, no inspiring soundtrack. Instead, there's only a pleasant-looking man, standing on a stage, expressing his views on education. As of the summer of 2013, the video had been viewed approximately 23,000,000 times. Clearly, people are hungry for creativity, even in – and *especially* in – academic settings.

In their book, *The Element: How Finding Your Passion Changes Everything*, Ken Robinson and Lou Aronica describe the current state of affairs in American education:

> We place tremendous significance on standardized tests, we cut funding for what we consider "nonessential" programs, and then we wonder why our children seem unimaginative and uninspired. In these ways, our current education system systematically drains the creativity out of our children. (Robinson and Aronica, 2010: 16)

Many school systems have moved in this direction for supposedly forward-thinking reasons, nudged (or pushed) by politicians who believe "that it's essential for economic growth and competitiveness and to help students get jobs" (*ibid*). Robinson and Aronica give these politicians a failing grade:

> …in the twenty-first century, jobs and competitiveness depend absolutely on the very qualities that school systems are being forced to tamp down…. Businesses everywhere say they need people who are creative and who can think independently. (*ibid.*)

In discussing the lamentable situation in primary and secondary schools, they say that "the academic culture of universities" is part of the problem, because this culture tends to "push aside any sort of activity that involves the heart, the body, the senses, and a good portion of our actual brains" (Robinson and Aronica, 2010: 13).

Robert Sternberg (Sternberg, 2006) believes that people can *decide* to be creative. As I read Sternberg's suggestions for acting upon that decision,[1] I think of many ways that we teachers can help our students develop their creativity:

- We can serve as role models by sharing our own writing and demonstrating our own writing processes in front of the class;
- We can devise playful activities that call on students to generate as many ideas as possible, no matter how outlandish those ideas might seem;
- We can encourage students to take "sensible risks" in their writing, using new ideas and new approaches and then selectively incorporating those into their written work for other classes;
- We can welcome ambiguity and difference in students' interpretations and responses;
- We can reward creativity in our students' work even when we might see flaws in other aspects of their work;
- We can help our students see that missteps can sometimes lead to breakthroughs;

- We can build teamwork into our course curricula;
- We can encourage intellectual growth by developing activities and assignments that require students to exercise not only their creativity but also intellectual capabilities such as logic, reasoning, analysis, flexibility, and adaptability.

Why should university faculty emphasize creativity in academic writing classes? Because, as vividly demonstrated by a school in Massachusetts, such an emphasis can help students develop emotionally, intellectually, and academically. Once "plagued by violence and disorder," this school was so academically weak that it ranked "in the bottom five of all public schools in the state of Massachusetts" (Tur, 2013). When the head of the school fired the armed security guards at his troubled school and "reinvested all the money used for security infrastructure into the arts," he helped show what can happen when a culture of conformity, rigidity, and fear is replaced by a culture of creativity (*ibid.*). Even the school environment has been reinvigorated: "Brightly colored paintings, essays of achievement, and motivational posters line the halls. The dance studio has been resurrected, along with the band room, and an artists' studio" (*ibid.*). Three years after the school's transformation, it has "one of the fastest student improvement rates statewide" (*ibid.*).

Keyvaughn Little, who attends this Massachusetts school, explains what he has learned as a result of the new emphasis on creativity: "There's no one particular way of doing something…. And art helps you…see that" (Tur, 2013). He goes on to say that this realization applies not only to academics but also to "anything else" (*ibid.*). Whatever the future may hold for this young man, I believe that he will benefit from learning the value of tapping into his creativity and being flexible in his thinking.

Much the same goal can be reached, I believe, in university classes that encourage students to write essays combining research with creative approaches. Students can learn that "there's no one particular way of doing something," a valuable lesson for those heading toward graduate school or careers. In this chapter, I first discuss the benefits of using creative approaches to research-based writing. Then I describe the approaches I have developed and describe the wide variety of papers that my students have written.

Benefits of Creative Approaches to Research-Based Writing

In my experience, even the strongest writers often struggle with traditional research papers. Perhaps because the word *research* intimidates students, many over-rely on their research sources. Perhaps because they believe research papers are *supposed* to be dull and dry, many students exclude information that is engaging and compelling. Perhaps because they find it difficult to reproduce the kind of formal papers that teachers often require, many students write sentences that are garbled and incoherent, filled with language that is clumsy, inaccurate, and pseudo-academic. And perhaps because they don't understand why or how they should "translate" information from their research sources into their own language and framework of ideas, many students plagiarize.

Using approaches that blend creativity with research can help students avoid some of these problems. These approaches can also provide additional benefits:

(1) They can help students overcome some of their fears about writing research-based essays;
(2) They can encourage students to experiment and take risks as writers;
(3) They can help students understand the need to consider key rhetorical concerns such as purpose and audience;
(4) They can help students write papers that are not only informative but also creative and genuinely engaging;

(5) They can help students feel validated as creative people, as thinkers, as researchers, as writers, and as producers of knowledge; and

(6) They can help students increase their involvement and investment in their topics and sources and thus develop an original voice and avoid over-reliance on others' ideas

What's more, students gain valuable practice for the writing they will do in college and beyond, because all of the approaches rely on essentials such as analysis, explanation, exemplification, and (of course) research. These papers involve creativity, but they *are* legitimate research papers.

All of the approaches that I advocate are, I believe, beneficial to those students who already consider themselves creative, as well as those who need to discover that they are more creative than they realize. These approaches are the *Personal/Traditional Blend*, the *Drama Approach*, the *Multi-Genre Approach*, the *20–25 Random Things Approach*, and the *On-Fire Approach*. Although the *Personal/Traditional Blend* involves creativity, it tends not to intimidate those students who feel comfortable with traditional approaches to research-based writing. The *Drama Approach* is especially well suited for argumentation papers. Both the *Multi-Genre Approach* and the *20–25 Random Things Approach*, which lend themselves to essays that are intended primarily to be informative or exploratory, are perfect for students who wish to work in pairs, as well as those who must work in short bursts because of busy schedules (or because of limited attention spans). The *On-Fire Approach*, which uses second-person pronouns, present-tense verbs, and compelling details, can be quite intense, helping writers and readers feel immersed in the subject. Since published articles often combine research with detailed examples and true stories, the *Personal/Traditional Blend* and the *On-Fire Approach* (and others) serve as valuable models for those students who hope to write for publication.[2]

Drama

In my experience, most students enjoy writing about controversial topics. Unfortunately, writing a *good* argumentation paper is far more difficult than they anticipate, and the papers that they write are often not only one-sided but also filled with ideas that are clichéd, illogical, and sketchily developed. The Drama Approach can help students realize the necessity to include multiple viewpoints and to treat all legitimate viewpoints fairly, carefully, and thoroughly. To write this paper, students create a cast of characters and have them debate the topic. Students use research and their own personal knowledge to ensure that their characters are well informed. To help make their plays entertaining, the students can also include a few dimwits for comic relief (just as Shakespeare did in his plays).

As we start the process, we read sample plays together and discuss the conventions of this genre (description of the setting, cast of characters, stage directions, and so on). I typically use plays written by students, as well as a play that I wrote about vegetarianism. As we examine the sample plays – and as we examine samples in all of the formats – we also make it a point to talk about things that the writers could do to improve their papers, including developing them more fully. Then we discuss controversial topics from which students can choose. I encourage my students to write about any topic which they find compelling, while explaining that it is best to stay away from topics which aren't genuinely arguable (those that are simply a matter of personal taste, for example).[3]

Below is an excerpt from a play written by a student named Jeb Lavender.[4] Set in a dining hall on a college campus, it opens with friendly chatter among the characters, then moves into a casually written but well-developed argument about the possible impact of video games.

...

Gary: [sticks his hand in the air] Hold on now. I said that *might* be smart. Why don't you want your kids to play video games?

Ash: [under his breath] Maybe she just wants to torture her kids.

Kairi: [shoves Ash out of the booth] No, I do not want to torture my kids. I think video games are bad for kids. Unhealthy, sometimes even dangerous.

Ash: [getting back into the booth] Whoa. Whoa. Name one time video games have been dangerous to kids.

Kairi: [matter-of-factly] The Columbine shooting.

Link: I heard about that. The shooters were influenced by violent video games, right?[i]

Gary: Almost. It was never proven that they were influenced by video games or music.[ii]

Kairi: What about the Washington Navy Yard shooting? I know for a fact I read somewhere that the shooter played "violent zombie video games for up to 16 hours at a time."[iii]

Gary: Yes, that is true, but again, it was never proven that video games were the real cause of the shooting. The shooter claimed he heard low-frequency electromagnetic waves. He said he was being controlled by them. Plus he had a mental illness. That illness, in tandem with violent video games, could have influenced him, but we won't ever know for certain. So technically, neither of those instances can be blamed on video games.[iv]

Ash: [sticks tongue out at Kairi] Ha! I told ya video games aren't bad for you!

Gary: Well… I wouldn't go that far, Ashyboy. While it's true those shootings might not be because of video games, there are still a lot of studies that can confirm video games are bad for kids. For example --

Ash: [interrupting] Here he goes again. [sarcastically] Where did you read this "fun fact of the day?"

Gary: [unfazed] I believe it was something by the American Academy of Pediatrics. Anyway, they said, and I'm quoting of course, "Exposure to violence in media, including television, movies, music and video games, represents a significant risk to the health of children and adolescents. Extensive research evidence indicates that media violence can contribute to aggressive behavior, desensitization to violence, nightmares, and fear of being harmed."[v]

Link: As annoying as this guy's eidetic memory can be, it's pretty dang impressive.

Ash: OK, I believe you got that information from a reliable source, and I have to admit that stuff sounds pretty reasonable, but I saw something this one time that I think is important in regards to this argument. And this is from a *really* good source!

Kairi: [rolling her eyes] Of course it is, Ash.

Ash: It is!! It's from CBS News! It was talking about a study this guy that worked for CBS had done about how video games might actually be good for kids....

Notes

[i]   "Columbine High School shootings." History.com. A&E Television Networks, n.d. Retrieved on 14 Nov. 2013. <http://www.history.com/topics/columbine-high-school-shootings>.

[ii]   *Ibid.*

[iii]   "Washington Navy Yard shooting: shooter allowed to buy gun despite mental issues, Navy misconduct." NY Daily News. N.p., n.d. Retrieved on 18 Nov. 2013. <http://www.nydailynews.com/news/national/navy-yard-gunman-struggled-mental-issues-officials-article-1.1458281>.

[iv]   *Ibid.*

[v]   "Washington Navy Yard Shooting Caused by Violent Video Games." Las Vegas Guardian Express. N.p., n.d. Retrieved on 17 Nov. 2013. <http://guardianlv.com/2013/09/washington-navy-yard-shooting-caused-by-violent-video-games/>.

References

"Are video games actually good for kids?" (18 Jan. 2011) CBSNews. CBS Interactive. 17 Nov. 2013. http://www.cbsnews.com/8301-501464_162-4453801.html.

"Columbine High School shootings" (14 Nov. 2013) History.com. A&E Television Networks. http://www.history.com/topics/columbine-high-school-shootings.

Ferguson, Christopher J. (April 2011) "Video Games and Youth Violence: A Prospective Analysis in Adolescents." *Springer's Journal of Youth and Adolescence* 40: 377-391. http://link.springer.com/article/10.1007/s10964-010-9610-x.

Guarini, Drew (7 Nov. 2013) "9 ways video games can actually be good for you." TheHuffingtonPost.com. http://www.huffingtonpost.com/2013/11/07/video-games-good-for-us_n_4164723.html.

Savastio, Rebecca (17 Sept. 2013) "Washington Navy Yard shooting caused by violent video games." *Las Vegas Guardian Express*. http://guardianlv.com/2013/09/washington-navy-yard-shooting-caused-by-violent-video-games/. http://guardianlv.com/2013/09/washington-navy-yard-shooting-caused-by-violent-video-games/.

"Washington Navy Yard shooting: Shooter allowed to buy gun despite mental issues, Navy misconduct" (18 Nov. 2013) NY Daily News. http://www.nydailynews.com/news/national/navy-yard-gunman-struggled-mental-issues-officials-article-1.1458281.

My students have written plays on topics including abortion, capital punishment, gun regulations, violent video games, voter fraud, prayer in schools, the legalization of marijuana, and the question of whether college athletes should be paid to play sports. They've set their plays in living rooms, dining rooms, secondary school lunchrooms, college cafeterias, nightclubs, and courtrooms. They've based their characters on family members, friends, classmates, TV or movie personalities, and even comic-book characters. Most of their plays have been well-balanced, thoroughly researched, and engaging. As a bonus, the best plays are so enjoyable that they can be performed in class, providing a valuable opportunity to recognize the writing done by students.

Multi-Genre

The Collected Works of Billy the Kid, an unconventional novel by Michael Ondaatje (Ondaatje, 1974) (Ondaatje, 1974), demonstrates that an assortment of genres can tell a story and paint a portrait of a character. In fact, Tom Romano, the author of *Blending Genre, Altering Style: Writing Multigenre Papers*, was inspired by Ondaatje's book:

> Ondaatje wrote about the last years of Billy the Kid's life in a style I'd never read before.... The book contained songs, thumbnail character sketches, poems, a comic book excerpt, narrative, stream-of-consciousness passages, newspaper interviews, even photographs and drawings. (Romano, 2000: 3)

What Romano says here is true of research-based essays in the multi-genre format. Each genre contributes information, adding up to a fairly detailed portrait of the subject. In addition, since multi-genre essays move from genre to genre without transitions or explanations, writer and reader are liberated from old-fashioned constraints. Obviously, the writers of these essays must take risks and exercise their own creativity. Another exciting advantage is that papers in this format require *readers* to be active participants.

My students have written multi-genre essays on an enormous variety of topics, including famous people from the present or the past, illnesses or conditions, rituals, holidays, hobbies, and societal issues. To create their multi-genre essays, they've written songs, poems, fairytales, letters, speeches, conversations, interviews, case studies, diary entries, brochures, newspaper or magazine articles, blogs, Facebook status updates, "tweets," and e-mails.[5] Of course, students must be warned against simply finding examples of these genres and pasting them into their essays. Their job is to write everything themselves, using their own knowledge together with information that they find in their research. The resulting essay is usually a fascinating "patchwork quilt" of genres, with each "square" contributing to the essay as a whole.

The On-Fire Approach

A breathtakingly intense essay written by a former firefighter named Larry Brown was the inspiration for the On-Fire Approach:

> You learn early to go in low, that heat and smoke rise into the ceiling, that cooler air is near the floor. You learn to button your collar tightly around your neck, to pull the gauntlets of your gloves up over the cuffs of your coat, that embers can go anywhere skin is exposed. You learn that you are only human flesh, not Superman, and that you can burn like a candle. (Brown, 1993: 167)[6]

As my students and I examine samples and discuss this approach, we examine the characteristics that make it distinctive: the use of the word *you* (a second-person pronoun) to replace the word *I* (a first-person pronoun); the use of present-tense verbs rather than past-tense verbs; and the intensity that results largely from the use of second-person pronouns and present-tense verbs, as well as the juxtaposition of day-to-day routine alongside life-and-death drama:[7]

> You learn every inch of your truck and you know which compartments hold the forcible entry tools, the exhaust fans for removing smoke from a house, the power saws, the portable generators, the pike poles, the scoops, the salvage covers, the boltcutters, the axes, the ropes, the rappelling gear. (Brown, 1993: 171)

When my students use the On-Fire Approach, their work is usually as impressively detailed and intense as Brown's. They've written about working in restaurants, retail stores, thrift shops, amusement parks, and daycare centers. They've written about being artists, cheerleaders, athletes, and members of the marching band. This approach is so versatile that it could be used in any discipline on campus. The On-Fire Approach would work well for a research-based essay on a career, such as "You Are a Neurosurgeon" or "You Are an Editor"; for a research report in a scientific setting, such as "You Encounter String Theory" or "You Discover Penicillin"; for an exploration of a medical condition, such as "You Have Polymyalgia Rheumatica" or "You and Your Migraines"; or for an informative essay about a societal ritual or tradition, such as "You Plan Your Traditional Wedding" or "You Celebrate Inti Raymi."[8] This approach could also serve as an inventive way to bring historical persons or historical events back to life, in an essay such as "You Are a Peasant on Bastille Day" or "You Are Aung San Suu Kyi." Teachers and students would want to work together to come up with a wider variety of titles than the ones above, but I have used these as a reminder that the heart of an On-Fire essay is the use of second-person pronouns and present-tense verbs.

Personal/Traditional Blend

In the Personal/Traditional Blend, students blend library research and online research with detailed examples and true stories from their own lives. The combination, I believe, adds color and vividness to their essays. Many students enjoy writing this kind of essay precisely because they have personal connections to the topics they have selected. They may also find it exciting to know that many published articles (whether online or in print) blend personal examples with research.

Below, I have included excerpts from a Personal/Traditional essay written by former student Hailey Dunavant.-

My Hero's Battle

Even though it was a school day, I was excited to wake up on this particular morning. I was in the second grade and I was going to "Doughnuts With Dads" at school. I was so thrilled that not only my dad was coming but so was my granddad, Pop Pop…. While we were enjoying our time together along with the doughnuts, I noticed that Pop Pop was eating rather slowly…. Being a curious seven-year-old girl, I asked, "Why aren't you eating more doughnuts?" Pop Pop smiled and simply said, "Oh, just a sore spot on my tongue that's hurting a little. Nothing to worry about, sweetie." So … I didn't worry and went on about my merry way. Little did I know things would change forever.

…In 2002, Pop Pop started noticing what looked like sores on his tongue. During his next visits to the dentist, he began to comment about the sores and how they were annoying him. Even though he had several sores during a period of about two years, the dentist never thought it was anything to worry about. Finally, there was a sore on the back left side of his tongue. The dentist tried to treat it by numbing it and scraping it down. The sore wouldn't go away. The dentist then decided Pop Pop should have it checked out by a medical doctor.

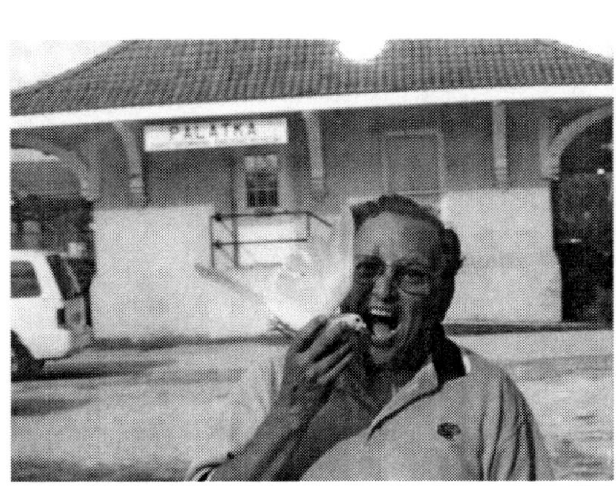

* * * *

Oral cancer includes cancer of the mouth, tongue, cheeks, lips, sinuses and throat…. The death rate of these cancers is higher than many cancers we commonly hear about, such as skin cancer and cervical cancer. 42,000 Americans will be diagnosed with oral cancer this year…. This rate is high because it is usually not discovered until late in its development, often not until it has metastasized to somewhere else in the body. Some symptoms of oral cancer include: lumps or bumps inside the mouth; white, red or speckled patches in the mouth or on the tongue; persistent sores on the mouth or neck that do not heal within two weeks time ("Oral Cancer").

Oral cancer can be dangerous because many times it is not noticed or detected in its early stages. Typically patients of oral cancer are over the age of forty, although there has been an increase recently in the number of patients younger than this. Men are at a higher risk than women and African-Americans are twice as likely as whites to have oral cancer. The survival rate for five or more years for this cancer is only fifty-five percent ("Oral Cancer Facts")….

****

The dentist referred Pop Pop to an oncologist. The doctor feared that the lesions on his tongue might have spread. He thought that the cells from the sore were more than likely cancer and that the cancer cells might be in the lymph node in the front bottom of his neck on the left side. It was recommended that he see someone at the Mayo Clinic for a second opinion. The doctor at Mayo recommended surgery. He also shared shocking news. He said, "If the biopsy comes back positive for cancer, you may only have a year left…."

****

Pop Pop will always be my hero because of the courage and fight he showed throughout his battle. He fought so that I would have many happy memories and pictures in my mind of how he wanted to be remembered – funny, happy and healthy. I know that my dentist checks his patients whenever they come in for signs of oral cancer. I hope that this is a trend that will increase and continue with all dentists and doctors. I hope that more screenings and education is brought to the public. My wish is that awareness will spare others from having to lose their "Pop Pop" or loved one.

References

"Chemotherapy" *Chemotherapy*. Oral Cancer Foundation, n.d. Retrieved on 04 May 2013.

"For the Dental Patient Detecting Oral Cancer Early" (May 2010) American Dental Association. Retrieved on 4 May 2013.

Göran Laurell, et al. (2012) "Morbidity of Supraomohyoidal and Modified Radical Neck Dissection Combined with Radiotherapy for Head and Neck Cancer: A Prospective Longitudinal Study." *Head & Neck* 34.1: 66-72. *MEDLINE with Full Text*. Retrieved on 29 Apr. 2013.

"Head and Neck Cancers" National Cancer Institute (01 Feb. 2013) Retrieved on 04 May 2013.

Jackson, Christopher R., Andrew G., Shuman, and Norman D. Hogikyan (2011) "A Critical Review of Head and Neck Cancer Screening." *European Journal of Clinical & Medical Oncology* 3.4: 33-41. *OmniFile Full Text Mega (H.W. Wilson)*. Retrieved on 27 Apr. 2013.

Lazarus, Cathy L., Jeri A. Logemann, and Barbara Roa Pauloski (2000) "Swallowing and Tongue Function Following Treatment for Oral and Oropharyngeal Cancer." *Journal of Speech, Language, and Hearing Research* 43.4: 1011-1023. *OmniFile Full Text Mega (H.W. Wilson)*. Retrieved on 27 Apr. 2013.

"Metastatic Squamous Neck Cancer with Occult Primary Treatment (PDQ®) (14 Jan 2013) " National Cancer Institute. Retrieved on 05 May 2013.

"Oral Cancer: Symptoms, Causes, Treatments, and More." WebMD, n.d. Retrieved on 28 Apr. 2013

"Oral Cancer Facts." Oral Cancer Foundation, n.d. Retrieved on 04 May 2013.

Popescu, B., Bertesteanu, S. V. G., Grigore, R., Scaunasu, R., and Popescu, C. R. (2012) "Functional Implications of Radical Neck Dissection and the Impact on the Quality of Life for Patients with Head and Neck Neoplasia" *Journal of Medicine and Life* 5.4: 410-13. Retrieved on 04 May 2013.

"Radiation Therapy." Oral Cancer Foundation, n.d. Retrieved on 04 May 2013.

In my view, Hailey's essay is a good example because it is thoroughly developed with both research and real-life stories; because it provides an opportunity to talk about rhetorical matters such as tone, purpose, and audience; and because it is engaging on an intellectual and an emotional level. However, teachers who would like their students to write less personal essays can simply explain their preferences to their students and show them models with a higher ratio of research to personal stories.

Segmented Essay

Hailey Dunavant's Personal/Traditional Essay is written in the "segmented" form, which is often seen in lengthy journalistic pieces and in creative nonfiction. A segmented essay (also known as a "lyrical essay," a "braided essay," a "snapshot essay," a "mosaic" essay, a "collage essay," or a "word portrait") is divided into sections, each of which is usually several paragraphs long. Each section features information that is relevant to the topic or depicts a "moment" that illuminates or illustrates the topic. To show where one section ends and the next one begins, the writer may use asterisks, hashtags, epigraphs, titles, or other signals. In Hailey's case, she used a combination of photographs and asterisks to signal the reader.

A segmented essay must have a focusing idea, but it will not necessarily contain overtly stated thesis statements or topic sentences. I encourage my students to use the segmented form because it allows them to move beyond the strict constraints of typical secondary school essays and because the "leaps" and "gaps" that characterize a segmented essay, along with the brief narratives and vivid descriptions, are often very engaging for readers. As seen in Hailey's essay, the segmented form can be used in combination with several of the approaches discussed here. Information on segmented essays, and samples of such essays, can be found online and in creative writing textbooks.[9]

20–25 Random Things

The 20–25 Random Things Approach resembles a bulleted list, but with fully developed paragraphs. A surprising number of students in my classes have been drawn to this approach, perhaps because it permits them to break rules that they find oppressive: they can leap in without an introduction or a thesis statement, they can forego topic sentences and transitions, and they can exit the paper without a traditional conclusion. As for me, I am drawn to it because of its potentially limitless versatility. Students could use this approach as an organizing principle for research-based essays in a variety of classes, including Biology, Chemistry, Physical Therapy, Nursing, History, Geography, Literature, and Information Technology. Interestingly enough, the Business School at Duke University now requires applicants to write essays in this format: "25 Random Things About Me" (Byrne, 2014). Perhaps the biggest benefit of this approach is that students *voluntarily* write more – more details, more examples, more explanations – than many of them have written in their entire lives.

An essay in this format should have an underlying focus, should inform and engage readers, and should use research in enlightening and responsible ways. Although students are often enthusiastic about the idea of being "random," I emphasize that the best examples of this approach are carefully orchestrated, not really random at all: more or less predictable paragraphs ("things") rub shoulders with startling ones, for instance, while humorous "things" hobnob with serious ones. Also, at least some of the "random things" should be analytical, rather than simply factual. Finally, the paper should end with a bang, not a whimper. Appendices A and B offer a sample rubric and grading system for these types of essays.

Most often, my students use this format for personal topics, but they've also used it to write research-based papers on subjects such as cars, music, celebrities, historical figures, scientific discoveries, and illnesses. One student wrote "25 Random Things About Mike Tyson" (a notorious American boxer), while another wrote "25

Random Things About Vlad the Impaler" (an even more notorious Romanian prince). I can envision "Random Things" papers on globalization, climate change, the essentials of caring for patients in an Intensive Care Unit, and many other subjects. Someday, perhaps, a clever student will write "25 Random Things About Chaos Theory."[10]

Concluding Thoughts

The process of teaching, reading, and grading research-based essays can be frustrating. But teachers who use creative approaches may find the grading process downright enjoyable. And, just as important, students may find it genuinely exciting to write research-based essays that allow them to meld their own knowledge, their own insights, and their own creativity with the knowledge, insights, and creativity of others.

Professors in a variety of departments may be open to creative approaches, so I encourage my students to muster the courage to propose such ideas. One of my former advisees asked her Justice Studies professor for permission to use the multi-genre approach for her research-based essay on community policing. To her delight, the professor welcomed the idea. Similarly, in a graduate-level Civil Engineering class, my husband, Mark Welford, once wrote about a very specialized and technical subject – how something called the Froude number varies during a flood event – but his approach was creative: he wrote from the point of view of a fish. His professor initially wondered if Mark's essay was meant to be serious, but once he saw that it was, he used it as a model in a subsequent class.

When my students submit their essays, they write a reflective letter in which they describe their processes of thinking, researching, writing, and revising their papers. I also include one question about what makes these *legitimate* research papers. In reply to this question, my students usually say that they've done "a ton" of research and that they've learned a great deal along the way. Most of them also note that they've found it difficult but at the same time enjoyable to write these papers.

In 2013, I presented these ideas in a workshop at the first annual Summer Institute on Creativity and Discovery in Teaching University Writing, held at City University of Hong Kong. As written in anonymous comments given on the workshop, one participant was pleased because the "topics [were] at the university level – complex, scientific, controversial, issues-based." This same participant wrote that she or he would "give students more options in their writing." Another liked the idea of "daring to be different and allowing students to break away from the norm occasionally." This participant also expected that students would be "delighted" to use the "unconventional genres suggested by [the] presenter." Others said that they would begin using student writing and their own writing as models in the classroom, and one thought that joining the students in a performance of a sample play could be a good way to build community in the classroom. One participant worried that the Random Things Approach might "encourage the current 'lack of focus,' attention-lacking culture" but said that s/he plans to try the approach nonetheless.

Although there can be no guarantee that these approaches will work in all settings or "pay off" for all students, I do believe that they come with real benefits, not only for writers but also for readers. And I believe that using these approaches can help students tap into abilities that they will appreciate as they move through their college classes, their careers, and their lives.

Notes

1   According to Sternberg (2006: 91), these are among the ways that we can all develop our own creativity: "(a) redefine problems; (b) question and analyze assumptions; (c) do not assume that creative ideas sell themselves: sell them; (d) encourage the generation of ideas; (e) recognize that knowledge can both help and hinder creativity; (f) identify and surmount obstacles; (g) take sensible risks; (h) tolerate ambiguity;

(i) believe in oneself (self-efficacy); (j) find what one loves to do; (k) delay gratification; (l) role-model creativity; (m) cross-fertilize ideas; (n) reward creativity; (o) allow mistakes; (p) encourage collaboration; (q) see things from others' points of view; (r) take responsibility for successes and failures; (s) maximize person–environment fit; and (t) continue to allow intellectual growth."

2   The journal *Creative Nonfiction* (http://www.creativenonfiction.org/), for example, publishes exactly the kind of work I'm discussing here: research-based essays with strong elements of creative writing (such as narrative, scenes, dialogue, and tension). The personal/traditional blend appears often in that journal, and more experimental types of essays appear on occasion.

3   It can also work well to have students write a problem/solution paper in the form of a play. In this case, the characters describe a problem (such as drunk driving) and then discuss the merits and drawbacks of possible solutions to that problem.

4   Because parenthetical citations within a play tend to be distracting, I encourage my students to create footnotes instead. They also create a References page. My students usually do their referencing in MLA format.

5   Helpful information and examples of multi-genre essays can be found online at the following websites: http://www.users.muohio.edu/romanots/mgrpapers.htm http://write-fromtheheartclasses.com/research-projects.php http://www.mrsjust-ersvirtualclassroom.com/Multi-Genre_Research_Paper.html http:// writing.colostate.edu/gallery/multigenre/introduction.htmhttp://writing. colostate.edu/gallery/multigenre/toc.htmhttp://theunquietlibrary. libguides.com/multigenre2011.

6   The essay, which is often anthologized under the title "On Fire," is actually an unnamed chapter in a book by Larry Brown called *On Fire* (Brown, 1993). It can be noted that Brown's essay has problems with parallelism and a few other stylistic matters, but his editor and countless positive reviewers obviously found these problems inconsequential. I do, too, especially when compared to the strength of the essay as a whole.

7   "The Man Who Sailed His House," by Michael Paterniti (Paterniti, 2011), uses second-person pronouns to address a specific person. Similarly, "The Miracles of Loss," by Joe Kovac, Jr. (Kovac, 2011), ~~also~~ uses second-person pronouns to refer to a specific person, while also using past-tense verbs. In all other ways, though, both of these essays serve as good exemplars of the On-Fire Approach.

8   Inti Raymi, an Incan Festival of the Sun, is still celebrated in Ecuador and other countries in which the Incan peoples lived.

9   Here's a website offering an interesting discussion of the segmented essay: https://www.creativenonfiction.org/online-reading/picturing-personal-essay-visual-guide.

10 In this variation on the "random things" structure, the author has used the English-language alphabet rather than numbers: http://www.sweet-juniper.com/2008/10/short-reading.html.

References

Brown, Larry (1993) *On Fire* 167–171. New York: Warner Books.

Byrne, John (2014) Duke asks applicants for 25 random things. *Poets and Quants*. Retrieved on 14 January 2014 from http://poetsandquants.com/2012/07/17/duke-asks-applicants-for-25-random-things/.

Kovac Jr., Joe (1999) The miracles of loss. Retrieved on 29 May 2013 from http://joekovacjr.blogspot.com/2011/04/carlene-tengelsen-story.html.

Ondaatje, Michael (1974) *The Collected Works of Billy the Kid*. New York: Norton.

Paterniti, Michael (2011) The man who sailed his house. Retrieved on 29 May 2013 from http://www.gq.com/news-politics/newsmakers/201110/hiromitsu-shinkawa-japan-tsunami-rescue-story.

Robinson, Ken (2006) How schools kill creativity. Lecture, TED Talk from TED (Technology, Entertainment, Design). Retrieved on 15 June 2013 from http://www.ted.com/talks/ken_robinson_says_schools_kill_creativity.html.

Robinson, Ken, and Aronica, Lou (2010) *The Element: How Finding Your Passion Changes Everything*. London: Penguin.

Romano, Tom (2000) *Blending Genres, Altering Styles: Writing Multigenre Papers*. Portsmouth, New Hampshire: Heinemann.

Sternberg, Robert J. (2006) The nature of creativity. *Creativity Research Journal* 18(1): 87–98. Retrieved on 15 June 2013 from http://people.uncw.edu/caropresoe/giftedfoundations/SocialEmotional/Creativity-articles/Sternberg_Nature-of-creativity.pdf.

Tur, Katy (Correspondent) and NBC News (2013, May 1) Principal fires security guards to hire art teachers – and transforms elementary school. *The Daily Nightly*. Retrieved on 15 June 2013 from http://dailynightly.nbcnews.com/_news/2013/05/01/18005192-principal-fires-security-guards-to-hire-art-teachers-and-transforms-elementary-school?lite.

Appendix A. Sample Rubric

Features of your paper	Awesome!	Good!	Needs work….	Not Acceptable….
<u>Focus, organization, & development:</u> Written in the form of a play, with a cast of characters, a setting, and stage directions showing us what the characters are doing as they deliver their lines. Clearly focused, with a stated or implied main idea. Organized and unified, staying on the focus. Informative and thoroughly developed with **relevant** details, examples, true stories, descriptions, facts, information from your own knowledge and from a variety of research sources. **Top score:** **50**				
<u>Audience awareness:</u>				
Engaging & potentially interesting to readers. Written with a lively & accurate vocabulary. Shows evidence of time, effort & intellectual engagement. **Top score:** **25**				
<u>Research:</u>				
Includes plenteous details from research sources, smoothly incorporated into your sentences. Features well-informed characters, using information from your own knowledge & from research sources. Features characters who thoroughly explain their own viewpoints, acknowledge the strengths of other viewpoints, offer counter-arguments, and so on. Uses correct number and combination of research sources. **Top score:** **25**				
<u>Editing:</u>				
Sentence structure, subject-verb agreement, pronoun usage, verb tenses, punctuation, spelling, etc.				

Appendix B. Grading System

HOW MY GRADING SYSTEM WORKS

For details about grammar, spelling, & punctuation,

see "The Secret Code" on earlier assessment sheets.

I'LL GIVE YOU A **NUMERICAL SCORE** FOR **CONTENT.** By that, I mean things such as focus, organization, details, examples, explanations, information, clarity, vivid language, audience awareness, and so on.

THEN I'LL **DEDUCT ONE POINT** FOR EACH GRAMMAR, SPELLING, OR PUNCTUATION ERROR. Actually, I ignore errors after the first time they appear – unless they're big errors like run-on sentences or subject-verb disagreements.

YOU ARE **REQUIRED** TO HAVE **FIVE OR MORE RESEARCH SOURCES.** If you have fewer than that, I **will deduct points** from your grade for this assignment. (If you have only four research sources, for example, I'll take off two points. If you have only three sources, I'll take off four points. And so on.)

YOU ARE ALSO **REQUIRED** TO HAVE **TWO OR MORE RESEARCH SOURCES THAT ORIGINALLY APPEARED IN A PRINT PUBLICATION**. If you have fewer than that, I **may deduct points** from your grade for this assignment.

<table>
<tr><td>YOUR GRADE FOR
ESSAY 3:

</td></tr>
</table>

At least one rough draft (can also include brainstorming and outlining): **Daily Grade**
Works cited page, complete and correctly formatted: **Daily Grade**
Copies or printouts of your research sources: **Daily Grade**
Finished paper: **Major Grade**
Cover letter: **Daily Grade**

7 Local Voices, Global Imagination

Using Ethnography as a Creative Approach to Student Research and Academic Writing

Pauline Burton

Introduction

Based on its etymology, *ethnography* means "to write about a people." This apparently simple formulation implies duality, as Roger Sanjek pointed out: "The word 'ethnography' has a double meaning in anthropology: ethnography as *product* (ethnographic writings – the articles and books written by anthropologists), and ethnography as *process* (participant observation or fieldwork)" (Sanjek, 1996: 193; original emphasis). In the characterization of Norman K. Denzin and Yvonna S. Lincoln, "Ethnography combines research design, fieldwork, and various methods of inquiry to produce representations of human group life" (Denzin and Lincoln, 2000: 372).

Although ethnography is historically associated with social and cultural anthropology, it is not a bounded academic discipline; rather, it is an approach (or perhaps, a set of approaches) and as such is defined largely by method. Approaches and methods in ethnography have been (and still are) hotly contested by anthropologists, sociologists, and practitioners in other fields. A working definition of ethnography could, however, be given as: *the small-scale study of cultures and subcultures through face-to-face interviewing and participant observation, resulting in communication shared with others – typically, in writing, but also through means such as speech, photography, sound recording, and film.*

This chapter explores ways in which students can use ethnography as a creative approach for both academic research (process) and academic writing (process and product) – that is, as a rule-governed, staged, and open-ended task in which students explore local discourse communities through small-scale interviewing and participant observation and then communicate their findings to an audience. Any enquiry that takes human subjects as its basis is, by definition, unpredictable; hence, student ethnography is a form of discovery-based learning, derived from the principles and practices of academic ethnography, as outlined below.

Ethnography as a Creative Process of Discovery

I would suggest that academic ethnography is a creative process of discovery, involving four stages: (1) preparation, (2) gaining access to the field, (3) data collection, and (4) writing up the findings and presenting them to others. In practice, these stages are recursive and overlapping, as with any creative task; what follows is an idealized model of the ethnographic process.

The first stage is preparation before entering the field: choosing the site of investigation for fieldwork, or being chosen by others to carry out a commissioned task; identifying problems and gaps in knowledge from existing literature and from others returning from the same field; and formulating possible questions for research.

The next stage is gaining access to the field: settling in and establishing an identity in the community, finding participants and interpreters, formulating interview questions, and gaining access to interviewees.

The third stage is the main phase of data collection: observing and taking notes about the physical features of the place to be studied such as a region, village, neighborhood, or notable gathering-place such as a local café or community center, and the day-to-day activities within the selected place; taking a census (population count, and household survey) of the inhabitants; and then gathering and recording data through face-to-face interviews and participant observation in key events, such as a ceremony, a regular group activity, or a shared meal. All of the observations must be carried out with scrupulous care and documented in field notes that can be shown to others – not only to show that the findings are genuine, but to open up the possibility of alternative interpretations by other observers and indeed by the participants themselves.

The final stage is writing up and publication, typically for a target audience of the writer's academic peers, though a wider audience might also be sought through writing a popular book (often related to a scholarly monograph) and through photography, videos, and programs for TV. The goal of classic ethnography is to give a holistic account of the people concerned and their way of life, and to achieve what Clifford Geertz referred to as "thick description" (Geertz, 1973):[1] that is, a representation of the layers of symbolic meaning conveyed through speech and action and informed by socially situated inference. In writing up, therefore, the ethnographer has to provide context and interpretation to make an unfamiliar way of life intelligible to the reader, rather than provide a raw record of observed behavior.

As Denzin and Lincoln (2000) observed, ethnography in the 20th century was mainly conducted in a colonial context, though not necessarily (one might even say, seldom) with a colonial agenda. Fieldwork usually took place among peoples who were far away from home to the researcher, geographically, linguistically, and culturally. In the greatest works written in this tradition (Douglas, 1963; Evans-Pritchard, 1940; Levi-Strauss, 1955; Malinowski,

1922; Richards, 1956), creativity is shown in the transforming imagination that gives people from other cultures a voice that can be heard: as Geertz (1973: 14) put it, "the aim of anthropology is the enlargement of the universe of human discourse."

This has continued to be the main aim of ethnography up to the present day, further informed by a reflexive awareness of the ways in which ethnographic discourse is constructed (Atkinson, 1990; Clifford and Marcus, 1986) and through the diffusion of ethnographic methods into other academic fields, notably sociology, sociolinguistics, and education. Through ethnographic studies carried out closer to home, such as Shirley Brice Heath's longitudinal study of the language practices of families in American communities and schools (Heath, 1983; 2012), it has become apparent that the "enlargement of the universe of human discourse" (Geertz, 1973: 14) can be achieved in local settings.

In any model of ethnographic enquiry, discovery of the other – other worlds, other cultures, other ways of living and thinking – is still at the heart of the enterprise. Since discovery is essentially a creative act, the staged process of a creative task can also be used as a framework for student ethnographic research and writing. Mihaly Csikszentmihalyi describes the creative process in terms of five steps: preparation, incubation, insight, evaluation, and elaboration. In practice, the steps or stages of creativity are recursive, rather than linear: insights can be small-scale and cumulative, feeding into further enquiry, rather than appearing as a single "Eureka moment" (Csikszentmihalyi, 1996: 79–80).

Writing about creativity in the classroom, A. J. Cropley adds additional stages to the creative process: communication and validation (Cropley, 1997: 88–90). In the concluding phase, students share their findings with others – teacher, peers, informants, perhaps a wider audience – hopefully learning how to "achieve effective surprise"(p. 89)[2] with their discoveries and receiving recognition for their work. How such "effective surprise" can be facilitated by the teacher is further discussed below.

Case Study: Learning about Culture

The case study of student ethnography presented in this chapter is drawn from a course in intercultural communication designed for second-year English major associate degree students at the Community College of City University in Hong Kong. This course – *Communicating across Cultures* – is a one-semester, three-credit course with a weekly one-hour lecture and two-hour tutorial over thirteen weeks, with (typically) twenty-five students in each tutorial section. In the mini-research project that formed the spine of this course, students worked in groups of three or four over an eight-week period to conduct and present an ethnographic investigation. The aims of this project were to enable students to do the following:

- Apply key concepts in the theory of intercultural communication (such as identity, socialization, subculture, stereotyping, ethnocentricity, discourse, discourse community) to their own experience and that of others;
- Practice academic research methods, such as topic-based searches in the library and online, critical reading, developing research questions, conducting interviews and observation, and recording data; and
- Practice academic writing, oral presentation, and discussion as a means of sharing their discoveries with others and reflecting on their own learning process.

Each group was instructed to choose a minority subculture in Hong Kong, and to explore within that subculture (a) a specific topic of their own choice, such as family, food, festivals, women's status, education, or employment; and (b) any stereotypes or misconceptions of the chosen group, and the quality of their communication with the majority or mainstream culture. Students were required to use a combination of secondary data (source material from books, articles, and documentaries) and primary data from their own investigation: a face-to-face interview with one individual member of their chosen subculture was essential, combined with participant observation of at least one key collective activity. The main phases of work through the semester, along with their written and spoken outcomes, are as described in the following sections.

Weeks 1 to 4: Preparation through Lectures, Reading, Video Viewing, In-class Discussion, and Writing about Culture from Personal Experience

The first individual written assignment was a 500-word essay about a critical incident in the formation of the student's sense of cultural identity, "Where do I come from?" This assignment was carried out through process writing with double drafting, a writing workshop, peer review, and consultations with the teacher. The final draft was posted on an online bulletin board at the end of Week 5.

The main aims of this preparatory phase were to familiarize students with the basic concepts of intercultural communication and to encourage them to reflect on their own experience in the light of some of these concepts. The students read materials to prompt their writing, including passages of creative non-fiction and essays by student writers. They discussed their initial ideas in class, along with doing short in-class writing exercises.

The first draft of the individual essay was an essential step in their writing apprenticeship: not so much (as they supposed) to check and correct their grammar, as to help many of them shed two major obstacles to reflective personal writing: either fixed beliefs about the kind of essay they "ought" to write (formal, balanced, impersonal, with a neat conclusion in the last paragraph) or the trap of defining their cultural identity through negative beliefs about others rather than writing directly about themselves. Looking again at the writing models and using the most creative parts of their own early writing as a starting point, students could begin to see how powerful it is to tell a story from one's own experience as truthfully as possible; to provide the key details of remembered experience that make that story live for the reader; and to incorporate the voices of significant others through direct speech and dialogue.

The essays that resulted were as varied and individual as the writers, yet expressed recurring themes: family life and the influence of parents and grandparents; family expectations and the pressure of study; family gatherings, shared meals, and favorite foods; community, neighborhood, and social change; coming to Hong Kong from Mainland China; family visits to Mainland relatives; school life and group formation; learning a new language, especially English; membership in churches and youth organizations; first experience of overseas travel; part-time and temporary jobs; foreign friends; and, for a few, living and studying overseas away from home.

Weeks 5 to 6: Incubation, Communication, and Validation

These two weeks marked a transition from individual writing to group work. The students had incubation time (time for reflection) before posting the final version of their first essay (Week 5). They were then required to read the writing of students from another class and respond to at least one posting by replying to the content and linking it with their own experience in 150 to 200 words. In addition to the required response, students were free to add comments to postings from their own classmates and friends, and many of them did so. This exercise provided students with an authentic audience and validation of their writing, in addition to the teacher's comments and formal assessment.

Weeks 5 to 8: Setting up and Conducting Group Mini-Research Project

Concurrently with posting and response to their individual writing, the students formed research groups and began discussing in and out of class which subculture each group might select for the main task of the semester: the mini-research project into a minority subculture in Hong Kong. Students were given multiple examples of possible choices, and their own initial choices gave rise to productive discussion on the nature of a subculture or discourse community. They also needed to consider the practical issue of access and were encouraged to use their personal connections as a starting point (though not to take the easy option of interviewing foreign teachers on campus). Once the subculture for investigation was chosen and approved, the students could begin to explore at the library and on the Internet for background reading, identify their special topic, negotiate access, and formulate questions.

Before carrying out fieldwork, the students had to submit a group research proposal of 250 to 300 words, stating their choice of minority subculture with a brief rationale for choosing it; their special topic, research question(s), proposed method, interview questions, and a short list of secondary sources relating to the lives of their chosen people in Hong Kong and (if relevant) in other countries. They were asked to provide at least one good source for each student in the group, including a mix of academic and general references. Although this proposal is short, it is a complex text; small-group consultations in Week 6 and 7 were used to help steer students through the process of formulating the terms of their enquiry and ensure that all group members were engaged.

Students were expected to carry out their field research – the interview, along with any participant observation they had planned – in Weeks 7 and 8. In practice, there was some flexibility about this: if students gained a fixed date with an interviewee that was earlier or later, or if they planned to attend an event or festival on a specific date, this could be accommodated – and any groups that experienced difficulties with gaining access, or with non-contributing group members, could be helped to find substitute interviewees, regroup, and catch up.

Weeks 9 to 12: Incubation, Communication, and Validation, Phase II

From Weeks 9 to 10, students were given time in class (around one hour a week) to help them prepare a group presentation of 20 to 25 minutes, depending on the size of the group. For their presentations, they were encouraged:

- to keep written text on PowerPoint slides to a minimum and to focus more on visual images;
- not to show more than one slide per minute;
- to use direct quotations from their interviewees (if need be, in translation);
- to incorporate their own photographs and short videos;
- to use role play, music, and any creative means they chose to convey the essence of their discoveries and engage their peers.

They were also encouraged to prepare notecards, rather than reading from a written script or reading aloud off text-based slides; and to rehearse outside class. Each group was asked to pick another group to serve as their discussants for a five-minute question and answer session at the end of each presentation.

Presentations were held in Weeks 11 and 12, with an "unlucky draw" at the beginning of class in Week 11 to determine the order in which groups would present. The aim of the presentation was for students to share their findings with the whole class and introduce an aspect of their chosen subculture, along with comments on the quality of intercultural communication with mainstream Cantonese-speaking culture and (if necessary) recommendations for improving that communication. When all of the presentations were complete, there was a whole-class discussion (moving around a seated circle, so that everyone spoke) on which presentation the students had liked best, and why. Finally, the students voted on their favorites with a show of hands, and their responses were taken into account in the assessment.

The final piece of work was the second individual written assignment: a reflective essay of 250 to 300 words discussing an observation from field research in relation to a relevant quotation from a single printed source, using correctly formatted APA referencing with in-text citation and a matching end reference. This academic writing – deliberately limited in scope and form – was almost the end point of the semester's work, though students had the opportunity to draw further on their field research experience in the final examination, in which questions based on key concepts typically carried the instruction: "Discuss with reference to your own reading, experience, or observation."

This course – which has evolved over several years – was well received by most of the students who took it in the years 2010, 2011, and 2012. One of the main learning outcomes was undoubtedly the enlargement of their universe of discourse not only through their own investigation, but through online postings and in-class presentations of a wide range of minority groups, reflecting the cultural richness and diversity of Hong Kong. Groups and topics chosen for investigation have included the following: Indian families and festivals, Pakistani and Bengali migrant workers, international and mainland Chinese students, the "Korean wave" in Hong Kong, Filipino and Indonesian domestic helpers, cosplayers,[3] gay men, lesbians, the blind, women footballers, evangelical Christians, heavy metal musicians, competitive swimmers, transgender and transsexual activists – a rich mix indeed. Even the weakest students had something of interest to say, and the strongest produced oral and written representations that succeeded in "achieving effective surprise" in their creative response to the lives of others.

Preparation for Student Ethnography

Careful and thorough preparation for student ethnography is essential to provide a firm basis for discovery learning, and rests on three main factors: *rich input, clear instructions* for all phases of the task, and *low-risk practice* in writing and discussion. Rich input can be given by relevant reading; for example, creative non-fiction, other students' writing, short academic texts, popular articles, current newspaper articles, blogs and forums, or documents/ websites from a particular discourse community. Such texts can be both print-based and online, with some provided by the teacher and some found by the students themselves through searches related to their chosen topics.

Listening and viewing are other sources of rich input: TV programs, films and documentaries, taped interviews, YouTube videos, artworks, and music can all help students grasp how local experience is linked with a wider world. For example, the music video "De Donde Vengo Yo" ("Where do I come from?") by the popular Afro-Colombian hip-hop band, ChocQuib Town (2010), exemplifies aspects of popular global culture as well as more traditional local customs and a sense of national identity. I played this video to my students in Hong Kong (and to the participants in my workshops at the Summer Institute) as an introduction to key concepts of culture; the infectious rhythms and lively movements of street dancers and musicians engage the students' interest, while the unfamiliar language of the Spanish lyrics leaves them the freedom to observe and draw their own conclusions from the visual images of Colombian culture.

Clear instructions for all tasks, explicitly linked to the desired learning outcomes, are essential for students to respond positively to the challenge of an ethnographic project. A creative task involves open-ended problem-solving, but this is always carried out under constraints – for example, constraints on time, resources, topic, and word counts in the instructions for a written assignment. If constraints are too tight, student creativity can be inhibited; if they are too loose, or absent, students become frustrated and demotivated. The right balance between freedom and structure has to be found anew for every class, and may still not be ideal for every student in that class.

In-class writing practice and discussion also helps students explore their own sense of cultural identity as a first step towards considering the identity of cultural others. Writing and discussion prompts can be used, such as this: "You have to put together a 'culture capsule' for Hong Kong in 2014, to be sealed for 50 years and then opened (or to be sent into outer space for beings from other worlds to find). Which six objects would you include in it, and why?" This prompt leads students into considering the relative symbolic value of objects that embody the material culture, history, and practices of their own community, and of the tension between the global and the local in the different objects that they choose. Through offering competing views and attempting to compile a master list in groups or as a whole class, students can begin to understand how much diversity can be found in the interpretations of others and how shared meaning can be constructed through dialogue.

Ethnography Revisited: Developing New Academic Literacies

From my own experience as a teacher, I would argue that the most important outcome of student ethnography as a method of teaching and learning is the development of new academic literacies, and that this outcome can be achieved by recognizing practical constraints and working within them. Clearly, the main constraint on any student project is time. Since this constraint also applies to professional fieldworkers – notably, teacher-researchers and those carrying out funded research in educational settings – it is worth considering what solutions they propose.

Educational researcher Karen Watson-Gegeo was critical of what she saw as the superficiality of some short-term ethnographic studies in which "the researcher 'dive-bombs' into a setting, makes a few fixed-category or entirely impressionistic observations, and then takes off again to write up the results" (Watson-Gegeo, 1988:

576). Watson-Gegeo went on to assert the key principles of ethnographic research, claiming: that ethnography focuses on groups and cultural patterns rather than on individuals; that it is holistic; that it is "guided by an explicit theoretical framework" (p. 578) from research literature; and, not least, that "each situation investigated by an ethnographer must be understood from the perspective of the participants in that situation" (p. 579). Indeed, taking the participants' perspective can be taken as a guiding principle in student ethnography, and it is a principle which students readily grasp; the issue of time limitation, however, still needs to be considered.

Jeffrey and Troman (2004: 544) provided a possible solution to the problem of "how to compensate for the lack of extensive time in the field": applying different "ethnographic time modes" (p. 538) in field research with different purposes and outcomes. One of these – "a compressed mode [which] involves a short period of intense ethnographic research" (p. 538) would appear to be well suited to undergraduate student ethnography. Drawing on their own research experience, Jeffrey and Troman challenged the view that every study needs to be holistic and carried out over an extended time period; they argued that different types of study can be complementary in building up a wider picture, and researchers can "use other relevant research studies as a broader context" (p. 544).

Another constraint is that of access to interviewees and sites of enquiry. Student ethnographers – especially those who aim to interview senior informants in academic or professional fields that they aspire to enter themselves – are often in the position of supplicants, requesting time for interviews or access to the activities of their chosen group. This situation can provide an opportunity for students to develop rhetorical strategies of explanation, persuasion, and request; they will need to find and open channels of communication with their interviewees and convince them that their participation in a student project is worthwhile. The teacher therefore needs to give enough time for access to be negotiated and to provide students with alternatives when (as occasionally happens) their first attempts are unsuccessful.

Writing a short proposal outlining the purpose and rationale of the research, and even submitting questions to interviewees in advance, are authentic writing activities that arise from the requirement to move outside the classroom and engage with human subjects. Even when access has been gained, research and interview questions need to be formulated with care and to be specific enough to delineate a particular line of enquiry, yet sufficiently open-ended to allow informants to express what they wish to say. Learning to ask questions that are searching without being intrusive is a real art – even more so, learning how to truly listen to a response and elicit further discussion when an interviewee raises an interesting or unexpected point (even a point that is outside the frame of the original question).

Bearing the practical limitations of student ethnography in mind, what guiding principles can be drawn from the practice of academic ethnography? Returning to Geertz's (1973: 14) comment that "the aim of anthropology is the enlargement of the universe of human discourse," it can be inferred that this is also the aim of ethnography, derived from its parent discipline; and that when students learn to bring ethnographic methods to bear on their early attempts at academic research and writing, it is their own universe of discourse that is enlarged. This is not to claim that student writing based on ethnographic principles lacks intrinsic value; when challenged by the complexity of real human experience, even on the smallest scale, students can surprise and delight their teachers (and each other) with their insights. It is probably true to say, however, that students using ethnographic methods in small-scale, short-term research and writing projects such as term papers are not "doing ethnography" but rather being shaped by it.

The product resulting from the process of ethnographic enquiry is therefore not so much the students' writing, judged by the standards of academic publication, as the development of new academic literacies and, along with that development, an enlarged capacity to benefit from further study. Dan Melzer's account of the academic discourse community mini-ethnography that he uses with first-year and second-year composition classes identifies student learning as the end product of the project: practicing rhetorical analysis and academic research methods, studying the differences and similarities among academic discourse communities of various disciplines, and developing the ability to "critically reflect on the nature of academic discourse" (Melzer, 2011: 203).

Such critical reflection includes the ability to engage with the academic conventions that govern second-language student writing: not only those that are imposed by the teacher or the academic institution (such as the requirement to use English as the language of teaching and learning, or the criteria for assessment) but those that are often expressed by students themselves; for example, the belief that a large-scale survey is more "scientific" than a single, carefully conducted interview; that academic objectivity requires them to mute any kind of personal response; or that findings that run counter to their expectations represent a kind of failure. Eliciting and discussing students' own beliefs, expectations, and fears in relation to the process of research and writing is therefore an essential aspect of the teacher's role in directing student ethnography.

The first and possibly the most important principle of ethnography is that participants are the subjects, not the objects, of enquiry. The basic requirement of any ethnographic research project, as Watson-Gegeo (1988: 579) argued, is therefore to understand a situation from the participants' perspective. In order to achieve this shift in viewpoint, students can be encouraged to examine their own preconceptions, stereotypes, and cultural biases, as well as to study relevant materials on their chosen (or allotted) group and topic. They also need to understand, and apply, ethical research criteria that respect the privacy and human dignity of their participants, and to be prepared both to explain the purposes of the research and share their findings with them.

The process of recording data can also draw upon the ground rules of classic ethnography: though "thick description" is the fullest sense may not be attainable, students can learn to set down their observations carefully, accurately, and as completely as possible, not excluding some unexpected piece of data because it does not fit with a preconceived schema or because it is difficult to interpret. Thus, they can begin to develop a sense of comfort with ambiguity and incompleteness, reflecting on the richness of human communication in even the briefest encounter: discovering that, in Geertz's (1973: 10) words, "Doing ethnography is like trying to read (in the sense of 'construct a reading of') a manuscript—foreign, faded, full of ellipses, incoherencies, suspicious emendations, and tendentious commentaries, but written not in conventionalized graphs of sound but in transient examples of shaped behavior."

In addition to constructing a reading of the data, expert and student ethnographers alike also construct writing (or other means of representation, such as oral presentation, film, artworks, or performance) in order to communicate their findings to an audience in an intelligible and persuasive form (Atkinson, 1990). This is the stage at which the teacher can do much to help students achieve a satisfying conclusion to their ethnographic enquiry: by giving them sufficient time and formative feedback to create work that they will enjoy sharing with others, and by providing platforms – such as in-class presentations and online bulletin boards – that give them an authentic audience. In this way, they can receive validation from their peers as well as from the teacher through further discussion of their discoveries and the revelation of any wider picture that emerges when the work of the class is seen as a whole.

Success Factors

I would offer the following factors as pointers to success in using ethnography as a creative approach to student research and writing, especially with students who are novices in both fields.

- Start with the self and personal experience;
- Provide rich input and relevant writing models;

- Provide clear guidelines and deadlines, but allow enough time and space for incubation of ideas;
- Control and monitor the process, but leave topic choice as free as possible;
- Help students gain access to informants and search for relevant secondary sources;
- Help students – especially those with lower language proficiency – formulate interview questions in English, even if they plan to conduct the interview in another language;
- Assign both group and individual work, and require work in and out of class and off campus;
- Insist on students engaging with live informants face-to-face;
- Encourage students to raise questions of each other and of themselves;
- Reward originality in assessment criteria, and involve students in the process of assessment.

Further Reflections based on Questions from the Summer Institute Participants

I owe a debt of gratitude to the participants in my two workshops at the Summer Institute in 2013, whose questions and comments led me to reflect on my own teaching practice and to consider further applications of student ethnography. In a lively discussion, we considered questions such as the following:

- How might the case study assignment be adapted outside Hong Kong?
- What problems might arise with ethnographic research, and how can they be resolved?
- How had participants used ethnography – or how might they use it – with their own students?

Several of the workshop participants were also teachers in Hong Kong; others came from Mainland China, Macau, and Singapore, and hence from settings in which teachers operate in a different cultural and linguistic environment from the setting of my case study example, and within a different set of constraints. One option which is available in Hong Kong – using English as a lingua franca to carry out research among members of non-Chinese speaking groups – is less possible in largely monolingual areas such as parts of Mainland China. In Singapore, one participant pointed out, linguistic minorities are relatively large and powerful, and would not be happy to be accorded minority status as a basis for ethnographic research; they would therefore need to be approached on their own merits, not as "minorities."

This comment raised the reflection that the approach taken with my own students in Hong Kong was formed by the context of situation, as well as by the focus of the course as a whole on intercultural communication. Even within the Hong Kong setting, students had explored a variety of different Cantonese-speaking discourse communities, including some to which they themselves belonged. Thus, while the diversity of an international city is particularly suited to ethnographic exploration, monolingual settings can also offer new worlds of discourse to discover. The workshop participants were active in discussing options for ethnography such as asking students to interview parents and grandparents to learn the stories and practices of the older generation, and using writing prompts as a means of encouraging reflection. Among the written comments I received after the workshops, one participant suggested that conducting original ethnographic research could help students avoid plagiarism. Another participant described student ethnography incisively as "discovering unheard voices and presenting them reflectively," and yet another summed up the main value of ethnography to student learning thus:

> Ethnography lends itself to discovery. By finding out about other people, or more accurately groups with a unique identity, students can learn about themselves by thinking about how similar or different they are from their informants.

Conclusion

What, then, can students gain or learn from carrying out ethnographic research and writing? I would argue that they learn not only research skills and practice in using academic conventions in the process of writing up their findings, but also creative and critical thinking. Student writing based on ethnography can create a bridge between writing for self-expression and writing as a means of constructing the external world and the lives of others. In faithfully recording and seeking to interpret local voices, students can begin to develop a global imagination.

Notes

1   A notion that Geertz acknowledged he had borrowed from the philosopher Gilbert Ryle (Geertz, 1973: 6).
2   Cropley attributes the concept of "effective surprise" to Jerome Bruner (Cropley, 1997: 89).
3   "Cosplay" is short for "costume play." It is a form of performance art derived from Japanese popular culture, in which participants wear costumes, make-up, and accessories to represent a particular character from comic books, video games, or animated films.

References

Atkinson, Paul (1990) *The Ethnographic Imagination: Textual Constructions of Reality*. London: Routledge.

ChocQuib Town (2010) De donde vengo yo? (Music video). Retrieved on 3 June 2013 from *www.youtube.com/watch?v=yb_jD–Yfp4*.

Clifford, James and Marcus, George E. (eds.) (1986) *Writing Culture: The Poetics and Politics of Ethnography*. Berkeley, Los Angeles, and London: University of California Press.

Cropley, A. J. (1997) Fostering creativity in the classroom: general principles. In Mark A. Runco (ed.) *The Creativity Research Handbook, Volume 1* 83–114. Cresskill, New Jersey: Hampton Press.

Csikszentmihalyi, Mihaly (1996) *Creativity: Flow and the Psychology of Discovery and Invention*. New York: HarperCollins.

Denzin, Norman K. and Lincoln, Yvonna S. (eds.) (2000) *Handbook of Qualitative Research* (2nd edition). Thousand Oaks, California: Sage.

Douglas, Mary (1963) *The Lele of the Kasai*. Oxford: Oxford University Press for the International African Institute.

Evans-Pritchard, Edward E. (1940)*The Nuer: a Description of the Modes of Livelihood and Political Institutions of a Nilotic People*. New York: Oxford University Press.

Geertz, Clifford (1973) Thick description: toward an interpretive theory of culture. In *The Interpretation of Cultures: Selected Essays by Clifford Geertz* 3–30. New York: BasicBooks.

Heath, Shirley Brice (1983) *Ways with Words: Language, Life and Work in Communities and Classrooms*. Cambridge: Cambridge University Press.

Heath, Shirley Brice (2012) *Words at Work and Play: Three Decades in Family and Community Life*. Cambridge: Cambridge University Press.

Jeffrey, Bob and Troman, Geoff (2004) Time for ethnography. *British Educational Research Journal* 30(4): 535–548. http://dx.doi.org/10.10 80/0141192042000237220.

Lévi-Strauss, Claude (1955/1961). *Tristes Tropiques* (trans. John Russell) New York: Criterion Books.

Malinowski, Bronislaw (1922/1978). *Argonauts of the Western Pacific*. London: Routledge and Kegan Paul.

Melzer, Dan (2011) Academic discourse mini-ethnography. In Martha Pennington and Pauline Burton (eds.) *The College Writing Toolkit: Tried and Tested Ideas for Teaching College Writing* 201–213. Sheffield, U. K. and Oakville, Connecticut: Equinox.

Richards, Audrey (1956) *Chisungu: A Girl's Initiation Ceremony among the Bemba of Northern Rhodesia*. London: Faber & Faber.

Sanjek, Roger (1996) Ethnography. In Alan Barnard and Jonathan Spencer (eds.) *Encyclopedia of Social and Cultural Anthropology* 193–198. London and New York: Routledge.

Watson-Gegeo, Karen Ann (1988) Ethnography in ESL: Defining the essentials. *TESOL Quarterly* 22: 575–592. http://dx.doi.org/10.2307/3587257.

8 Reconsidering the Essay's Definition in the University Classroom
Writing, Disjunction, and the Active Nature of Thought

Olivia Archibald

And when I return to write, will I be able to reshape the form so more of this world falls on the page?
— Susan Griffin, "Red Shoes" (1993: 11)

Introduction

In a 2003 article on education philosopher John Dewey's (Dewey, 1933/1998) views on creative expression, Nathan Crick uses Dewey's ideas to construct a perspective of writing "as a constitutive and ongoing practice whose purpose is not to transmit static ideas in language but to transform our lived experience in time" (Crick, 2003: 259–260). To encourage this successful transformation of "lived experience," Crick (2003: 273) interprets Dewey's philosophy to suggest that writing practices consider "a philosophy of Becoming that recognizes the importance of time and transaction in the act of writing." [1] In Crick's Deweyan paradigm, writing reinterprets and extends the writer's experiences. Both writer and reader change in a relationship that stresses the primacy of the writer's experience and involves the active, dynamic nature of thinking and reflection in the writing process. As opposed to being a vehicle to represent fixed, preconceived, static thoughts, writing becomes a process that reflects the active nature of thinking.

Dewey (1933/1998) examined in detail this dynamic, active nature of thinking and the importance of making meaning from our lived experiences in his book *How We Think*. [2] He described thinking by situating it into categories such as stream-of-consciousness thought, set beliefs, and reflection, with the act of reflection viewed as the highest form of thinking (Dewey, 1933/1998: 1–9). Reflective thought, according to Dewey, is not a fast-paced process, but a slow, rigorous, systematic one, rooted in both emotion and cognition. Reflective thinking occurs through an "[a]*ctive, persistent, and careful consideration of any belief or supposed form of knowledge in light of the grounds that support it and further conclusions to which it tends*" (Dewey, 1933/1998: 9; original emphasis). The reflective act, as Dewey scholar Carol Rogers explains, is an inquiry-based process that allows a growth in knowledge (Rogers, 2002). Growth through reflection connects "one experience of the learner to the next" in steps similar to the scientific method in order to make meaning that gives "direction and impetus to growth" (Rogers, 2002: 850). In such a paradigm, writing that evidences reflective thought can function to transform not just the writer, but also the reader. Transformation takes place through experiences of finding connections for discovery and insight – an impressive aim in Dewey's notions of education's role in society.

The significance of Dewey's philosophy and its relationship to writing has had a notable place in composition studies, visible especially in scholarship about language, student-centered education, writing in the disciplines, and discussions of expressionism versus constructivism. Dewey's (1933/1998) perspective on thinking and reflection offers us an interesting place to begin when we consider creativity and discovery in essays that are typically assigned in the university classroom. We want to see ideas in students' essays that have been synthesized, reinterpreted, and extended through Dewey's (1933/1998) "careful consideration" of their lived experiences – whether these experiences come from their encounters with texts and/or come from their personal relationships with others and the world beyond. We hope for papers with evidence of meaning-making in deep, rich, creative ways that enact the process of a mind at work and present insights that represent a growth in knowledge about what is being examined. But what happens to these goals when the writing form we ask our students to use is limited to the standard thesis+support type of essay? Why do many professional essayists view the traditional thesis-driven form as one that can limit representation of ideas? Why then is the typically dry, objective-sounding, thesis-driven essay privileged in educational contexts over more creative, reflective, personal-voiced writing forms?

Often called the thesis-driven essay, thesis-supported essay, expository essay, or "academic essay," the thesis+support pattern of writing conveys one central idea directly expressed in the opening paragraph(s) in the form of a thesis statement. The thesis statement is supported with reasons, examples, and details in each subsequent paragraph of the body of the paper. These paragraphs, cohesively held together by clear, logical transitions, develop the thesis by supporting, demonstrating, and proving the paper's central idea in a concise, systematic way with "no room for the student's thoughts to wander or stray from his or her purpose" (OWL, 2014). A conclusion offers closure to the essay and expresses in some manner that the writer has proven the paper's thesis. The tone – the writer's attitude toward the subject – is typically presented in a seemingly objective, nonpersonal voice with minimal or no use of pronouns other than third person. The thesis+support pattern is the conventional writing structure in university classrooms, typically the assumed form to use in when assignments ask for reports, position papers, critical analyses, argumentative essays, and research papers.

Rather than serving as a structure for discovery and creativity, the exclusive use of the conventional thesis-supported essay form can become one that restricts thinking, boxing in the writer to limited subjectivities, and encouraging static rather than dynamic, discovery-oriented, inquiry-based thinking. This chapter examines the history of the essay and the beginnings of the composition course at the university level to address why current composition practices privilege explicitly thesis-driven writing forms. I focus on a particular kind of Montaignian essay called *the disjunctive essay* as an example of essay forms that exemplify additional structures for university writing beyond the type of essay that is built on a thesis stated explicitly early on, illustrating how I teach this essay form in four different literature and writing courses.

My purpose here is to call for a reconsideration of the essay in university classes and an expansion of current composition practices to include writing assignments in forms that are in addition to the conventional thesis-driven essay. An expanded understanding of the essay in writing instruction that includes alternative, Montaignian forms within the essay's definition and in classroom practice can offer writers rich possibilities to express critical inquiry, creativity, and difference.

The Essay in History

Copious amounts of writing have been published and continue to be published under the name "essay." Many essayists and essay theorists have attempted to define it, if only to acknowledge that the form is, as Annie Dillard describes it, "all over the map" (Dillard, 1995: 16); so various in construction that, as Justin Kaplin declares, "all you can safely say is that it's not poetry and it's not fiction" (Kaplan, 1995: 8). Since so many definitions of the word "essay" exist, Ruth-Ellen Boetcher Joeres and Elizabeth Mittman observe in *The Politics of the Essay: Feminist Perspectives* (Joeres and Mittman, 1993), anyone researching interpretations of what the genre is could easily conclude that everyone at some time or other has written about it.

With so many possibilities of essay definitions available, one has to wonder why university classrooms have narrowed the term "essay" primarily to mean a piece of writing with a directly stated thesis, followed by supporting evidence and a conclusion, especially when considering the beginnings of this writing form. The self-reflexive 16th century Frenchman Michel de Montaigne was the first to use the word "essay" to describe his writing (Montaigne, 1575/1965) and for this reason is often called the "Father of the Essay." Montaigne (1575/1965) gave his collection of 107 chapters the name *Essais*, a French word that means "trials" or "attempts." His essays are personal, tentative, loosely structured, and digressive as he puts on "trial" his ideas and "*essaies*" his reflections, while often contradicting himself on the way to discoveries. Indeed, Montaigne's explorations take the reader on his journeys of discovery while he processes his lived experiences and skepticism on subjects such as fear, sleep, death, cowardice, idleness, education, cannibals, war horses, and "to live more at leisure, and at one's ease" (Montaigne, "On Solitude," 1575/1965: 175).

Montaigne's style of writing is so rambling that a reviewer of the Donald F. Frame translation of the *Essays* (Montaigne, 1575/1965) once described Montaigne's pieces as "a jungle of digressions, quotations, and literary allusions" (Brake, 1969: 237). Montaigne's explorations, as he states in his essay "Of Vanity," include ample "lusty sallies" (Montaigne, 1575/1965: 761) that he sprinkles about in his essays, the digressions simulating a mind at work. We readers of Montaigne's *Essays* are gifted with experiencing with Montaigne his mind at work on his pathways to discovery – his pathways of thought – and we too experience his ideas, emotional responses, and reflections seemingly as they come to him.[3] In such a form, we readers witness the writer Montaigne being transformed – a transactional act that can result in growth for us readers while we experience the writer's critical inquiry and reflective thoughts.

The form that Montaigne invented is, as essay theorist Carl Klaus describes it, an "anti-genre" rather than a genre, given Montaigne's tendency to push against systems and genres that would stipulate the writer follow a system of rules (Klaus, 2010). Montaigne's essays and exploratory structure, Klaus (2010: 10) argues, are "an open form of writing at odds with systematized bodies of knowledge and systematized modes of transmitting knowledge." Michael L. Hall has noted that Montaigne's exploratory structure reflects the age when the writer lived (Hall, 1989), the time of the Renaissance which was marked with a multitude of discoveries and changes that stretched geographic and scientific knowledge, modified educational and economic practices, and altered for some Europeans an understanding of self-worth and individuality.

Montaigne – as do *all* writers when they are exposed to new ideas and new subjectivities – needed a writing form that could represent new subjectivities and question prevailing truths. The new form of writing that Montaigne called "essay" gave him "a kind of prose composition particularly suited to the examination of conventional wisdom, the exploration of received opinion, and the discovery of new ideas and insights – a kind of written discourse which allowed the author to think freely outside the constraints of established authority and traditional rhetorical forms" (Hall, 1989: 78). Rather than a static structure that could limit discovery and creativity, Montaigne's *Essays* provided the writer an open structure to explore his ideas and capture the active act of thinking.

Another writer of the Renaissance, the Englishman Francis Bacon also sought a writing form that would allow him to explore opinions and existing beliefs of his time. For that exploration, he also wrote a collection of writings that he called *Essays* (Bacon, 1592/1996), publishing his book seventeen years after Montaigne's first edition was published. But, rather than write his essays in a form and style that captures the active process of thinking, Bacon chose to write his pieces in a form and style that allowed him to declare the *products* of his thoughts, not the *process* of how he arrived at them. While writing on such topics as "men's depraved judgments" ("Of Truth"), love's "mischief" ("Of Love"), or an atheist's hypocrisy ("Of Atheism"), Bacon presents to his readers rules of behavior and general truths in a very impersonal style and a methodically analytical form – in "preacher prose" (Archibald, 2009: 27). The authority that such prose brings to the text comes from the writer's position above the reader, the author positioned on a platform high above to posit truths in a seemingly objective, impersonal voice that masks the writer's subjectivity.

This habit of discourse is the faceless, textbookish, encyclopedic voice of prose that gleans its authority by giving us the facts without showing us the path of discovery the writer traversed to arrive at them. It is often the voice of the conventional thesis-driven essay. It is the typical prose we encounter in textbooks. It is the directive that Sergeant Joe Friday gives to the women whom he interviews on the early radio and television drama *Dragnet*: "All we want are the facts, ma'am."[4] Just the facts. It is the very controlled oral prose I often hear in fast-paced university committee meetings when the speaker asserts a "fact" with little or no explanation of the process used to arrive at the assertion.

Unlike the form and style found in the tentative, self-reflective, loosely structured essays by Montaigne, Bacon's essays reveal a writer using a very controlled prose form that offers the reader no glimpses of his voyages to discover the truths he shares. Yet Bacon's essays do demonstrate, as Hall (1989) argues, "*a* process of discovery, carefully re-presented to the reader, allowing the reader to experience the movement of the author's mind and to examine the premises upon which his conclusions are founded" (Hall, 1989: 83; original emphasis). As we readers move from maxim to maxim, we can experience growth in knowledge and be moved into action to accept and/or reflect on the themes and truths posited. Bacon's essays, although not written in the open, "anti-genre" form of Montaigne's, are constructed to allow for some discovery and to suggest further reflection, thus also giving that "direction and impetus to growth" (Rogers, 2002: 850).

Authority and Creativity in the Essay

The two distinct forms and styles of essays written by Montaigne and Bacon have given subsequent generations of essayists two distinct approaches for the essay and two methods of discovery to choose from. Essayists such as E. B. White, George Orwell, Alice Walker, Annie Dillard, Scott Russell Sanders, and Susan Griffin write in forms and styles that reflect the Montaignian tradition of the essay. The "European essay" and essayists such as Susan Sontag and Stephen Jay Gould exemplify forms and styles closer to the Baconian tradition. Essayists such as Nancy Mairs and Joan Didion offer some of both styles and forms. When considering how these two traditions are represented in essays after Montaigne and Bacon, Philip Lopate reminds us that we typically find vestiges of both Montaignian and Baconian approaches in many essays (Lopate, 1994), both styles thus offering to nonfiction writers a spectrum of approaches and a rich smorgasbord of subjectivities, thanks to the two originators of the essay.

Despite these possibilities, when universities began to include composition as part of their curriculum, the Baconian essay – with its habits of assertion and authority through a seemingly objective, impersonal voice, and its method of exploration through premises and conclusions – became the preferred form and style to use in writing assignments, especially in the composition classroom (Archibald, 2009: 20). Added to this style and voice was a rigid formulaic thesis-driven structure that mirrored the classical rhetorical conventions of analysis and argument (Spear, 1997: 322–323). As a result, Montaigne's style and form were overlooked in essay definitions and writing practices in the university classroom.

This dearth of Montaignian approaches to the writing form we call *essay* is particularly puzzling if we consider the purpose of a liberal arts education and its aim of exposing students to problem-solving skills in order that they may function successfully in our complex, diverse, ever-changing world. To meet that goal, it would seem that our students need writing forms that allow them to capture complexity, contradiction, and diverse ways of knowing. It would seem that students need teaching and learning practices involving a multiplicity of writing structures that allow them the room and freedom to fully discover and analyze ideas.

The necessities at the university level for creativity, discovery, and innovative inquiry were reinforced in the United States recently when the Association of American Colleges and Universities [AACU], a national higher education association committed to highlighting and guiding the importance of liberal learning in the 21st century, launched a series of "Valid Assessment of Learning in Undergraduate Education (VALUE) Rubrics" (AACU, 2013) to evaluate intellectual skills, articulate curriculum, and measure students' progress through their university education. Creative thinking skills were deemed essential proficiencies by the AACU. The AACU's Creative Thinking VALUE rubric specified such competencies as taking risks, solving problems, integrating divergent ideas, and transforming these ideas into something new – competencies that echo the Deweyean paradigm of "slow, rigorous, systematic" (Dewey, 1933/1998: 9) inquiry-based thinking.

The typical absence of Montaignian essay forms in the university classroom is also perplexing when considering the very messy, risk-taking nature of discovery and creativity. Rich, creative ideas often come from disorder, as noted, for example, by the writer Henry Miller when he discusses his creative process in "Reflections on Writing": "I began in absolute chaos and darkness, in a bog or swamp of ideas and emotions and experiences" (Miller, 1941/1952: 178). These descents into "chaos and darkness," American poet Brewster Ghiselin argues, require reconsideration of existing conventions in order to support the creative process since "the creative order, which is an extension of life, is not an elaboration of the established, but a movement of it and often of elements not included in it. The first need is therefore to transcend the old order" (Ghiselin, 1952: 14). How then can we transcend the "old order"? How can we, as Susan Griffin asks in her essay "Red Shoes," "reshape the form so more of this world falls on the page?" (Griffin, 1993: 11). To address that question, rather than using conventional writing forms, Montaigne invented a form to represent his discoveries and enact the active nature of thinking, reshaping the form so more of his lived experiences in his world could be captured.

The general absence of Montaignian forms in university level classrooms is also mystifying if we examine the practices of professional writers. Since the early 1970s, composition studies made a habit of investigating professional writers' practices to discern their writing processes and find approaches that can improve student writing. This research ushered in pedagogical methods that include such innovative techniques as writing groups, writing conferences, and revisions. In the same investigative spirit of making student writers more successful, a worthy inquiry to make when critically examining our pedagogical practices in writing at the university level is to scrutinize how professional essayists define their writing form. Composition and essay theorists such as Stephen M. North (North, 1987) and Carl Klaus (Klaus, 1989) assert that, when professional essayists talk about the essay and their experiences of writing in this form, they view their practice differently from the way composition textbooks approach writing an essay. For example, Klaus (1989) discovered in a review of 40 essays from different periods of the essay's history that professional essayists typically view the essay as a form of freedom beyond what is permitted in systematized forms of discourse and composition textbooks: "I repeatedly found them invoking images and metaphors suggestive of the essay's naturalness, openness, or looseness as opposed to the methodicality, regularity, and strictly ordered quality of the conventional prose discourse" (Klaus: 1989: 156).

How do professional essays talk about their form? Essayist Philip Lopate describes the essay as a nonfiction genre that "possesses freedom to move anywhere, in all directions" (Lopate, 1994: xxxvii). Such a notion of the essay hails from the Montaignian tradition, a perception that moves essayist Edward Hoagland to describe it as "the human voice talking, its order the mind's natural flow" (Hoagland, 1982: 25). In the same tradition, essayist Scott Russell Sanders describes an essay's structure as a form that simulates the discovery process of being lost in a forest "without being quite sure what game you are chasing….You sniff down one path until some heady smell tugs you in a new direction, and then off you go, dodging and circling, lured on by the sounds of unfamiliar birds" (Sanders, 1989: 34).

"[F]reedom to move anywhere;" "the *human* voice talking;" "some heady smell *tugs* you in a new direction, and then off you go, dodging and circling" – such notions of the essay which capture the active nature of thinking are not the descriptions of the essay form often found in typical composition textbooks. Montaigne himself repeatedly within his essays writes about his writing style as he seeks to express his ideas, particularly his tendency to "ramble" by "scattering a word here, there another, samples separated from their context, without a plan and without a promise" (Montaigne, 1575/1965: 219). This tendency toward digressiveness within the essay's form, this writing to simulate the mind's movement, this "dodging and sniffing," feasibly provoked Samuel Johnson to define the essay in his famous *Dictionary* as "a loose sally of the mind" (Johnson, 1755/1805) – a loose sally of the mind "dodging and circling" in an open form to seek discovery and creativity.

The Essay Redefined

Elements of Joeres and Mittman's (1993) definition of the "essay" that they present in *The Politics of the Essay: Feminist Perspectives* and Joyce Carol Oates' description in her "Introduction" to *The Best*

American Essays 1991 (Oates, 1991), comprise my definition of the essay, a definition that allows for both Montaignian and Baconian traditions and that is the basis of my pedagogy:

Working Definition of the Essay

An essay is a flexible nonfiction form of writing which "has at its core an argument that welds its various parts together" (Joeres and Mittman, 1993: 16), evidences a process of discovery, and is marked with the ability to "transcend [its] data, or transmute it into personal meaning" (Oates, 1991: xxii).

My evolution to this encompassing definition has been, during my years as a writer and teacher, a gradual one, with roots in the Baconian form that I used as a student and faithfully taught in my classrooms for several years. I began to realize that my singular fidelity to this form needed to be revisited when I noticed how much the form could limit students' thoughts, even subverting their attempts into deeper considerations of their subjects, "undermining their ability to render in a thoughtful way their ideas and restraining the act of discovery" (Archibald, 2000/2004). Conversion to my present conception of the essay reached passionate levels after a Conference on College Composition and Communication nearly 25 years ago when I heard Rebecca Blevins Faery read a disjunctive essay entitled "On the Possibilities of the Essay: A Meditation" (later published in *The Iowa Review*; Faery, 1990). Faery had artfully juxtaposed alongside an academic argument that called for wider acceptance of the personal essay, a personal story enacting her thesis via narrative and metaphor. The memory of Faery's (1990) rhetorical power from fusing both essay traditions has remained with me through the years. With characteristics that include the conventional "academic essay" form combined with other modes such as narrative, and with an organization that is both logical and "methodically unmethodical" (Adorno, 1984: 161) – the disjunctive essay form and its possibilities for discovery, expression, and creativity have offered me an alternative form to the standard essay structure and style in the courses I teach and for my own writings.

The disjunctive essay is an essay that is presented to the reader in three or more distinct segments of prose, usually separated on the page by spacing, numbers, and/or asterisks. Sometimes called the "collage essay" because of its visual characteristics, each segment of a disjunctive essay enriches and complicates the other sections with its new layer of meaning. For example, George Orwell's disjunctive essay entitled "Marrakech" (Orwell, 1939/1946) is a series of five scenes, each scene giving us another side to the ugly faces of poverty and imperialism in a country with ideologies that effectively interpolate the Moroccans into compliance with this colonial secret. As many of her essays are, Joan Didion's "On the Road" (Didion, 1979/1990) has a disjunctive structure with jump-cutting images and reflections that give us a cultural criticism of America as Didion describes in chronological order a book promotion tour across the country. Howard Moss's "Jean: Some Fragments" (Moss, 1979) is an essay in 23 fragments, each fragment told in past tense and organized in chronological order as Moss narrates his personal experiences with the extraordinary woman and writer Jean Stafford.

For the writer of disjunctive essays, the essay's line spaces can become another means of signification within the text that impel the reader to inject meaning into the silences of the spaces. We as readers enter a disjunctive essay via its first section, colonize it to make meaning, and leave. Then we see another piece of prose, but to get there we must negotiate mute space. It's a jump between two different textual mountains, and we're often without a bridge. Reading such an essay, moving from section to section, we discover that our journey becomes a continuous process of adjustments to a fluid, changing sense of meaning. In our journey we enact the transactive process of "Becoming" that Crick (2003) describes as essential to Dewey's concept of learning and as applicable to a philosophy of composition pedagogy that Crick constructs.

Although I use the personal essay form, with its narrative possibilities of discovery and argumentation, in two of my three writing courses (see e.g. Archibald, 2011), it is the disjunctive essay that I use most often in my courses. Students in many of my courses are given an opportunity to write a disjunctive essay as one of their writing assignments. For the remainder of this chapter, I share steps I have used and experiences I have encountered when I assign a disjunctive essay to four distinct populations of students in four very different writing and literature courses.

Description of Activity: Teaching the Disjunctive Essay

This series of assignments is developed for: first-year students enrolled in the initial composition course of a year-long university writing program; sophomore-level students taking a general education literature course; upper-class (i.e. 3rd and 4th year) students who have elected to take a creative writing course; and English majors taking a literary criticism course.

Students in these courses are typically traditional-aged college students. The composition and general education courses reflect the overall population of the school, which has a diverse student body, with almost 30% coming from various ethnic groups – primarily Latinos/Hispanics, Asians, Pacific Islanders/Hawaiians, and African Americans. For many years, the creative writing and literary criticism courses were less ethnically diverse than the composition and literature classes, whereas in the past two years these courses now also reflect the overall population of the university as more ethnically diverse students become English majors and writing minors. The average gender composition in the four courses approximates equal numbers of males and females. The average number of students in each course ranges between 10 (literary criticism) and 25 (general education literature).

All courses meet for 50 minutes three times per week. The activity, from the first assigned reading to the final draft of the assigned essay, takes two weeks of class time in the composition and creative writing courses and 2–3 classes in the literature and literary criticism classes. Despite the differences in the courses, I follow essentially the same steps for each class.

Step 1: Using Professionally Written Disjunctive Essays as Models (2–4 classes)

To illustrate what a disjunctive essay is, I begin the activity by assigning at least two professionally written essays that illustrate the form. Students in all classes are assigned Alice Walker's "Beauty: When the Other Dancer Is the Self" (Walker, 1983) and Annie Dillard's "Death of a Moth" (Dillard, 1976) to read since these pieces represent two very different kinds of disjunction. My objective when I assign these two essays is to familiarize students with how the disjunctive essay provides writers with an alternative architecture for composing writing assignments by the use of space, that graphic quality that marks off the disjunctive essay's segments. Walker's (1983) "Beauty" is a disjunctive essay in nine sections relating her attempts to come to terms with the blindness in one of her eyes. Most of the segments in the essay are chronologically structured. Disjunction is represented through a series of vignettes that illustrate Walker's journeys of suffering and acceptance as she comes to terms with the blindness and initial visible disfigurement that challenge her conventional notions of beauty, love, and self. In discussing this essay with classes, I emphasize that spacing can become another form of punctuation, a textual marker like a period or comma, signaling important structural and intertextual information such as a change in focus, tense, or writing style.

I assign Dillard's (1976) "Death of a Moth" to exemplify another kind of disjunctive essay whose prose segments differ in such ways as topic, time, place, mode, point of view, or even prose style. "Death of a Moth" is a disjunctive essay in three prose segments of differing lengths, subject matter, and style. The first section callously describes a spider living behind the narrator's toilet and its habit of feasting on insects. The second section is an intensely emotional narrative relating a mystical experience Dillard encounters while camping one evening in the Blue Ridge Mountains of Virginia. In the last and shortest section, Dillard gives her impressions of living alone. The first and third sections are written in the present tense and are situated in her house. The second section is written in the past tense and takes place in the woods. Each section, thus, is separated from the others not only by textual space, but by other features as well. When students discuss this essay, they often note the "extreme disjunction" that they feel, unlike the experience of reading the Walker essay. As the reader moves from section to section, the cuts, the stops, and the pauses between the prose sections often fracture attempts at finding cohesion. Students, especially in my creative writing and literary criticism courses, will frequently talk about how they become in some ways co-creators of the text as they are woven into its textual web, its architecture demanding that they too become an author in the text's "writing."

In the writing courses, especially the creative writing class, I assign additional essays beyond "Beauty: When the Other Dancer Is the Self" and "Death of a Moth" to read as models of the disjunctive form. Through the years, these other essays have included Dillard's (1982) "Living Like Weasels," Didion's (1979) "On the Road," Griffin's (1993) "Red Shoes," Dillard's (1982) "Teaching a Stone to Talk," and Woody Allen's "Random Thoughts by a Second-Rate Mind" (Allen, 1990). The criteria used to choose representative disjunctive essays generally depend on the variety of a piece's disjunctive moves alongside the essay's abilities to evidence artful ways to present both details of the writer's experiences and the writer's reflections on these experiences, two essential components that I want to be in evidence in the student-written essays I will receive. Both realms – the "outer" story of detail and the "inner" story of thought – are typical requirements for any essay I assign in my courses (Archibald, 2011).

In the literary criticism and general education literature course, the disjunctive essay is an option to writing a conventionally structured essay on literary interpretation. Even though not all students will choose to write in a disjunctive form, I always assign the disjunctive essays "Beauty: When the Other Dancer Is the Self" and "Death of a Moth" as reading assignments for all students.

Step 2: Giving the Writing Assignment (1 class)

After students have read and discussed at least two disjunctive essays, I distribute a handout detailing specifics about the assignment of writing a disjunctive essay that will be at least 1300 words. In the literary criticism and general education literature course, I suggest to students who have elected the disjunctive essay that they may perhaps want to interweave or frame their literary criticism piece with one or more personal stories that somehow connect to the literary work(s) they plan to analyze. Or, I suggest, perhaps they may want to use other genres like poetry or letters to create disjunction in their papers.

In the two writing courses, writing a disjunctive essay is a requirement, and it is typically the last essay I assign. Students are asked to write about an important experience in a disjunctive style with the goal to "tell your story(ies) with enough detail and evaluation for us to understand why this event or person is important to you, and to 'complicate,' enrich, play with ideas – deepen our understanding of your essay – by using disjunction to 'thicken' the paper's meaning."

Evaluation criteria listed on the assignment sheet in my writing courses state:

1. How well have you followed the requirements of the assignment?
2. How well is your paper supported with detail?

3. How well does the paper provide depth of thinking and evaluation of detail?
4. How well does the paper evidence creativity?
5. How well does the paper evidence risk taking with disjunction?
6. How well does the paper synthesize ideas into a coherent theme?
7. How well does the paper provide an organizational structure and signals that assist the reader to "move" through the paper in ways that, although disjunctive, allow her/him to understand the essay?
8. To what extent does the text reveal evidence of editing, crafting, and proofreading?
9. How well have you handled the "process" of writing this essay, including participation in writing/editing workshops and meeting all deadlines?
10. How well does the essay demonstrate a command of standard writing conventions?

Evaluation criteria listed on the assignment sheet in my literature courses will include all criteria given in the handout for writing courses, and also will include additional criteria focusing on the specific assignment that deals with literary analysis.

Step 3: Peer Group Workshop and Writing Conference (for writing courses, 1–2 classes)

In my writing courses, peer review writing workshops are held during class time a week before the final drafts are due. Students in my composition course meet in groups of four to five students in library study rooms adjacent to my classroom. Students in my creative writing class meet in similarly sized groups in lounge areas near my classroom. For the two writing courses, I create peer groups before class begins, provide reader response sheets to be completed for each paper read, and visit each group briefly one or two times during the activity. After the workshops, I schedule student writing conferences to give further feedback on students' disjunctive drafts.

I do not generally schedule writing workshops for peer reviews of drafts when I assign essays in my literature and literary criticism courses. I do, however, make an exception for students who choose to write a disjunctive essay. Any student who elects to use a disjunctive form is required to meet with other students who have also elected to write in this form. I have never had more than three students choose this style of essay; perhaps because the conventionally structured thesis+support form is so embedded in student writing practices, students cling to the "familiar" rather than challenge themselves by crossing over to a novel writing structure. Since so few students choose the disjunctive essay, assisting students to organize a peer review workshop outside of class a week before the final paper is due is relatively easy. I also require these students to meet with me for a writing conference immediately after their peer review work for additional comments.

The disjunctive essay has always been a part of my writing assignments in creative writing, a course that I have taught since 2000. In 2009 I began assigning for the last paper disjunctive essays in my first-year composition class. Only recently have I begun to provide the choice of a disjunctive essay in lieu of a conventional essay in the general education literature and literary criticism courses.

Reflections and Recommendations

When Canadian artist Emily Carr writes about the creative process in her pithy memoir *Hundreds and Thousands: The Journals of an Artist*, she advises creators to"[e]xtravagantly play with your idea, keep it fluid, toss it hither and thither, but always let the *idea* be there at the core" (Carr, 1966: 33; original emphasis). The disjunctive essays I receive from my students so regularly reflect Carr's advice for discovery and creativity that what began in my creative writing courses as a teaching strategy to deepen students' understandings of creative nonfiction forms I now continue to use more and more often in literature courses and other writing courses.

I have found that students are more engaged with the assignment and express the hope to be able to have this opportunity again in future courses. I have also discovered that students can present both inner and outer story realms in a manner that allows for more possibilities of reflection – Dewey's (1933/1998) highest category of thinking in his categories of our thought processes. This style of the essay offers students new ways of making meaning from experience, the form allowing them to appear to capture the nature of thinking by *simulating* stream-of-consciousness thought. Yet the simulation is only an illusion when we read their finished products. Their finished essays evidence the art and craft students have used to organize a "captured stream-of-consciousness" appearance in their essays by the means of innovative thinking and creative connection and risk-taking, perhaps pulling from both Baconian and Montaignian traditions in these Montaignian structures of disjunction.

Problems I have encountered in my attempts to assign the disjunctive essay fall primarily in the areas of instructional time to teach the disjunctive essay's form, especially in my literature courses, and the relative lack of experience students have with this writing style. The steps I use to teach the disjunctive essay in literature classes are designed to balance minimum writing skill instruction with content specific to the courses. The writing courses allow for much more classroom teaching than what I can provide in my literature classes.

Because of the problems with time and novelty of form, I view both peer review workshops and faculty–student writing conferences as crucial to my practice of assigning disjunctive essays. Alongside the importance of students being able to see how their peers approach the assignment in writing workshops, the conferences I hold with each student allow me to encourage more disjunction, more risk-taking – in short, more potential strategies to move their often still very connective essays into the realm of creativity, complexity, and rich inquiry-based pieces. Since I expect each of their essays to have "at its core an argument that welds its various parts together" (Joeres and Mittman, 1993: 16), I also use these conferences as opportunities to stress the importance of having, even in a disjunctive essay, a controlling theme or thesis in order to "always let the *idea* be there at the core" (Carr, 1966: 33; original emphasis). In keeping with Dewey's (1933/1998) philosophy of reflection as the highest form of thought, I seek in disjunctive essays a rigorous, careful consideration of theme or thesis presented to enact discovery and insight within the discontinuous segments, disjunction thus serving to capture the dynamic nature of thinking in ways that are "methodically unmethodical" (Adorno, 1984: 161).

As I plan for future courses, I am in the process of constructing a rubric to more systematically assess creativity and critical thinking in the disjunctive essay. Drawing from the excellent AACU (2013) VALUE Rubrics, I will have a rubric that can measure such competencies as integrating contradictions, depicting "new knowledge that crosses boundaries," taking risks, and thoroughly analyzing assumptions.

I am also modifying my practice of making a disjunctive essay an option for essay assignments in my literature courses. This elective component is in itself creating a "disjunctive" facet in these classes. I plan to require all students in my next iteration of a literary criticism course to write a disjunctive essay when the course focuses on poststructuralist literary theories, a strategy that can bridge this content-heavy course with writing skill instruction.

Conclusion: Beyond the Thesis+Support Essay Form in University Writing

Are there other writing forms and writing styles – forms and styles other than the standard thesis-supported essay – that can be viewed as legitimate in higher education? In other words, can students present evidence, and reflect on, analyze, or play with that evidence through writing forms and writing styles other than the conventional thesis essay in the university classroom? My answer to such questions is a fervent "yes." Defining the university essay beyond standard thesis+support forms unlocks the potential for writing assignments that represent the Montaignian tradition of the essay. The disjunctive essay is one way to bring Montaignian forms of the essay into the university classroom, and adding it to my teaching has offered me new dimensions for using writing as a tool for learning and discovery in my university classes. I have found the disjunctive essay so flexible in form and style that I have been able to successfully use it in many of my courses, much because of its ability to encompass both traditions of the essay while providing students with an open structure to encourage and also make it possible for them to demonstrate their discoveries and creativity. In the spirit of Dewey's social ideals for education, I have discovered that the disjunctive essay is rich in possibilities to foster reflection and transformation through deep learning.

Notes

1   In his article, Crick takes on current composition studies debates on expressionism and constructivism, and, using Dewey's theories, attempts to construct a composition pedagogy without "metaphysical mind–body dualism" (Crick, 2003: 265). In my chapter, I am interested in Nathan Crick's provocative insights on writing and its relationship to Deweyean ideas of thinking and transformation. Crick develops his ideas on Dewey and the concept of Becoming further in later writings, particularly in *Democracy and Rhetoric: John Dewey on the Arts of Becoming* (Crick, 2010).

2   Dewey's first version of *How We Think* was published in 1910. In 1933, he published another version of *How We Think* with many changes. My chapter uses his second version.

3   Montaigne's meandering form gives the impression that his writing is just a rendering of stream of consciousness thoughts that occur in his rambling mind, but he is very clear in acknowledging that his apparent artless organization is a literary convention, and, as with any other literary technique, involves craft rather than "carelessness" – craft that deliberately arranges the text's materials in ways other than the structure and coherence found in more systematized methods of discourse. See, for example, his essays "Of Presumption" and "Of Vanity."

4   A famous statement often uttered by Sergeant Joe Friday, a character played by Jack Webb, in the popular *Dragnet* series on American radio (1949–1957) and early television (1951–1957). Any time a female character being interviewed by Sergeant Friday appeared to wander from the question he asked, Friday would say, "All we want are the facts, ma'am."

References

Adorno, Theodor (1984) The essay as form (trans. Bob Hullott-Kentor) *New German Critique* 32: 151–171. http://dx.doi.org/10.2307/488160.

Allen, Woody (1990) Random reflections of a second-rate mind. *Tikkun* 5(1): 13–15,71–72. Retrieved on 18 December 2013 from file:///C:/Users/mcpenn/Downloads/13Allen.pdf.

Archibald, Olivia (2000/2004) *Sleeping with Bacon; Waking with Montaigne: Letters to Bacon.* Paper presented at the Annual Conference on College Composition and Communication, Minneapolis, April 2000. Paper and workshop presented at the Fifth International Conference on Self-Study of Teacher Education Practices, SIGN of American Educational Research Association, Herstmonceux Castle, East Sussex, England, June 28, 2004.

Archibald, Olivia (2009) Representation, ideology, and the form of the essay. *Writing & Pedagogy* 1.1: 11–36. http://dx.doi.org/10.1558/wap.v1i1.1.

Archibald, Olivia (2011) The personal essay as a tool to teach academic writing. In Martha C. Pennington and Pauline Burton (eds.) *The College Writing Toolkit: Tried and Tested Ideas for Teaching College Writing* 21–40. London: Equinox.

Bacon, Francis (1592/1966) *Essays.* New York: Oxford.

Brake, Robert J. (1969) *Review of The Complete Essays of Montaigne* by Michel Eyquem de Montaigne: Donald M. Frame. *Philosophy & Rhetoric*

2(4): 237–241. Retrieved on 18 December 2013 from http://www.jstor.org/stable/40236687.

Carr, Emily (1966) *Hundreds and Thousands: The Journals of an Artist.* Toronto: Irwin Publishing.

Crick, Nathan (2003) Composition as experience: John Dewey on creative expression and the origins of "mind." *College Composition and Communication* 55(2): 254–275. Retrieved on 18 December 2013 from http://www.ncte.org/library/NCTEFiles/Resources/Journals/CCC/0554-june04/CO0554Index.pdf.

Crick, Nathan (2010) *Democracy and Rhetoric: John Dewey on the Arts of Becoming.* Columbia: University of South Carolina Press.

Dewey, John (1933/1998) *How We Think: A Restatement of the Relation of Reflective Thinking to the Educative Process.* Boston: Houghton Mifflin.

Didion, Joan (1979/1990) On the road. *The White Album* 173–179. New York: Simon & Schuster.

Dillard, Annie (1982) Living like weasels. *Teaching a Stone to Talk* 11–16. Boston: McGraw Hill.

Dillard, Annie (1976) Death of a moth. *Harpers* 252 (May): 26–27. Retrieved on 18 December 2013 from http://harpers.org/archive/1976/05/the-death-of-a-moth/.

Dillard, Annie (1995) On the essay. In Robert Atwan (ed.) *The Best American Essays, College Edition* 8–16. Boston: Houghton Mifflin.

Faery, Rebecca Blevins (1990) On the possibilities of the essay: A meditation. *The Iowa Review* 20(2): 19–27. Retrieved on 10 December 2013 from http://www.jstor.org/stable/20152987.

Ghiselin, Brewster (1952) Introduction. In Brewster Ghiselin (ed.) *The Creative Process: A Symposium* 11–31. Berkeley: University of California Press.

Griffin, Susan (1993) Red shoes. In Ruth-Ellen Boetcher Joeres and Elizabeth Mittman (eds.) *The Politics of the Essay: Feminist Perspectives* 1–11. Bloomington: Indiana University Press.

Hall, Michael L. (1989) The emergence of the essay and the idea of discovery. In Alexander J. Butrym (ed.) *Essays on the Essay: Redefining the Genre* 73–91. Athens: University of Georgia Press.

Hoagland, Edward (1982) What I think, what I am. *The Tugman's Passage* 24–27. New York: Random House.

Joeres, Ruth-Ellen Boetcher and Mittman, Elizabeth (1993) An introductory essay. In Ruth-Ellen Boetcher Joeres and Elizabeth Mittman (eds.)

The Politics of the Essay: Feminist Perspectives 12–20. Bloomington: Indiana University Press.

Johnson, Samuel (1755/1805) *A Dictionary of the English Language in Which the Words are Deduced from their Originals, and Illustrated in their Different Significations by Examples from the Best Writers to Which are Prefixed, a History of the Language, and an English Grammar.* London: Longman, Hurst, Rees. Retrieved on 10 December 2013 from http://www.ucalgary.ca/~smit/Scholarship/SamJohnson.htm.

Kaplan, Justin (1995) On the essay. In Robert Atwan (ed.) *The Best American Essays, College Edition* 8–16. Boston: Houghton Mifflin.

Klaus, Carl H. (1989) Essayists on the essay. In Chris Anderson (ed.) *Literary Nonfiction: Theory, Criticism, Pedagogy* 155–76. Carbondale: Southern Illinois University.

Klaus, Carl H. (2010) *The Made-up Self: Impersonation in the Personal Essay.* Iowa City: University of Iowa Press.

Lopate, Phillip (1994) Introduction. In Phillip Lopate (ed.) *The Art of the Personal Essay: An Anthology from the Classical Era to the Present* xxiii–liv. New York: Doubleday.

Miller, Henry (1941/1952) Reflections on writing. In Brewster Ghiselin (ed.) *The Creative Process: A Symposium* 178–185. Berkeley: University of California Press.

Montaigne, Michel de (1575/1965) *The Complete Essays of Montaigne* (trans. Donald M. Frame). Stanford: Stanford University Press.

Moss, Howard (1979) Jean: Some fragments. In Maureen Howard (ed.) *The Penguin Book of Contemporary American Essays* 221–30. New York: Penguin Books.

North, Stephen M. (1987) *The Making of Knowledge in Composition: Portrait of an Emerging Field.* Upper Montclair, New Jersey: Boynton Cook.

Oates, Joyce Carol (1991) Introduction. In Joyce Carol Oates (ed.) *The Best American Essays 1991* xiii–xxiii. New York: Ticknor & Fields.

Orwell, George (1939/1946) Marrakech. *A Collection of Essays* 180–187. Orlando, Florida: Houghton Mifflin.

Rogers, Carol (2002) Defining reflection: Another look at John Dewey and reflective thinking. *Teachers College Record* 104(4): 842–866. http://www.tcrecord.org ID Number: 10890.

Sanders, Scott Russell (1989) The singular first person. In Alexander J. Butrym (ed.) *Essays on the Essay: Redefining the Genre* 31–42. Athens: University of Georgia Press.

Spear, Karen (1997) Controversy and consensus in freshman writing: An overview of the field. *The Review of Higher Education* 20(3): 319–344. Available at http://muse.jhu.edu/journals/review_of_higher_education/toc/rhe20.3.html.

Walker, Alice (1983) Beauty: When the other dancer is the self. *In Search of Our Mothers' Gardens* 384–393. New York: Harcourt Brace Jovanovich.

9 The Wide World of Nonfiction
Breaking Barriers of Form to Empower and Improve Student Writing

Sonya Huber

Introduction

To teach nonfiction writing, we have broken this wide field down into component parts and various subgenres: business writing, narrative writing, persuasive writing, and many others. This is not a bad approach, and it is often a necessary one. Mastery of genre distinctions is a literary approach that is often assumed to be one of the main tasks for student writers; but distinguishing a genre by its "rules" and separating modes of writing often has the effect, in my experience, of freezing students' natural discovery processes and creativity and even restricting their ability to use their own experience as a resource for research. My aim here is to explore the unintended consequences of this categorization specifically as it relates to students' understanding of the choices available in writing nonfiction and to suggest specific remedies to allow for flexibility in voice and mode of discourse. In particular, I will offer an overview of a "family tree" of nonfiction forms, with question-asking as the "trunk" that unites these various forms.

A Problem in the Teaching of Nonfiction

As a writer of nonfiction in the genres of journalism, academic prose, memoir, literary essays, and commentary, I find that my writing projects in these various genres are intimately connected. The impulse for one approach or topic comes out of a problem raised in another genre: an insight that emerges in a commentary piece provides a new insight into pedagogy, and a work of memoir will require research and persuasive writing. I draw from my own writing process to explain the cycle of writing from inspiration to final product (and I call it a cycle because a final product will naturally lead to the next source of inspiration). In observing the fact that genres – while meaningful – work best when they are seen as approximations, not final goals, I began to wonder whether I was explaining this adequately to my students.

It is a standard approach in the teaching of writing to show students models that demonstrate characteristics of a subgenre or form, such as the persuasive essay, the personal essay, or the editorial. As we do this, we confront a chicken-and-egg problem of product versus process. Ideals of a form are essential to show students what good writing looks like and to reveal the possibilities for expression among writers with different goals, voices, and audiences. Yet each piece of writing presented as an ideal invites the type of imitation that focuses on identification of necessary qualities and criteria for that ideal, which often implicitly excludes invention or transgression.

We who teach writing at university have in mind the ideal qualities of the essay, the newspaper article, the research paper, and other generic forms which we teach our students. Due to time constraints, we might show students a few examples that express these ideal characteristics. What I am most interested in here is the unintended effect for our students, who are asked to read and then mimic these multiple forms. A final assignment may often ask students to collect multiple finished products in a portfolio, and each of these assignments is assumed to be the students' best attempt to follow genre conventions in a specific subform of nonfiction. The final goal of collecting finished products in multiple genres may be sending the message to students that the rules and finished products – in other words, demonstration of knowledge of those forms and their conventions – are more important than the open-ended questions of research and inquiry that reach beyond each of these finished products.

This, after all, is what unites nonfiction – not the forms or the products, but the questions pursued. While mimicry of subgenre conventions is an excellent way to practice writing skills, I believe we need to also offer an alternative that reveals to maturing writing students the ways in which effective writing breaks rules and conventions of form as often as it adheres to them. This should not be communicated as simple permission to "break the rules" occasionally for the sake of calling attention to one's writing, but based on the fact that the history and development of nonfiction writing is one of wide and overlapping forms that of necessity influence one another according to the aims of the individual author. We can teach students a wide range of strategies for approaching their nonfiction writing tasks that come not out of thin air but out of the rich history of nonfiction writing. In the process, we will prompt them to analyze how various moves might be useful in their own work. We can also – as I have tried to do in my classes recently – give students assignments that confound genre and ask them to make connections beyond and between nonfiction forms.

This separation from fluidity in nonfiction isn't accidental. Within the field of nonfiction, our sense of what nonfiction writing is on an abstract level has ossified over time. Writers such as Bishop (2003) and Stuckey-French (2011) address the history of composition and describe how "the essay" as we think of it in college/university composition courses in the United States emerged through a kind of winnowing-out process as other forms (business writing, creative writing, journalism) were parceled off to their own departments. In the composition classroom, the stripping away of narration and imagination followed the dictates of academic and practical subdivision of tasks, with composition set up "as a training regimen for school and vocational skills," as described by Douglas Hesse (Hesse, 2010: 44). Many authors locate this transition as happening as the U.S. economy expanded after World War II and greater numbers of office workers were needed to serve as middle managers, and also in earlier decades to acculturate immigrants with English as their second language into the U.S. workforce. In the process of formulating composition:

> Exposition and argument were left to us, not narration and description, which were ceded to creative writing. And much of our instructional effort was grounded in further subtractions as we lost or abandoned business writing, reporting, technical writing. Containment and teachability resulted in an eviscerated type of essay, not personal writing (too easy, too dangerous), not professional writing (too challenging), but school writing and research papers. (Bishop, 2003: 265–256)

This simplified form of the research paper, as one example, is a standard requirement in most departments at the university level in the United States, and the benefit of this standardization comes in the ability for colleagues to share best practices and textbooks to address a common task. On the other hand, some teachers including myself struggle with its limitations and the implicit expectations in the form. It seems that the ideal form, when taught without nuance and under the time constraints of a class, is often reduced to a one-sided and long-winded barrage of sources that strangely fails to engage either the writer or the reader. William Zeiger describes such work as based on "a premise, implicitly or explicitly, with which presumably the audience agrees" within a paper that "then attempts to transmit the force of that agreement to a conclusion with which, presumably, the audience would not have agreed initially" and in a voice of "intrusive rigidity" (Zeiger, 1989: 236).

The deployment of persuasion is important for scholarly argumentation, workplace functions, and also for civic engagement. In order to take part in community debates and in conversations inside or outside of their future workplaces, students should be able to advocate clearly for a position. Yet as I have explored in other works (e.g. Huber, 2011), persuasion as a primary emphasis makes little sense if it is presented as the main goal of nonfiction, especially if this form is assigned before a student writer has been prompted to discover standpoints about which he or she feels passionately. In other words, we put the persuasive cart before the exploratory and engaged horse. And as teachers of writing know, reading a persuasive essay on a topic chosen out of desperation by a disengaged student will persuade the reader of only one thing: the persuasive essay sometimes just doesn't work to engage students in the act of writing. Instead, it can even alienate students from their own writing and discovery processes.

In an introductory-level writing class at the college level, an instructor might turn to the type of writing traditionally classified as the "personal essay" as a warm-up or first unit before asking students to work on the "research paper" and the "persuasive essay" in a composition class. In this first unit, the personal essay might include a few acknowledged classics such as E. B. White's "Once More to the Lake" (White, 1994) or George Orwell's "Shooting an Elephant" (Orwell, 1946/1981). The troubling implicit argument in this arrangement is that one progresses from the personal to the academic, with a concomitant rise in complexity. Yet the two forms are, obviously, very different – so different in rhetorical strategies that shifting gears from the personal essay to the research paper often produces a sense of disjuncture, as the "self" and the reflection present in the personal essay do not seem to transfer into the persuasive or research papers. In this way, presentation of a few samples as ideal types – so far separated from each other – can frustrate students who might feel themselves pulled from one extreme to another in terms of formal conventions without any way to bridge that gap.

One way to address this disjuncture, for me, has been to give students in this transition a snapshot of the sweep of nonfiction's history in order to emphasize its literary, meditative, informational, rhetorical, and other purposes and written modes and thus to point students in the direction of creating texts that follow the method by which texts have been created over time. This is not a traditional framework in rhetoric and composition programs nor in literature departments. The former has focused on argumentation and generation of text within discourse communities, while the latter focuses on output of specific examples of literary work rather than invention, most often in genres other than nonfiction. By offering a bit of the lineage of nonfiction writing, I hope to emphasize not only the artfulness and literary quality of the genre and its range, but also to demonstrate for students and fellow teachers the ways in which our common forms – research presentation and persuasive writing – occupy a small part of the overall history and presence of the genre. Ultimately, one of my aims is to open a conversation about how students can be encouraged to write in forms that widen beyond the overly persuasive and thus overly narrow voice into nonfiction writing that is exploratory, meditative, and more useful for readers who are already overwhelmed with persuasive arguments and salesmanship from every side.

Classroom Application

I first began to discuss the wide range of types of nonfiction with my undergraduate students in a memoir-writing workshop that included both English majors and non-majors. In the context of memoir specifically, this genre history was necessary to demonstrate that memoir is not a new fad driven by sales forces in publishing but is instead one of the oldest forms of writing. I slowly began developing a "family tree" of nonfiction forms based on the characterizations of memoir by Ben Yagoda (Yagoda, 2009) and G. Thomas Couser (Couser, 2012), both of whom delve deeply into the history of forms of first-person nonfiction such as the confession or spiritual meditation (St. Augustine's *Confessions*), the diary, the captivity narrative, the slave narrative, and the conversion narrative (John Bunyan's *The Pilgrim's Progress*; Bunyan, 1678/1966), in order to understand modern forms. Like the old forms of the essay by Michel de Montaigne (Montaigne, 1575/1965), the popular form of readable book-length nonfiction with narrative and research elements written for a general audience – Rachel Carson's *Silent Spring* (Carson, 1962/2002) and Rebecca Skloot's *The Immortal Life of Henrietta Lacks* (Skloot, 2011) are two examples among thousands – is personal and compelling, often interweaving research with personal stories and essayistic meditation that grapple with spiritual, philosophical, or ethical issues. This approachable nonfiction form works to connect with readers because it is the expression of a personally engaged and invested author who also has enough distance and curiosity to pursue other perspectives and outside information.

This family tree (included in Figure 1) developed as I read the work of Yagoda and Couser and filled in the branches to try to include as many sub-forms as I could think of. After using a first version of it with my memoir students, I then shared an expanded version of the family tree (Figure 1) with my students in composition, many who have been raised on the so-called "persuasive essay" or "argument essay," to open a conversation about writing nonfiction and to show visually that strongly worded arguments have not traditionally been the mainstay of the entire field of nonfiction. I also developed this to affirm for myself that a non-traditional nonfiction assignment I had developed (discussed below) was historically well within the bounds of nonfiction writing.

As I began talking about nonfiction writing with my Introductory Composition students (first-year students across many majors and many undeclared), I had the aim of discovery as a primary goal.

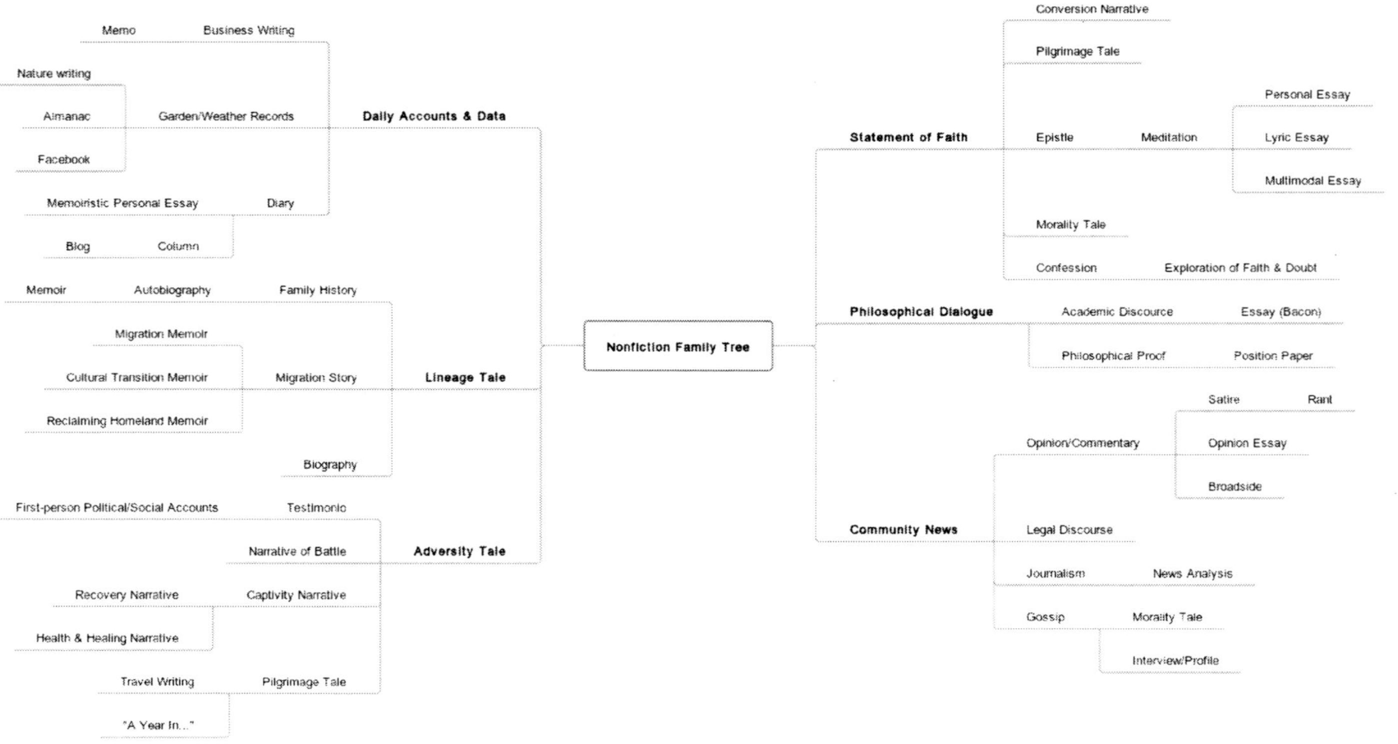

Figure 1. Nonfiction Family Tree

I found myself first referring briefly to our tasks as writers in the context of nonfiction's history, which has long included the creation of texts that exist to provide a space for personal meditation and reflection, or that help an author drawing together notes for the purpose of further examination, and the keeping of records. These specific forms include the lineage tale or multi-generational family history, the spiritual meditation, and the accumulation of records in the form of diaries. Because of our contemporary bias in seeing nonfiction as inherently functional and informational and therefore not literary, we rarely discuss the fact that the diary/life-history craze in Daniel Defoe's time directly led to his experimentation with semi-fictionalized nonfiction forms (*Journal of a Plague Year*; Defoe, 1722) and fictionalized diaries (*Robinson Crusoe*; Defoe, 1719/1862), which led to the canonized literary form of the novel (Yagoda, 2005: 45).

An important argument for looking at the nonfiction family tree is to understand that persuasion is not the function of most writing within the history of nonfiction. Instead, nonfiction forms have evolved and proliferated, some emerging from functional roots (such as business records or agricultural diaries) and developing specializations that other authors have turned into literature. Still other forms can be argued to be simultaneously functional and meditative, such as Rachel Carson's *Silent Spring* (Carson, 1962/2002), which both provides information and deeply engages with the subject matter of environmental concern, inviting the reader to engage with the subject as personally as the author has. These nonfiction books are united not by an ideal form but by the motivation of the author in finding new hybrid forms to convey information and pose questions to connect with a reader while also meeting the needs of the writer.

I would argue that the family tree of nonfiction is united by its focus not on outcomes such as persuading or informing but on the unifying "trunk" of asking questions. The personal essay pursues a question or experience in order to ask about its multiple interpretations. The practice of journalism is an obvious record of asking questions and seeking answers. Research in most academic disciplines presents the evolution of a researcher's questions over time. A diary involves a call-and-response between the data presented by the world and the writer's reaction to what is observed or noticed. Beyond nonfiction, even a short story can be seen as an exploration of the question of what happens when a character is placed in a challenging situation. Many theorists in the field of rhetoric and composition (most importantly many works by Peter Elbow (e.g. Elbow, 1995) have highlighted the degree to which writing is a question-asking and recursive discipline. As a writer commits a sentence to paper, that writer learns and reveals what is unknown or half-formed. As writing teachers, we then should pay attention to and value what students don't know, including the successful exercising of the questioning impulse in our grading and formal evaluation of multi-phase writing projects.

Examining the range of artful and effective writing in nonfiction reveals that the most skillful forms are not Platonic ideals but always innovations developed by merging forms, bending parameters, and combining techniques. As in other genres of literature and art, this blending and pushing at the edges led to the evolution of forms over time. I decided to put the theory of mixed nonfiction genres to the test in my Fall 2011 and Spring 2013 composition classes at Fairfield University. I have asked students to use journalism, creative writing, research, and scholarly writing approaches, often braiding several together into a single final project. In Fall 2011 my first-semester composition students worked on a multi-phase investigation centered around a group activity to design a blog focused on a campus issue they chose as significant. I chose the blog because of its ease in allowing for writing collaboration among members of the group, the ease of including images and hyperlinks, and for the real-world audience of a blog that often adds a sense of urgency and relevance for students in their writing process. After identifying and researching this issue as a group, students individually chose a person on campus that they would interview related to the topic, then analyzed and reacted to the interview transcript. The complete list of steps followed is included below:

1. A rant to locate personal interest in the area of "life on campus"
2. A group blog project to choose a group interest to research and investigate
3. Raising questions
4. Researching and writing for background
5. Individual phase of project: Interviewing and taking notes or recording
6. Individual creation of interview transcript and reflection on the interview
7. Transcript analysis: commentary by student on types of arguments and appeals made by speaker in interview, types of evidence provided, logical fallacies, and other elements of rhetoric
8. Research for context
9. Raising questions
10. Final essay

Although this project took the whole semester, individual components had specific due dates, goals, requirements, and outcomes. Rather than gathering evidence in order to "make a case" or to convince an audience about a position on a pre-determined thesis, my students were required at several points to return to their initial assumptions and topic in order to raise additional questions before engaging with the next phase of the task. In addition to teaching students through doing that writing and research are multi-phase recursive projects, this approach exercised the mental muscles used in many modes of nonfiction as practiced historically.

As one example, the "rant" was an initial brainstorm that allowed students the luxury of being as irrational and subjective as they wanted in their associative wanderings about a topic. I assigned this initially on a whim, based on seeing the typical grousing by students that a reading was "stupid" and "boring." I hoped that by using the rant, they would blow off steam and then we could get to the serious work. However, several students reported to me that the process of the rant itself allowed them to connect their first reactions to a text or topic with later focused questions. In some cases, they were able on their own in the space of a few sentences to perform the recursive act of examining their own assumptions and then changing or modifying those initial assumptions. After this experience, I began to think about the rant in its genre context. Nonfiction is the place of screeds and broadsides, and I expected the students' rants to conform to the broadside's tone. However, my initial expectation was proven false, and students in this rant assignment were sometimes able to use the form of the essay as first practiced by Michel de Montaigne in the 16th century (without being introduced to it) to wander from one position to another (Montaigne, 1575/1965). This examining and self-arguing is also familiar to anyone who has kept a journal. The rant, then, has become a larger part of my nonfiction toolbox, because it allows students to record and reflect on the fact that they might have multiple responses to a text. Some of these responses are even contradictory, and those moments of contradiction or discomfort raise questions that are perfect for research and further engagement.

In my second multi-genre experiment in composition, I ran a composition class this year with a service-learning component in which students were trained to provide tutoring and then served as writing tutors in the public high schools of Bridgeport, Connecticut, a mid-sized city north of New York City that has fallen on hard economic times as manufacturing jobs have departed in the last 30–40 years. The service learning orientation is one which students both provide concrete assistance to others but also engage in inquiry about the meaning and context of their experiences as well as learning about the implications of traditionally paternalistic service projects. The service learning orientation aims to develop a mutually beneficial and long-term relationship between service partners, and this class was part of a larger partnership between Fairfield University and the Bridgeport Public Schools. Our lens for the class was public primary and secondary education in the United States as it expresses the persistent theme of income inequality. Because students all had K–12 experiences themselves, I began the class by having them write about their own schooling experiences, and this theme of self-reflection then continued throughout the course. Their tutoring experiences then gave them another personal connection and direct experience to the subject matter. In addition, we used literature about K–12 education, including memoirs, news articles, and novels, to see how different writers explored this social issue. Students tutored high school students in selected classes at the 9th and 11th grade levels, returning repeatedly over several visits to the same classrooms to work with students on writing assignments that had been assigned by their teachers. They read students' drafts and gave feedback, often engaging in the kinds of conversation common in writing centers, as a writer talks through doubts and questions with a tutor to locate relevant subject matter, focus, and evidence. Between our tutoring visits, we analyzed literature, wrote personal narratives, and engaged with literary and news sources on the topic of income disparity in K–12 education. My goal was to have students constantly weaving back and forth between their own experience when they were in K–12 schools – whether public or private – and their tutoring service experience, their reading in literature, and their reading in informational texts.

The students' final papers contained a summing-up component that required them to make four moves: (1) to look back and reflect on a journal they kept of their service assignment; (2) to weave in research on an issue they chose to explore related to income inequality in education; (3) to pull in quotes and reflection on several works of literature we read related to this theme, including *Prep* by Curtis Sittenfeld (Sittenfield, 2005), *Teaching in the Terrordome: Two Years in West Baltimore with Teach for America* by Heather Kirn Lanier (Lanier, 2012), and selections from *Literature, Class and Culture: An Anthology* (Lauter and Fitzgerald, 2000); and (4) to integrate their personal K–12 experience in some way. Given these requirements, their final papers, of course, veered far from the research paper format expected as a final project in most English classes. I initially worried a bit that this final project assignment was not "academic" enough; later reflection and examination of the students' final projects revealed its rigorous academic components, including deep engagement both with secondary and primary sources. Although students were not modeling their work after a finished genre form based on specific models given to them as Platonic ideals of that genre, they successfully blended genre requirements and united these elements with the strength of a balanced, reflective narrative voice. Despite their many formal requirements and the challenge of switching modes, I found the papers to be highly readable prose employing multiple rhetorical strategies to connect with a reader. Moreover, this merged-genre nonfiction is not foreign to the average reader because of nonfiction's wide background and many functions.

Finally, I have found that the question-asking referenced above as the "trunk" of the nonfiction family tree and the use of multiple modes of nonfiction writing go hand in hand. I believe this is because the nature of the assignment asked students to develop the voice of an essayist or researcher who is aware of communicating his or her own thought process in the writing of complex texts that charted not only increased understanding of problems in K–12 education but also changes in understanding their own educational history, changed life goals (including many students' interest in staying involved in urban education in some way), and increases in the ability both to express opinions and to simultaneously acknowledge uncertainty about larger solutions to the problem of income inequality. Additionally, this process required a great deal of both primary and secondary research. Students read a novel and a memoir as well as journalistic and academic views of K–12 education as secondary sources, and also created their own primary texts: first, a personal essay on their K–12 experiences and, second, a record of their service experiences throughout the semester. They then used these two primary texts in the creation of the final project. I had them draw their own experience into every paper and constantly make connections between their own life experience and the subject matter that was the focus of the course. I employed this same approach for a paper about *Prep* (Sittenfield, 2005), a novel about a girl from a middle class background who attends an East Coast boarding school. In the paper assignment, I asked students to make similar connections between texts in multi-genres and emphasized the question-asking requirement (included in the Appendix).

Discussion

As an essayist, my underlying orientation is toward a question-asking text, which engages me on multiple levels as a reader. As a teacher, I quickly tired of reading research essays written in the traditional "academic" voice, which often makes its rhetorical argument for its own reliability and objectivity, based not on the moves made in the writing and research itself but based on the performance of a persona with certain circumscribed rules: no "I," no personal experience, and a single focus on the goal of building an argument structure. In student writing, attention to the performance of this persona often overshadows the quality of the research and the engagement with sources, especially when students are overwhelmed by requirements to practice multiple levels of skills. They often default to the surface-level require-ments of performing this persona and do not deeply practice the engagement with sources and questions. Despite the multiple tasks given to them in their paper assignments, my students' multi-genre papers had several qualities of "readability" that I was pleasantly surprised to encounter, including clear structures, a strong sense of voice, clear transitions, and unstilted prose.

Serious inquiry in and of itself is not a problem, nor is the scholarly convention of removing the first-person pronoun from prose. The posturing and artificial persona of the scholar, however, may not always be appropriate for beginning researchers, and the performance of this persona may take so much of a students' energy that they misunderstand their writing task and see this performance as their ultimate goal. While Enlightenment values might say that the visible "I" makes a text unreliable, more sophisticated post-Enlightment understandings of texts have moved beyond the dualism of objectivity vs. subjectivity to recognize that each account is situated. This is a stance which, while moving away from classical, context-free definitions of reliability, does not at all descend into solipsism or nihilism. Rather, it recognizes – like peer review in academia – that communities are built not only on shared values but on overlapping perspectives that correct each other and develop into larger conversations.

Traditionally, rhetoric examines the degree to which a text makes an effect on a reader. Richard Filloy writes that Aristotle's concept of *ethos* is grounded in a narrator's communication of his or her "good sense, virtue, and goodwill" (Filloy, 1989: 55). Yet in the traditional conception of an academic essay, the academic persona demonstrates through its moves a certain argument of disinterest, then asks the reader to transfer these moves to the assumption that the narrator is reliable and therefore believable. Today, however, the average reader is a savvy consumer of this persona performance of the "expert" intent on persuading a reader. A narrator who comes on strong with surface arguments for his or her reliability and virtue and who enacts a strong persuasive case may be in fact less persuasive when encountered by a skeptical or media-savvy reader who has seen too many iterations of this performance. Such an association can paradoxically reveal the narrator to be less self-critical and therefore less reliable than one who admits his or her own experience, questions, and even vulner-abilities as a starting point.

As a counterexample to the strong and unified rhetorical performance of persuasion, Filloy (1989) uses the example of the essays of George Orwell, who Filloy identifies as using a rhetorical strategy of self-effacement, presenting himself as non-exceptional: "in doing so, he turned the classical theory of ethos on its head" (p.

57). Filloy describes Orwell as persuading the reader by beginning with his "individual thoughts and feelings which were then adjusted, altered, even abandoned, to fit political principles. But as any reader of Orwell knows, the sense of the individual, of the person struggling with social justice and political necessity, is never lost" (p. 53). What we follow, and what transforms the reader, is the encounter with Orwell's changing rather than static viewpoint on a topic, tracked throughout the course of an essay: "The narrator's character thus becomes the chief means of persuasion" (p. 54).

This insight explains the persuasion enacted in essays that are not structured in the genre of persuasion and highlights the fact that reflection can be highly effective rhetoric. This builds upon a discovery-oriented approach to research writing, as seen in the valuable "I-Search" approach introduced by Ken Macrorie, in which students track their own questions as they navigate a research project (Macrorie, 1988). However, in the example I have provided from my own classes, the questions and reflections pursued by students can reach beyond students' initial personal interest and into multiple subjects linked in some way to their personal past or present experiences (Macrorie, 1988). I found, in my students' writing in a merged genre that required reflection integrated with research, a readable prose in which students were often able to integrate doubt, acknowledge limitations, and use questions as a means of scaffolding their own critical and creative thinking, integrating a reflective voice more fully into formal documents produced for class assignments.

Composition Studies has traditionally had an uneasy relationship with the personal narrative, using it as a stepping stone to more complex assignments. Writing from the first-person perspective has been excluded to challenge students to reach beyond a limited personal reference point and rigorously examine texts and ideas without falling back on simplified responses to texts such as "I didn't like it." But writing from life itself remains useful, and a complex level of analysis and synthesis can be achieved by asking students to weave life experience with research and reflection on readings in order to challenge students to connect to reading material at a deeper level. The self-persona as presented on the page can be a complex filter through which students generate knowledge and track their changing reactions to texts. I would argue that this mode of writing is a more accurate fit with the daily practices of research in various fields and is also in keeping with the long history and legacy of nonfiction writing. For developing writers, allowing a persona of researcher and question-asker to be expressed on the page does not demand the creation of a false academic persona, which I believe sets up an artificial alienation from writing and inquiry.

Towards a New Sense of the Writerly "I"

We currently offer students two choices in nonfiction writing – "I" and "no I" – but we might go beyond this, using the history of nonfiction to steer us, in developing students' awareness of a "Fluid I," that of a flexible narrative persona. The "Fluid I" can give student writers a greater sense of movement within the "I," beyond the dualism of subjective and objective and into the realm of the intersubjective. This might also release students from the incorrect assumption that a "Hidden I" equals formal writing and objectivity whereas an "Explicit I" equals informality. Ultimately, I believe the doubts and questions of the narrator and writer are the centerpieces of good rhetoric *and* good research. In an effort to stop students from rambling on about unfounded opinions, the response of some teachers appears to be to take students' selves completely off the page. I am arguing here that we should put students back on the page as knowers who are also questioners and doubters in order to show them how persuasive and thoughtful nonfiction writing has been created for centuries.

References

Augustine, Saint (2002) *Confessions* (trans. R. S. Pine-Coffin). New York: Penguin.

Bishop, Wendy (2003) Suddenly sexy: Creative nonfiction rear-ends composition. *College English* 65(3): 257–275. http://dx.doi.org/10.2307/3594257.

Bunyan, John (1678/1966) *The Pilgrim's Progress* (ed. Roger Sharrock). London: Edward Arnold.

Carson, Rachel (1962/2002) *Silent Spring.* New York: Houghton Mifflin.

Couser, G. Thomas (2012) *Memoir: An Introduction.* New York: Oxford University Press.

Defoe, Daniel (1719/1862) *The Adventures of Robinson Crusoe.* London: S. O. Beeton.

Defoe, Daniel (1722) *Journal of a Plague Year*. London: E. Nutt.

Elbow, Peter (1975) *Writing Without Teachers*. New York: Oxford University Press.

Filloy, Richard (1989) Orwell's political persuasion. In Chris Anderson (ed.) *Literary Nonfiction: Theory, Criticism, Pedagogy* 53–68. Carbondale: Southern Illinois University Press.

Hesse, Douglas (2003) Who owns creative nonfiction? In Teresa Enos and Keith Miller (eds.) *Beyond Post-Process and Post-Modernism: Essays on the Spaciousness of Rhetoric* 251–266. Mahwah: Erlbaum.

Hesse, Douglas (2010) The place of creative writing in composition studies. *College Composition and Communication* 62: 31–52. Retrieved on 30 January 2014 from http://www.ncte.org/library/NCTEFiles/Resources/Journals/CCC/0621-sep2010/CCC0621Place.pdf.

Huber, Sonya (2011) *The Backwards Research Guide: Using Your Life for Reflection, Connection, and Inspiration.* London: Equinox Publications.

Lanier, Heather Kirn (2012) *Teaching in the Terrordome: Two Years in West Baltimore with Teach for America.* Columbia: University of Missouri Press.

Lauter, Paul and Fitzgerald, Ann (2000) *Literature, Class and Culture: An Anthology.* New York: Longman.

Macrorie, Ken (1988) *The I-Search Paper*. Revised edition of *Search Writing*. Portsmouth, New Hampshire: Heinemann.

Montaigne, M. de (1575/1965) *The Complete Essays of Montaigne* (trans. Donald M. Frame). Stanford: Stanford University Press.

Orwell, George (1946/1981) Shooting an elephant. *A Collection of Essays* 148–156. New York: Harcourt.

Sittenfeld, Curtis (2005) *Prep.* New York: Random House.

Skloot, Rebecca (2011) *The Immortal Life of Henrietta Lacks.* New York: Broadway Books.

Stuckey-French, Ned. (2011) *The American Essay in the American Century.* Columbia: University of Missouri Press.

White, E. B. (1994) Once more to the lake. *The Art of the Personal Essay: An Anthology from the Classical Era to the Present* (ed. Phillip Lopate) 533–538. New York: Doubleday.

Yagoda, Ben (2009) *Memoir: A History.* New York: Riverhead Books.

Zeiger, William (1989) The personal essay and egalitarian rhetoric. In Chris Anderson (ed.) *Literary Nonfiction: Theory, Criticism, Pedagogy* 235–244. Carbondale: Southern Illinois University Press.

Appendix

EN 12, Spring 2013
Major Paper 2 * Sonya Huber
Personal Reflection and Analysis
Draft Due: March 27
Final Paper Due: April 4

Your second paper will use your personal experience in high school to compare and contrast with the experiences portrayed in *Prep*. First, develop a thesis – just a statement of what you will focus on – that explores *one specific* theme brought up in *Prep* that you can connect broadly to education and specifically to your experiences. Why do you find this connection interesting? Why should it matter to the reader? Can you make the case for why this is relevant to consider in light of the debates about education in the United States?

Second, provide evidence from your own experience to give concrete examples, scenes, images, and memories that compare or contrast with specific moments or images in *Prep* (with quotes). For each, you will be doing more than a "compare and contrast." You will use each piece of evidence to offer an interpretation, analysis, reflection, or question that pursues some larger issue related to education, access, and/or social class.

Third, raise questions. You don't have to solve the school funding crisis. Just mull it over – evidence of thought is more important than an over-confidence thesis.

Fourth, a conclusion. How might this element/theme connect to larger questions we have considered so far in class about education, access to education, and messages about expectations? In this section, use a quote from any other reading we have considered in the class so far.

An "A" paper will:

1. Correctly include quotes within the text
2. Incorporate the quotes and have a *conversation* with the quotes
3. Go beyond simple "compare and contrast" to raise the stakes, connect to larger issues, and bring up complexity.

Papers must have these qualities to get a "C" or better:

1. A separate works cited page
2. A logical structure with introduction and conclusion
3. Transitions & clarity
4. Four or more quotes from the book
5. A thesis – this can be a QUESTION you investigate
6. At least **five** double-spaced pages
7. Formatted with 12-point font, page numbers, spelling and grammar proofread adequately.

Part 3
Applying Techniques from Creative Writing and Literature to University Writing

10 The Creative "I" Workshop

Xu Xi

Introduction

For over a decade, I've taught creative writing workshops in fiction and creative nonfiction to Masters of Fine Arts (M.F.A.) students. M.F.A. programs develop serious literary writers, and in the United States, where the degree was first established, such programs have become the training ground for many writers who go on to win major national and international literary awards in fiction, poetry and literary or creative nonfiction. The workshop model, originally pioneered at the University of Iowa's Writer Workshop some seventy years ago, is a rigorous one. The class usually meets weekly (or daily in the case of low-residency programs), and the students whose piece will be "workshopped" in that session must submit their manuscript in advance for the rest of the participants in the group and the faculty leader to read. A typical workshop session (which usually lasts around an hour per manuscript) involves group members each critiquing the manuscript for issues of writing craft, directed by a faculty writer. Generally, the workshop is unique to the genre of the students; poets are workshopped only with other poets, fiction only with fiction writers, etc.

This standard workshop teaching approach can be daunting for the writer whose work is critiqued; M.F.A. students often refer to such sessions as ones where they get "torn apart"; the literary work and its writer's ego are inextricably linked among such advanced creative writing students. Although this model is adapted and used for all kinds of university writing teaching, the M.F.A. workshop retains a kind of mystique (rightly or wrongly) among would-be poets and writers, and "survival" of the experience is a rite of passage, given the competition for acceptance into the most prestigious M.F.A. programs and the even more competitive odds of subsequently pursuing and establishing a successful literary publishing career.

For the 2013 Summer Institute on Creativity and Discovery in the Teaching of University Writing held at City University of Hong Kong, I taught a highly modified version of the standard M.F.A. writing workshop which was titled *The Creative "I."* The modification was designed for beginning writers or academic writers or college teachers of writing. The audience in mind is one that may not necessarily have previously written creative literary work or those who have never written or desired to write such work, unlike an M.F.A. workshop of those accepted for study in graduate level creative writing programs. The objective was to introduce some of the approaches and thinking which creative writers use in M.F.A. teaching to this audience in order to give them new tools that might be usefully applied to the teaching of various other forms of college writing. Here is a brief description of the aims of the workshop:

> All human beings have a story to tell. It may be a story from life, or one that is imagined, but storytelling is a basic human impulse and desire. Language evolves because we need to "talk-story" (講故事), this Chinese-English term popularized by the Chinese-American author Maxine Hong Kingston. In this workshop, Xu Xi will exercise your creative "I" through language. She will show you how to give voice, through writing, of the stories inside you. There will be in-class reading and writing exercises to help you read and think like a writer. She will also talk about ways to develop your writing life. Participants should come with an open mind and a

willingness to tap into their creative "I" through language. Bring either a laptop or good old-fashioned paper and pen.

Essentially, what this workshop tried to do was introduce the idea of writing personal stories by learning to think and read like a writer. Writers read with an eye towards how a story is constructed, in other words, the technical issues of *craft,* such as the architecture of the plot, the choice of point of view, the reason for the sentence or paragraph structure, how characters are introduced, and the consciousness of the protagonist, among many other craft issues. In other words, it is to read the *how* of the narrative, the artifice behind it that the author has chosen, in order to understand why it works as a story. This is different from the more typical experience of those who read for enjoyment or knowledge or, for example, in a literature class (the experience for many in their secondary or university education), where the main focus is on literary criticism and the theoretical framework to inform such reading.

Workshop Activities

There was a pre-workshop reading assignment which introduced two narrative genres, fiction and creative nonfiction. These were "The New Year," a short story by Pamela Painter (Painter, 1999), and "Leap," a creative nonfiction essay by Brian Doyle (Doyle, 2002). Both pieces could be classified as either short-short or flash narratives, meaning work that is usually under 1,000 words. The terms "short-short" and "flash" are used almost inter-changeably in contemporary literary publishing, although "flash" generally denotes very short work, even as short as a sentence or paragraph. Also included was a short excerpt from *The Mindful Writer* (Moore, 2012) to set the tone for how writers think about and experience the creative process for producing their work. In particular, the quote from Thomas Mann, that "a writer is someone for whom writing is more difficult than it is for other people"

(Mann, 1947) offers a perspective about what writing is or can be. University writing teachers must try to encourage their students *not* to find writing too difficult because they need to learn to write, whereas no M.F.A. student needs to be told to write, as that person already chooses to do so and is driven by whatever passions drive this. University writing students generally must learn to write in order to turn out essays or research or academic papers, and some would probably never write if they didn't have to. It is likely easier to learn to write an undergraduate essay or paper passably well than it is to make a commitment to being a writer and coming to terms with the idea that nothing you write is or ever will be "good enough." Hence Thomas Mann's perspective.

That no one *needs* to write a poem or memoir or novel is something a creative writing workshop asks participants to consider, and it therefore shifts the paradigm for what it means to call yourself "a writer." As Moore (2012) points out, the reason writing is more difficult for a writer is "because we care about finding the right word, the clearest expression, and we understand that a thought needs to be revised tens or hundreds of times before we find the perfect way to say what we really mean." Moore is himself a highly acclaimed creative nonfiction writer and essayist, known for his short, pithy work and precision of language. The discussion generated from the pre-workshop reading assignments provided a way to talk about the writer's passion, persistence, and art; and how writers approach their work may prove helpful for those who need to encourage and motivate their university writing students.

The workshop was structured around two main handouts of first lines and first paragraphs of fiction and creative nonfiction. Participants read these during the workshop and were asked to choose only *one* that each felt s/he would want to continue to read on the basis of that first line or paragraph. Discussion then centered around the why of that choice, as invariably, different choices were made by individuals in the group. Since this is a format I've long used for either beginning writing workshops or for one-off workshops at literary festivals or conferences, I generally always include a few choices that have proven over time to be "hot favorites." A good example is the opening line "I steal" from the short story, "Lawns," by Mona Simpson (Simpson, 1984). For one thing, few members of such audiences ever recognize it (whereas many fiction writers already know this story). Also, its brevity always startles and intrigues participants, and in some rare cases, moral judgments are levied by less imaginative readers who respond with the likes of "I would never read that because stealing is wrong," or "such a person is bad." Two other contrasting examples include the opening of an essay – "When the weather is good, or when I'm tired of having seven million neighbors, I drive north from downtown Beijing" (Hessler, 2007) – and the opening of a piece of flash fiction: "There's a bomb on this plane" (DeMarinis, 1996).

These opening lines and paragraphs are first given to participants without attribution so as not to prejudice their thinking. The idea is to get them to look closely at the language of storytelling, that is, the nuts and bolts of creative work, without concern for how famous a writer is or even what genre the piece might be; fiction and creative nonfiction were mixed in order to prompt discussion of genre. As a contrast to the first part of the reading exercise, participants were also asked to choose the opening line or paragraph that would least make them wish to read on. The fact that one person's favorite choice would be another one's least favorite highlights the difference between readers, and invites participants to read like writers, rather than merely as readers whose tastes may be due to unpredictable and inconsequential reasons for the writer or the work. This aspect of the workshop is usually what surprises participants the most, as their judgment is challenged if, for example, one person loves an opening line because she or he can relate to the situation of the piece or is intrigued by the mystery, whereas another says that same opening is boring or uninteresting or that it suggests an inconsequential story. We usually examine the *why* of each person's choice, and it's startling how otherwise intelligent participants suddenly can only say something as mundane as "well, I just don't find that subject interesting" but are unable to offer any reason why. This allows a discussion about language, emotional responses, preference for one kind of story over another or of nonfiction over fiction, and the reasons for those preferences. In other words, we look at the text itself to unlock the reason for the reaction, which focuses the participants on how to read beyond subjective preferences, *and to try to see instead what the writer of the piece is attempting to achieve.*

A writer's primary tool is language, and this workshop tried to show participants how to pay close attention to ways of manipulating language in storytelling. Only after the reading exercises were completed did the participants receive a handout with a key citing attribution for the examples used. (See the Appendix for a few examples included in the handouts.) The reason for this approach is that anonymity focuses the group on just the words themselves, out of the context of what these lines and paragraphs are supposed to be. After all, reading literature requires a "willing suspension of disbelief," and this is a variant of that suspension. Participants are often surprised by which ones were fiction and which nonfiction, and in cases where they recognize the author, this may cause them to reflect on how their opinions are formed. Secondly, first lines take on new meaning when participants see the rest of the paragraphs that follow, as this can confound their original expectations. Notably, some participants revise their chosen first lines when they see the paragraph, as a gripping first sentence may or may not live up to its promise, while a rather ordinary or bland first sentence might actually follow with a far more compelling story.

In between the reading exercises, participants were asked to write first lines and paragraphs of a story they wish to tell. They were then asked to revise these after the reading exercise and discussion around why certain opening lines and paragraphs work better than others. This reading exercise acts as a prompt for the participants to think about why a writer chooses a certain word or sentence or sequence of sentences for an opening. It is, essentially, showing non-writers how creative writers think. Given the size of the Summer Institute workshop, the writing exercises were private to each individual. For those interested in actually pursuing creative writing, this gives them a starting point that may be the genesis of a piece. For others, such as the Institute's teachers of university writing, this put them in the student's role of having to write in a form that might be unfamiliar or new – an experience that their own students might find themselves in.

To conduct the workshop, I used a PowerPoint presentation showing the sequence of the writing exercises. The closing section of the workshop included a few slides about the writer's life.

Reflections on the Workshop

This was a successful workshop as the participants were willing to speak up and offer opinions about why some opening lines worked better than others. As these were all teachers of university writing, they were used to the idea of discussing language and style, even if this was in fiction and creative nonfiction as opposed to an academic essay or a research paper. As the majority had read the pre-workshop assignment, this allowed for a more fruitful discussion.

In similar workshops for beginning creative writers, I modify the format so that the group is firstly much smaller and secondly, time is built in to allow the students to share their first lines or paragraphs by reading these aloud. As the Summer Institute workshop was essentially a one-off session, similar to the kind I conduct at conferences, book fairs, or festivals for large audiences, where no limit is placed on the number of participants, sharing individual first lines or paragraphs would take too long.

Although this is a successful way to introduce some fundamentals of creative writing, I should emphasize that this format is not in any way what an M.F.A. creative writing workshop demands. However, it is possible to adapt the approach used in M.F.A.

creative writing programs by creatively structuring a workshop that is fun, educational, and inspiring as well. Several participants indicated that the workshop was an inspiration and gave them ideas of how to introduce some of these elements into their own teaching. For one thing, the handouts with the reference information gave all participants a significant amount of reading material that, for the most part, was completely new to them. This could be useful reading material for anyone teaching narrative writing of any kind, literary or otherwise. In all of the years I've taught variations of this basic format, it has never happened that any participant in such non-writer workshops can identify all of the first lines or paragraphs, or have even heard of the authors included – although several on the lists are fairly big names. Other participants say that the activity of having students respond to first lines in terms of "which one would you choose to read" and choosing only one reflects the kind of judgment any writer, creative or otherwise, needs to make when selecting the right turn of phrase, or word, or image for her or his own work. This can easily be adapted to any form of writing that needs to be taught. Finally, asking students to think in terms of genre for this exercise – the differences and similarities between creative nonfiction and fiction – can be applied to other forms of writing where comparable genres or categories must be learned.

References

Dawson, Jill (2011) *Lucky Bunny*. London: Hodder and Stoughton.

DeMarinis, Rick (1996) Your fears are justified. In Stern, Jerome (ed.) *Micro Fiction: An Anthology of Really Short* Stories 36. New York: W. W. Norton.

Doyle, Brian (2003) *Leaping: Revelations and Epiphanies*. New Orleans: Loyola Press. Retrieved on 1 May 2013 from http://www.pbs.org/wgbh/pages/frontline/shows/faith/questions/leap.html.

Hessler, Peter (2007) Walking the wall. Letter from China. *The New Yorker*. May 21, 2007. Retrieved on 1 May 2013 from http://www.newyorker. com/reporting/2007/05/21/070521fa_fact_hessler. Also available at http:// www.thegreatwall.com.cn/en/tot/topic/topic05/.

Langomarsino, Nancy (2005) *Light From an Eclipse*. Buffalo: White Wine Press.

Mann, Thomas (1947) *Essays of Three Decades*. Westminster, Maryland: Random House.

Moore, Dinty W. (2012) *The Mindful Writer: Noble Truths of the Writing Life*. Boston: Wisdom.

Painter, Pamela (1999) The new year. In *The Long and the Short of It*. Pittsburg: Carnegie Mellon University Press.

Simpson, Mona (1984) Lawns. *The Iowa Review* 14(3): 80–98. Retrieved on 1 May 2013 from http://www.jstor.org/stable/20156080.

Vaswami, Neela (2010) *You Have Given Me a Country*. Louisville, Kentucky: Sarabande Books, Inc.

Appendix

Four examples of first lines out of 18 given to the workshop group:

1. "Lately, for some strange reason, I've been wondering which of his three daughters he will forget first."

   Light From an Eclipse by Nancy Langomarsino (Langomarsino, 2005; conf/memoir)

2. "There's a bomb on this plane."

   "Your Fears Are Justified" by Rick DeMarinis (DeMarinis, 1996; fiction/flash fiction)

3. "I steal."

   "Lawns" by Mona Simpson (Simpson, 1986; fiction/short story)

4. "When the weather is good, or when I'm tired of having seven million neighbors, I drive north from downtown Beijing."

   "Walking the Wall" by Peter Hessler (Hessler, 2007; cnf/essay)

Two examples of first paragraphs out of 16 given to the workshop group:

1. Queenie's not my real name, of course. The name I was given at birth is plain enough, well known, and easily looked up. Queenie's the name I took, chose for myself. Only the best for me, I remember thinking at the time: the Queen of everything. A cracking name. I wanted it, I took it, I made it mine. As there might be some proper consequences attached to my real name, it wouldn't be right to set my given name down. I shouldn't even call that one my real name because, now I think of it isn't that the point? Queenie's real, to me.

Lucky Bunny by Jill Dawson (Dawson, 2011; fiction/novel; copyright © Jill Dawson 2011; reproduced by permission of Hodder and Stoughton)

2. At Dum Dum Airport, Calcutta, the hot air is fluffy with mosquitoes that hover but do not bite. My mother gives me a candy cane wrapped in plastic. "Little bit of Christmas," she says. The air blooms with zinnia-colored saris and flashes of gold. Doors, windows, flung open to the long dark hem of horizon, the sun rising like a bloody egg. A woman sweeps the floor with a broom of sticks, moving in a squat like a crab. Two policemen with black guns lean against a wall. I tighten my fingers around my father's pant leg. He looks down at me and says, "Calcutta," his loss, joy, mingled.... Just past the baggage claim, the clan stands shoulder to shoulder. My father waves and nineteen hands wave back…. I am comforted by the faces and bodies like mine. The stories come true. Everyone speaks like my father, a jumble of Sindhi, Hindi, English.

You Have Given Me A Country by Neela Vaswani (Vaswami, 2010; cnf/memoir; reprinted by permission of the author and Sarabande Books, Inc.)

11 Travel Writing without Leaving Home

Robin Hemley

Introduction

In order to write travel literature, the natural prerequisite would seem to be the ability and financial means to board a boat, plane, train, or automobile, and take one's preferred conveyance to some distant land, some exotic shore. One writer, Phillip Graham, claims that all writing is a form of travel literature, the notion that a good essay, poem, or story takes the reader on a journey. To some extent, I agree, but I believe that travel writing should involve some sort of nonfictional exploration of a place, and should seek to understand this place in relation to the writer and her/his audience. This requirement doesn't necessarily involve travel as such, but requires a perceptive eye, and also a desire to see the familiar and the unfamiliar with the eyes of an explorer.

A hundred years ago or so, travel writing, much like anthropology, had a Eurocentric bias, a case of *Us* (Western Civilization) versus *Them* (the Mysterious Orient, Darkest Africa). There were exceptions, but the audience was assumed to be the folks back home. When the explorer and translator, Sir Richard Burton, disguised himself as an Arab trader and infiltrated Mecca, he wasn't writing as an Insider, but as a spy, fluent in Arabic, who could divulge the exotic secrets of the Arabs to a group of London gentleman of the same socioeconomic background and ethnic background.

> A crowd stood gathered round the Ka'abah, and I having no wish to stand bareheaded and barefooted in the midday September sun. At the cry of 'Open a path for the Haji (pilgrim) who would enter the House!' the gazers made way. Two stout Meccans, who stood below the door raised me in their arms, whilst a third drew me from above into the building. At the entrance I was accosted by several officials, dark-looking Meccans, of whom the blackest and plainest was a youth of the, Ben!l Shaybah family, the true blood of the El Hejaz. He held in his hand the huge silver-gilt padlock of the Ka'abah, and presently, taking his seat upon a kind of wooden press in the left corner of the hall, he officially inquired my name, nation, and other particulars. The replies were satisfactory, and the boy Mohammed was authoritatively ordered to conduct me round the building, and to recite the prayers. I will not deny that, looking at the windowless walls, the officials at the door, and a crowd of excited fanatics below...my feelings were of the trapped-rat description.... A blunder, a hasty action, a misjudged word, a prayer or bow, not strictly the right shibboleth, and my bones would have whitened the desert sand. This did not, however, prevent my carefully observing the scene during our long prayer, and making a rough plan with a pencil upon my white *ihram*. (Burton, 1857/1964: 206–207)

While Burton was more respectful of cultures different from his own than the average Victorian gentleman, Orientalism was the norm, and the idea of travel writing was not to examine one's own culture but to unveil the mysteries of another culture, often with the subtext of "This is another reason why we are civilized and they are not."

A little earlier than Burton's forays into Africa and India, directly after the Napoleonic Wars, the Continental Tour was the rage. Before the wars, continental touring had been the province of wealthy men and women, but later such touring of Europe became as common as Junior year Study Abroad is now in universities across the United States. This created a different kind of travel literature, a literature of the beaten path in which writers chronicled their adventures with the same impulse as current travelers might have to post photos on Facebook and to update their status to brag where they've been. These 19th century continental travelers often wrote about the familiar in a familiar way, reinforcing the beauty of Florence, Venice, and Athens. As one contemporary critic complained: "It is certainly somewhat extraordinary that of the great number of travelers sent forth by the peace from this country, with the design of recording their adventures, so few should have deviated from the most frequent routes" (Craven, 1821).

Travel writing today is a more sophisticated business for the most part, and more complex. Gone are the days when writers can assume that their audience is made up entirely of people just like them. As much travel writing is written for the Internet, the audience is even broader. Today, if Richard Burton were writing about Mecca, he would understand that it would be a certainty that his audience would in part be made up of readers from the Arab nations who would scrutinize and potentially criticize his observations of them. Some of the authority he could claim as an English Explorer would be eroded by the fact of his Outsider status.

Likewise, rehashing the same old routes is something that might work occasionally in airline magazines, but not for the serious travel essayist. Does this mean that we are not allowed to write about the familiar, that everything which could possibly be said about, say, Venice, has already been said? Of course, one of the tasks of the writer is to make the familiar unfamiliar.

Today's travel writer must be mindful that his or her audience will not necessarily look like her, and must also shift her gaze to look inward as much as outward. The travel writer of today writes as much about the world within the writer as the writer in the world. One's assumptions about a place must always be in question, so that the piece becomes as much about the shifting perceptions of the writer as about the destination. Horace wrote: "Those who cross the sea, change the sky but not their soul."[1] Perhaps that was true of

Horace, but it's not an assumption we can make today. One reason to travel is to shift the sky within the viewer – differences in culture and perception create shifts in the way we perceive ourselves as well as our homelands.

But the question remains, How far do we need to travel in order for it to be travel? In the 18th century, Xavier de Maistre answered this question decisively in his volume, *Journey Around my Room* (de Maistre, 1794/2004). De Maistre, sentenced to several weeks of house imprisonment for participating in a duel, spent his time in confinement meditating on his surroundings and writing both an homage to and a satire of more conventional books of exploration that were popular at the time. He treats his room as though it's an unexplored continent, exploring paintings and furnishings with the kind of attention one might lavish on the dusty interior of a Pharaoh's treasure room. When it came time for de Maistre to leave his prison, he felt somewhat reluctant to leave. The attention he had given his surroundings turned his imprisonment into a voyage of discovery.

> My chamber forms a square, round which I can take thirty-six steps, if I keep very close to the wall. But I seldom travel in a straight line. I dislike persons who are such masters of their feet and of their ideas that they can say: "To-day I shall make three calls, I shall write four letters, I shall finish this work that I have begun." So rare are the pleasures scattered along our difficult path in life, that we must be mad not to turn out of our way and gather anything of joy which is within our reach. (de Maistre, 1794/2004: 7)

Something similar happened in the case of the Argentinian writer, Julio Cortázar, who in the early 1980's decided with his wife, Canadian Carol Dunlop, to embark on an adventure that, at first glance, might seem just as mundane and daft as circumnavigating one's room. On a road trip between Paris and Marseilles, they had counted some seventy "aires" or rest stops, and they hit upon the idea to visit every one of them. Most people would not see rest areas as destinations, but Cortázar and Dunlop devised a plan to spend a month traveling the A7 autoroute, stopping at two rest stops per day, one at lunch time and one for the evening. They didn't allow themselves to leave the autoroute at any time during the course of their journey and were resupplied by friends who agreed to help along the way. They wrote a book about their travels in tandem and it's often difficult to tell who wrote which passage – the result was a quirky but ultimately wrenching meditation on ephemerality and love: *Autonauts of the Cosmoroute: A Timeless Voyage from Paris to Marseilles* (Dunlop and Cortázar, 1982/2007). They couldn't have anticipated this when they began the trip, which started as a lark, but Dunlop was suffering from what would turn out to be terminal cancer, and she didn't live to see the book in print, and Cortázar lived for only another three years. But their book brims with life. Much as de Maistre didn't want to leave his room at the end of his imprisonment, Dunlop and Cortázar felt bereft when they reached the last rest stop:

> Sadness: that's what there was. A sadness that began two days before the arrival, when at the Senas rest area we looked each other in the eye and for the first time fully accepted that the next day we would enter the final stage. How can I forget Osita [his nickname for Carol] saying: "Oh, Julio, how quickly the trip went by...." How can I forget that at the moment we read the sign announcing the end of the autoroute we were so filled with anguish we could only combat with an obstinate silence, which accompanied us till we entered the clamour of Marseilles, looked for an empty spot in the Vieux Port and put our feet on land that was no longer Paris-to-Marseilles land. A triumph clouded by tears we dried in a café, drinking the first *pastis* and thinking that this very afternoon we would drive up to Serre for a few days' rest.... (Dunlop and Cortázar, 1982/2007: 347)

In a way, their month-long lark had become a haven of magical thinking and became transformative for them as well as for the reader: the most banal of physical spaces, the highway, turned into a series of, well, oases (Dunlop and Cortázar, 1982/2007: 337).

Description of Activity and Strategies for Implementation

With these works in mind, I started off my Summer Institute session by some discussion with the participants regarding their notions of travel. These were largely Asian university teachers, many serving communities of students with English as a second language. I never addressed ESL in my session as I believed that the teachers in attendance could adapt my exercises as needed, and in any case, the exercises themselves require only brief responses and seemed to me tailor-made for ESL students as well as students whose mother tongue is English.

I started by asking participants what they considered might be some differences between travel writing now and a hundred years ago. The question provoked a lively discussion of about fifteen minutes in which we discussed the idea of Insider versus Outsider status, the problems and inevitabilities of exoticizing the Other, at least in one's first moments in a foreign land, as well as how first impressions are valuable, but then need to be mostly cast aside as one gains familiarity with a place.

We discussed the ways in which a travel writer needs to take his or her own pulse frequently. In other words, we need to be self-conscious when we enter a place for the first time. We need to keep track of our stereotypes and attempts to generalize, as in a statement that one of my graduate students on a study abroad trip who'd never been outside of the United States made after twenty-four hours in the Philippines: "All Filipinos are so friendly." This is more of a tourist's observation than that of a traveler – a tourist makes surface judgments while a traveler (and the travel writer) examines details, goes beyond the surface, and examines things that might otherwise escape the notice of the average tourist.

That's not to say that the travel writer can ever truly find the "Authentic" Philippines or Authentic Burma or Authentic Italy, though the authentic experience is the Holy Grail for tourist and traveler alike. The canny traveler understands that authenticity itself is an illusion, that it's most often a dream of some static and pure state of culture which doesn't exist, and which is altered simply by the presence of the tourist/traveler/viewer.

Still, one's writing can *approach* some notion of authenticity by focusing on the details, by sticking to one's own experience and critiquing oneself and one's own culture at least as much as one tries to critique the people and places of one's travels.

First and foremost, the travel writer needs to be a good observer. To that effect, I asked the participants to close their eyes and not open them until I told them to do so. Then I asked them to recall one-by-one the visual details of the room. What does the floor look like? What color is the carpet? What does the door look like? How many windows are in the room? What about the lighting? In the course of this exercise, I told participants they should feel free to disagree with one another. And disagree they did. While they could agree on a number of the major details of the room – that it was uncarpeted, for instance – they disagreed on some major points as well: the color of the floor tiles, whether the door had a window in it, whether there was a rubbish bin at the front of the room (there wasn't).

As simple as this exercise is, it's one of the most effective exercises for showing how we filter our surroundings, taking in some details and imagining the rest, relying on our memories as much as our sight. As soon as we've left a place, turned our back, closed our eyes, or walked away, it becomes a site of imagination and memory, and we can and do place anything within this imagined space, whether it truly exists or not. Invariably, people place all kinds of objects in the room that are not in fact there, and they change the size and number of windows and doors, the colors of walls and carpet.

I wrote down participants' responses on the white board and only after we had exhausted all of the details in the room that they had noted (there were some light sockets and such that had escaped their attention completely), I asked them to fix in their mind the room as they saw it. Afterwards, I counted to three slowly and asked them to open their eyes. This is always my favorite part of the exercise, seeing people's wide-eyed expressions as they notice, as if for the first time, the classroom in which they've been sitting. Before the image from their mind's eye dissipates, I ask them to jot down the differences between what they imagined to be there and what was there in actuality. This precipitated a conversation on the lessons of the exercise – how we can only take in so much detail, how our imaginations and memories dictate our realities as much as what we see, and this then leads to a discussion of "salient details," the details that are most evocative and important in describing any given place.

I asked: "If you were to describe this room to a person ten thousand miles away, what 3 or 4 salient details would you choose to evoke how you feel about this place?" Again, we went around the room and listened to the individual choices of salient details as well as the reasons for these particular choices.

After this, I introduced the participants to the concept of the *lapidary*. The term is traditionally used to describe the polishing of gem stones, but it has an alternate meaning: a formal etching in stone as in an epitaph. Victor Hugo adapted the term *lapidary*[2] and turned it into a writing exercise of sorts. Hugo was intrigued by the notion of "automatic writing," a kind of quick, impressionistic writing that was seen as a kind of dictation from a place beyond human ken, the spirit world. His idea, as I understand it, involved a quick notation, a kind of first impression unhampered by reason in which one allowed the force of the place encountered to dictate the words as it were. These quick first impressions would be polished later into something more formal. I'm not certain if any of Hugo's lapidaries survive, but for me at least, that's not of primary interest. I have long been interested in the pedagogical uses of such an exercise for students today, as a way of teaching imagery, salient detail, revision, and concision.

For my purposes, a lapidary should be twenty-five words or so, no more than fifty, and should try through salient detail to capture some essence of a place. Roland Barthes writes in his book *Camera*

Lucida (Barthes, 1981) of the "punctum" and "studium" of a photograph, the studium being the intellectual appeal of an image, its composition for instance, the punctum being the "wound" of the photograph. When we look at a particular photo, occasionally a detail jumps out at us that pierces us emotionally in a personal way. You might see punctum in a photograph where I see only stadium – the image of a boy's crooked teeth in a photo of smiling children.

I believe that punctum can be conveyed in language as well, through description. That's not to say that lapidaries should all be poignant, but that the most effective lapidaries will create in much the way that a haunting photograph creates or a poem creates through precise detail and ambiguous meaning, an experience that suggests something ineffable and beautiful in its ephemerality. I often use as an example of the punctum of an image, Ezra Pound's famous poem, "In a Station of the Metro":

The apparition of these faces in the crowd;
Petals on a wet, black bough. (Pound, 1913: 12)

I don't expect students to write something as refined as this. In fact, I don't want them to even consider their word choice when they first write their lapidary. It's only upon reflection, later that evening, that I want them to go about polishing their first impressions. Of course, we only see Pound's finished poem here, not his initial jottings, which might have been wordier and sloppier than what he wound up with.

I asked the Institute participants to take this notion of the lapidary and wander the halls of the building in which we sat. I wanted them to find several different locations about which to write lapidaries, asking them to notice minutia or angles and perspectives they might not normally notice. I gave them approximately half an hour for this exercise, after which we were to reconvene and share our observations.

Admittedly, half an hour is not enough time in which to satisfactorily complete such an exercise, but the participants were able to at least get a taste of the way this exercise should develop. Normally,

I ask students to write several lapidaries a day and then to share several they have written over the course of a week. In a recent course I taught on Flash Fiction and Nonfiction, the lapidaries students created were the favorite aspect of the course for many of the students. Their lapidaries became by the end of the semester a kind of fragmented text, a record of the salient details of their lives over a period of several months.

Outcomes and Recommendations

All of the participants from the session seemed quite engaged with the exercises and seemed to benefit from the session. One participant described the session as "a mind opener" and another deemed the session her/his "favourite session of the institute." The participants also felt that the exercises would be useful in their own classrooms, with or without modification.

As I had hoped, the participants saw the value of close observation in a number of different classroom settings, one participant stating that s/he could even see the value of using these techniques in grammar lessons. Another thought that the techniques didn't need further adaptation, and that they could be "really useful for Hong Kong learners."

Both lapidaries and the room observation exercise seem useful to me in a variety of situations for learners at all levels. I've yet to encounter a situation in which lapidaries failed to intrigue and engage most students. Critiquing of the lapidaries in class should focus on specifics: which images seem most evocative? What is the attitude of the speaker of the lapidary towards the place being described? What word choices seem most effective in setting the tone of the lapidary? One might discuss, for instance, why Ezra Pound chose the word "apparition" rather than "ghost" or "phantom" or "specter."

Over time, if the class generates many lapidaries, the class could hold a lapidary reading, each student choosing her/his strongest four lapidaries to share with an audience. One might also collect the lapidaries in a printed or online text. Together, they might comprise a fragmented and poetic travel essay of sorts.

Notes

1   Quoted from Pearce (2005: 103).
2   See Hamon (1992) Parts I and II, for discussion of this term as applied to written works by French writers; and for specific reference to Hugo, see especially pp. 53ff.

References

Barthes, Roland (1981) *Camera Lucida*. New York: Hill and Wang.

Burton, Richard Frances (1857/1964) *Personal Narrative of a Pilgrimage to el Medinah and Meccah* Vol. 2 (ed. Isabel Burton). New York: Dover.

Craven, Sir Richard Keppel (1821) A tour through the southern provinces of the Kingdom of Naples. *Edinburgh Review* 36 (October 1821). Reprinted in Benjamin Colbert (2005) *Shelley's Eye: Travel Writing and Aesthetic Vision*. Cornwall: MPG Books.

de Maistre, Xavier (1794/2004) *A Journey around my Room* (trans. Andrew Brown) London: Hesperus Classics.

Dunlop, Carol and Cortázar, Julio (1982/2007) *The Autonauts of the Cosmoroute: A Timeless Voyage from Paris to Marseilles*. New York: Archipelago. Originally published in Spanish as *Los Autonautas de la Cosmopista*. Buenos Aires: Muchnik Editores.

Hamon, Philippe (1992) *Expositions: Literature and Architecture in Nineteenth-Century France* (trans. Katia Sainson-Franck and Lisa Maquire), Part I: Texts and Architecture 15–52; Part II: Texts and Their Monuments, Chapter 1: Ruins and glass houses 53–93. Berkeley: University of California Press.

Pearce, Philip L. (2005) The role of relationships in the tourist experience. In William F. Theobold (ed.) *Global Tourism* (3rd edition) 103–122. New York: Routledge.

Pound, Ezra (1913) In a station of the metro. *Poetry* 2(1): 12.

12 May the Farce Be With You

Reflections on "Extreme Puppet Theater" as a Vehicle toward Something Else

Mark Spitzer

Introduction

Puppets are often considered silly. This is a given. Still, they offer a creative way to communicate, research, present findings, and stimulate discourse and debate. In academia, puppetry is rarely used as a mode for discovery. Up until now, that is.

The inspiration came to me nearly a decade ago, when I was teaching a sophomore-level course in American Literature at Truman State University in Missouri. I was looking for an innovative way to encourage group work. I wanted students to be engaged in the process of analyzing a series of short stories by William Faulkner, so I took a risk and debuted what I jokingly termed "Extreme Puppet Theater." After putting students in small groups, I charged them with the task of putting on a puppet show that would examine plots, characters, themes, metaphors, and the underlying messages in Faulkner's stories. Students were given a list of criteria to satisfy. Their puppet show should be five to ten minutes long, it should incorporate relevant research or criticism, an excerpt from the text should be performed, and ultimately, a group opinion should be offered. Props and music were optional. Students were given class time to work on this project and were expected to bring art supplies to make puppets while brainstorming a script.

Predictably, the groans arose. But in the next class, students got to work with paper bags and random socks, glue, buttons, yarn, etc. We all knew this process was ridiculous, but what we found in the ensuing week was that serious research could be conducted through a forum usually reserved for children. For these young adults, this investigation proved to be an unusual, visionary learning tool, in which intensive dialogue and hands-on experience promoted cooperation and creative problem-solving. In contrast to writing boring college papers that regurgitate information, this process allowed students to create something new – and, as it turned out, something valued by all those involved.

As the years went on, I incorporated this kind of guerilla puppetry into many of the other classes I taught. At the University of Central Arkansas, I had first-year students in composition courses work together to stage talk-show-type puppet shows in which characters debated local environmental issues (see Assignment 1 in the Appendix). In essence, these productions illustrated a new twist on the outdated five-paragraph-essay format; the talk-show host would present the problem (the introduction), the opposing parties would argue different sides of the issue (pros vs. cons), and then the host would provide a closing statement (the conclusion). The result was a highly memorable process of investigation unlike any college experience they had ever had before. And because of their direct involvement with issues like preserving the Ozark hellbender (a giant salamander threatened by extinction), or protecting the controversial (perhaps nonexistent) ivory-billed woodpecker from encroaching development, these students were not only better equipped to envision potential structures for college papers by fleshing out their most important arguments, their investments in their productions supplied them with studied perspectives on topics of current relevance that informed them as citizens as well as scholars.

After years of experimentation with this process, I eventually integrated Extreme Puppet Theater into both graduate and under-graduate creative writing courses. In my Creative Nonfiction Workshop, I used this method in the form of author presentations. In my Ecopoetics course, a fusion of puppetry and poetic license was employed to deconstruct and re-imagine more advanced environ-mental issues like hydraulic fracking and the use of dispersants for cleaning up oil spills.

The idea of using puppets to develop students' writing was working, and evolving. Students were using creative techniques to make sense of texts, and they were discovering meaning through improvisation, analysis, and writing. They were developing skills that would be applicable to further studies and careers.

Because I still felt the need to make sense of the process, I wrote an article entitled "Extreme Puppet Theater as a Tool for Writing Pedagogy at K–University Levels," which built on established theories in writing pedagogy posited by and François Camoin (Camoin, 1994) and Stephanie Vanderslice (Vanderslice, 2006). Their argument is that when a text becomes an event, it turns into "something else." This generic term for an elusive concept is intentionally meant to suggest that texts can become something more than just words. Furthermore, this *something else* can be something useful, something fun.

From this, I extrapolated that works of prose, like works of drama, have the potential to be transformed into moments of action, or interaction. Thus, the experience of creating *something else* can be applied not only as a dramatic teaching tool for evolving writers, but as a highly effective, interactive teaching tool.

Given that group research is also a core part of the interactive process in Extreme Puppet Theater, I began to envision *something else* as a semi-living thing. Since it mimics life, in a sense, and since humans have a natural desire to create (consider the word "procreation"), it seemed to me that Extreme Puppet Theater provided the illusion, if not the actuality, of bringing something to life. That's why I wrote that as "an interactive learning experience, this *something else* can test the boundaries of traditional pedagogy [and that]... students can be the creators of that *something else,* which is not only engaging and empowering, but a lot of fun as well" (Spitzer, 2014: 122).

A few months later, I was en route to conduct workshops in Extreme Puppet Theater at the City University of Hong Kong, where the English Department was hosting a Summer Institute on "Creativity and Discovery in Teaching University Writing." Hence, it was time to see if the philosophy behind this pedagogy was actually applicable to the vast range of ages and academic subjects I claimed it to be. I was glad to have the opportunity to put my concept to "the scientific test." By subjecting it to such scrutiny, I figured that if my audience could find any weak spots in my approach, then that would be the equivalent of disproving the theory. If the theory was found faulty, then I'd have more work to do to. If it couldn't be disproved, then I'd be reassured that I was headed in the right direction.

However, as I was to discover (in a forum focused on discovery), putting my method to the test was a moot point, since the concept had already been accepted by the community I was flying toward. I didn't know it at the time, but the participants who had signed up for my workshop were already motivated by the idea of messing around with puppets in the classroom, and many colleagues I hadn't yet met were anxious to learn more about this unconventional pedagogical approach.

Description of Activity and Strategies for Implementation

I had no trouble getting through Customs with my suitcase full of glues, paints, scissors, markers, yarn, ribbons, pipe cleaners, buttons, sewing kit, googly eyes, paper bags, fabric scraps, and "slightly defective" dollar-store socks. I was also prepared with handouts (included in Appendix) and a lecture plan. On the day of the first workshop, I entered the room and met the class. They saw my suitcase full of stuff, they were there to make puppets and be creative, and an eager instructor immediately asked, "When can we start?"

Laughter arose, setting the tone. I then introduced myself, talked a bit about my experience with this teaching tool, and passed around the handouts to provide an outline of the process. I went through the argumentative assignment meant for first-year composition students, and pointed out the criteria I graded by. I explained that if students worked together to perform their show within the time limit while presenting information from authorities, and that if they each operated one puppet and had their arguments and their introductions and conclusions in order, and if they were entertaining (which they always are), then they would get an "A" grade. I added that in all my years of assigning puppetry as a mode of investigation, no group had ever gotten less than an "A." That's why, after performances happen in class, I'm prone to announce, "A's for everyone!"

Chinese students being somewhat conservative and serious about their studies, this led to some questions on how the grade for this particular project can affect a student's overall grade: if everyone gets "A"'s, what's the point?

The point, I explained, is to collaborate and have fun learning something that makes everyone involved a more critical/creative thinker. The fact that the group grade only accounts for five percent of the overall grade, I continued, means that not much is at stake. That the activity accounts for only five percent also means that the project isn't threatening, since it would be highly unlikely that a few percentage points could make or break a grade. The point is to play, to create, to "think outside the box" as a way to approach organizing writing ideas.

I also explained that I usually schedule these assignments at the end of the semester, when minds tend to be fried by academic pressure. In this sense, Extreme Puppet Theater is meant as a form of relief, which is why I usually schedule performances on the last day of class – at which time I bring in soda pop and donuts and we have a party, because "American students just love donuts!"

To give an idea of what was possible, I then showed the workshop a video made by upper-level undergraduates in an Ecopoetics class. The assignment (Assignment 2 in the Appendix) noted criteria and a timeline for making puppets, drafting a script, and scoring extra credit points by working as a group outside of class (as documented by their sending me a cell phone jpg of their group's creative process).

The concept of "extra credit" involved a bit of explaining, since it wasn't a concept at some Chinese universities. As I'd been told, students in Hong Kong are assigned work and expected to do it, end of story. This whole conference, however, was about applying innovative teaching methods in order to foster creativity and discovery, so I addressed the concept briefly by stating that this extra credit option is an incentive to encourage students to get together outside of class and rehearse in order to be prepared for their shows. I added that doing extra work together builds strong bonds and relationships, which results in more cohesive and imaginative productions.

This is where the *something else* that Camoin (1994) and Vanderslice (2006) talk about comes in. When groups create an event that they are excited about, individuals are naturally inspired to take off on their own. At this point, students become their own teachers and have little use for the teacher except as a symbolic deadline-enforcer whose grading mechanism is hardly as important as bringing their visions to crystallization. This is exactly what I'm aiming for: turning a mundane task into a self-propelled celebration that comes with its own momentum.

The video which I showed in the workshop and which is accessible on YouTube, entitled "In the Hot Tub with Sheila

Tubman" (http://www.youtube.com/watch?v=yrJ-oX16aYc), is pretty dang silly. It's a debate between an ExxonMobile executive and an environmental hippy over the recent Mayflower oil spill in Arkansas, near my university. Through the course of the semester, both graduate and undergraduate students in that class had been reading eco-nonfiction philosophy, then responding via poetry. It was unfortunate to have an environmental disaster in our midst, but it was also a vivid eye-opener for many of the students in that class. Our own patch of nature had been defiled, and the students in one particular group felt compelled to express their disgruntlement.

This video made for a good example of Extreme Puppet Theater, especially since the puppets were large and colorful and looked good on the projection screen. The people behind the foldable four-by-eight-foot puppet stage (which I constructed from 2 x 4s and purple fabric) were even more colorful. They had music and props and a talk-show format in which puppets holding opposing viewpoints supposedly met in a hot tub forum moderated by a sassy host. The students who planned and performed the show had equipped themselves with sophisticated arguments. At one point the petrochemical CEO held up a graph showing tornado damage in the United States in comparison to damage from oil pollution and then asked, "Mother Nature, Exxon... who's really on your side?"

Finishing up the video, I then went to the whiteboard and wrote the following talking point on it: "IN EXTREME PUPPET THEATER, RIDICULOUS ARGUMENTS ARE OKAY." This act, in a sense, made it official that students don't have to draft their scripts according to the expected language of academia, and that they can use their poetic license and imagination to order arguments according to what they want to express – which is a highly freeing process. Whereas one of the goals of the first-year composition assignment was to help students envision the structure of a basic paper, this assignment (much like "slam poetry," which relies on fiery expression as a performance technique) was geared toward utilizing emotional language as a political tool.

The message I was sending was that it's not only okay to take risks in creating biased puppet productions, it's encouraged. Being a creative writer at heart, my goal, in academic writing as well as in creative writing, is to promote discourse that strays from *the formal* and connects through *the informal*, an area where discourse is accessible to vast and diverse audiences. Because imaginations tend to connect at the informal level, where expected genre conventions aren't so important, risk-taking voices that speak to readers through *emotion combined with information* are often effective in providing perspective. Take hip-hop, for example, or punk rock, as practical modes of communication, especially as acts of protest.

Some of the workshop participants clearly understood the value of using alternative forms of discourse in academic situations. I could see it in their eyes – most of which were focused on the suitcase. The participants were ready to dive in and get cracking. Still, there were a few participants in the room who were having difficulty envisioning how to articulate what they wanted to express through playful tactics. One of the participants related that she was having trouble resolving how to unlearn the formal structures she had been trained to employ in teaching writing. Nevertheless, she was intrigued.

The next talking point I wrote on the board was this: "CRAPPY PUPPETS ARE OKAY." The reason I strove to make this official also has to do with risk. First of all, if students know that their art skills won't be judged, they can quickly get past this self-conscious hurdle and get on to mapping the specifics of their puppet's agenda, which they might be more adept at. And secondly, I like to think of Extreme Puppet Theater as a type of "outsider art" that's open and accessible. This means you don't need to be Jim Henson to make a puppet. All you need to do is to have been a kid at some time in your life, so that you can call upon that vestigial innocence and wonder we all recall, in order to apply it to the discovery process of learning from creative play.

I then put the workshop participants in groups of four so that they could jump straight into the process using puppets, and see, firsthand, how it's applicable. As usual, I dictated who would work with who and charged each group with coming up with an issue in which a talk-show host would moderate two puppets with differing views. This left each group in the position of trying to figure out a role for the fourth member, so they had to come up with a creative solution.

This is what Extreme Puppet Theater is all about: suddenly being charged with a mission, then looking for creative ways to transform discourse into something authentically *something else*. And that's what happened in that workshop. Some participants went directly for the supplies, while others pulled their desks together to powwow about issues and brainstorm ideas for character positions.

The participants had one hour to come up with a show. Essentially, I was giving them sixty minutes to come up with what I usually give my students a week to accomplish. And so the mad scramble was on for each group to come up with a five-minute talk show based on a real issue.

I went from group to group as they worked and asked them about their subject matter. As examples of their topics, one group chose obesity, another chose online dating, and another chose to look at the "fast fashion" retailer Topshop. Ten minutes into it, each group was working away, laughing out loud, and helping each other with gluing on eyes. I had told them to start with the eyes, since the glue would need time to dry. (In fact, I'd brought along a hair dryer from the hotel to speed up this process)

Toward the end of the workshop, I brought a table in from the hallway and set it up on top of the table at the front of the room so that the table top faced the audience. This was their makeshift stage – which they soon got behind, and, like adults reverting back to childhood, presented sophisticated arguments through a ridiculous medium. The participants were animated, excited, and communicating with sincerity and optimism. Everyone had a knee-slapping time, and when the class was over, half of the participants stuck around to discuss ways to apply Extreme Puppet Theater to other areas of study – like business, and even math.

Two days later, I conducted the same workshop again with the same inspired results, including one that I didn't expect: When I left the room, I was buzzing hard, totally pleased with the enthusiastic response I had received and the interest there was in applying this alternative pedagogy to extremely different disciplines. It's a feeling teachers rarely experience, when they feel they've made an impact not just on their students, but on themselves. Be it pride, a sense of accomplishment, or satisfaction in having successfully met a challenge, I felt an incredible self-indulgent rush, to have reproduced my pedagogical genes – which is the most that any educator can ask for. When work turns into something that's driven by *something else*, it turns into something progressive, something validating, something transcendental. And that's what we're all striving for, consciously or not.

Reflections and Purpose

Due to the dramatic interaction that naturally occurs with Extreme Puppet Theater, one suggestion offered by workshop participants in their evaluations was to implement this assignment at the beginning of a semester, rather than at the end. This would make the assignment operate as "an icebreaker" that could help introduce students to each other and promote a spirit of cooperation in the classroom. Several of the other overwhelmingly positive workshop evaluations also mentioned that Extreme Puppet Theater could work well to "jumpstart" more formal academic paper-writing assignments – which sounds good to me, if it works for the instructor's vision.

The way I see it, Extreme Puppet Theater is a flexible method that can evolve with the needs of any course. I offer my own version as a prototype to be tweaked by other teachers according to their instincts and agendas. What works for me may not work for others, and vice versa. Different subject matter might require different criteria, or more background in certain areas before implementation.

As an exercise in creative problem-solving, I recommend that students be charged with at least one problem or mystery to solve. For example, if all roles for a discourse have been claimed by student puppeteers, what type of supporting role can an additional group member take on in order to play a valuable part in the event? Perhaps there are components of technology that could add to the understanding of the discussion if incorporated in a creative manner. Or maybe the dialogue should touch on specific keywords or scholars to make the investigation of an issue more focused.

I've found that time is not a pressing factor. Whether students are provided an hour or a week to satisfy their objectives, they'll get the job done if the deadline is reasonable. Not only that, they'll go out of their way to get their supplies, and they'll even meet outside of class to iron out the details. Being accustomed to homework, students can predict what's required to get the job done. And since it's common knowledge that groups rely on individuals to literally play their part, everyone involved recognizes their level of responsibility, and what is required of them.

Of course, the question remains of whether or not slackers will act on what they know is expected. From what I've seen, this doesn't matter. In every group there are always those who take on leadership roles, and there are always those who remain more reserved or less engaged. The benefit of staging these shows later in the semester is that it allows the instructor to gauge who the most ambitious personalities in the class are, so that groups can be organized with a balanced number of "go-getters" in each one. But that's not my point here. My point is that because Extreme Puppet Theater is an amusing group project, I've rarely seen students not play their part. Sure, some students might miss a class or two during flu season, when viruses are going around, but for the most part, these teams develop organically and members carry their weight due to the inherent playfulness of the mode. Members of the group become invested in the process because they want to see what whacko form it will take in the end. The fact that they get only one chance to see the amusing efforts of their labor, and the fact that they will also get to see others in the same bizarre situation, pretty much guarantees that they will approach this process with more interest than class presentations in which droning monologues are the norm.

There's a big difference between mind-numbing class presentations and dramas that rely on enhanced visual and oral elements derived through spontaneous play, which is why Extreme Puppet Theater is appealing to the imagination. In other words, the unpredictable nature of the process makes the ride a suspense-packed odyssey, which, to quote my own article, allows university students to tap into something they "want to do as they enter adulthood: they want to take their youth with them, and they want to play along the way, in ways that make intellectual sense" (Spitzer, 2014: 125).

This brings me to my final talking point. For the same reason I established that ridiculous arguments and crappy puppets are okay, I hereby proclaim that because it's impossible for instructors not to fly by the seat of their pants when assigning such a surreal, childlike process, "EXTREME PUPPET THEATER MUST BE A HALF-BAKED & LUDICROUS EVENT TO BE EFFECTIVE."

My advice, therefore, is to not even try to bake it all the way. Don't spoil it by preparing highly detailed lesson plans, assessment rubrics and the like. Just let it rise and see where it goes, and adjust your expectations as you go along. Because that's what your students will be doing as well, and they'll work with you to figure it out.

As an educator, if this logic is perplexing to you, Extreme Puppet Theater might not work for you. But if the baking metaphor above seems clear, or at least puzzling in a not unpleasing manner, then you have the sense of humor it takes to guide students through academic investigations via the machinery of absurdity – so go for it. And may the Farce be with you!

References

Camoin, François (1994) The workshop and its discontents. In W. Bishop and H. Ostrom (eds.) *Colors of a Different Horse: Rethinking Creative Writing Theory and Pedagogy*, 3–7. Urbana, Illinois: National Council of Teachers of English.

Spitzer, Mark (2014) Extreme Puppet Theater as a tool for writing pedagogy at K–university levels. *Writing & Pedagogy* 6(1): 121–125. doi: 10.1558/wap.v6i1.121.

Vanderslice, Stephanie (2006) Workshopping. In Graeme Harper (ed.) *Teaching Creative Writing* 147–57. London: Continuum.

Appendix

Assignment 1.

WRTG 1310: Composition and Rhetoric, Spring Semester 2008 Persuasive Argumentative Puppet Talk Show Group Project

Here are the new groups:

Nikki	Kara	Howard	Bryce	Rebecca
Portia	Kristy	Cameron	Joe	Sharon
Steve R	Stephen H	Mary	Justis	Howard
Jonathan	Lauren	Chloe	Bethany	Jackie
Alex				

Each group will be given an issue which I want to hear about. On **Tuesday October 9** you will get together in class and split your group into two groups. One group will be the research group, which will go to the library and rustle up information on the issue (get on the computers, use Google, use the databases, ask a librarian) and be back by 3:40 with info that can lead to more insight on the dynamics of the problem. The other group will be the art group, which will make a list of what you guys need to make puppets and props for your production. This group will stay in the room and discuss how to approach the show.

Expectations

On **Thursday October 11** you will meet with your group in class, make silly puppets and props, and begin drafting a script for your five- to ten-minute puppet show. There should be one puppet for each group member, including a talk-show host, a puppet representing one side of the issue, a puppet representing the other side of the issue, and one or two puppets for additional guests. Basically, the talk-show host should introduce the issue (the introduction) and then the puppets with opposing views will debate the issue. Each debating puppet should present three informed arguments that try to persuade the audience. The talk-show host will then make a closing statement (the conclusion). To get out of the classroom, you must show me your puppets and a rough draft of your script. If you want to kick butt on this assignment, you will meet on your own before Tuesday the 16th and rehearse your five- to ten-minute puppet show (send me a cell phone jpg of your group at work and I'll give you **extra credit**). Your group will perform its puppet show on **Tuesday the 16th**.

Grading

50% of the grade will be in the category of entertainment/ workability. This means that half of your grade will depend on how well you engage your audience, how well you present both sides of the issue and inform your audience, and how well your show works overall. I will be looking for you to present serious issues through a ridiculous medium. The specific criteria are:

- the show should be five to ten minutes long
- an authority (critic, author, reviewer, reporter – but not *Wikipedia* or reader reviews from sources like Amazon) should be quoted
- three different aspects of the issue should be debated
- the host should supply statements that work like intros and conclusions
- each group member should operate one puppet

The other 50% of the grade will be technical. You will give me a typed and double-spaced copy of your script which has been worked on and proofread by everyone in your group. This script should have everyone's name on it and be free or errors. And don't forget to title it and staple it.

Additional Info

We will tip the table at the front of the room on its side to create a stage. Props add to the experience. So does music (or any other type of appropriate multi-media component) and food – so bring snacks if you like & we will kick it old school.

Assignment 2.

WRTG 4324 and 5324: Ecopoetics, Spring Semester 2013
Extreme Puppet Theater Ecologue Assignment

Yep, that's right: You'll be working in groups to put on silly puppet shows to be performed on the last day of class. The idea is that your group will decide on an environmental issue for puppets to debate through a talk-show format. As I noted at the beginning of the semester, an ecologue is a fifteenth-century poetic dialogue between shepherds on the subject of stewardship. Therefore, for the purpose of this class, we will envision the *modern ecologue* as a conversation between differing parties, written in verse, about some sort of contemporary eco-subject or philosophy. Here's what you need to know and what you will do:

Group #1	Group #2	Group #3
Joseph	Courtney	Chelsae
Lisa	Erica	Chase
Alissa	Jessica	Scotty
Kaleb		

Everyone should be involved and present for every class. Your group will work for a group grade of 3 homework points (each) that will be judged by the following criteria:

- your performance must be 5 to 10 minutes long
- everyone operates at least one puppet
- timely and relative research is presented
- it's informative and provokes people to think

- it's entertaining (meaning you amuse your audience and there's lots of action)

Music and/or props are permissible and will be factored into your grade if they add to the experience.

Thursday April 18: You will get together, decide on a topic, brainstorm approaches, then decide what supplies are needed and who brings what next time.

Tuesday April 23: You will make puppets in class and draft a script.

Extra Credit: If you can meet outside of class after April 23 and before April 25, and if you can send me a cell phone jpg of your group rehearsing and/or fine-tuning your performance, each group member will receive extra credit.

Thursday April 25: Come to class prepared to perform. I'll have a puppet stage (4 feet tall, 8 feet wide) set up for you and ready to go. Feel free to bring drinks and snacks and we'll kick it old school, yo.

13 Highways and Sinkholes
Incorporating Creativity Strategies in the Writing Classroom

Shirley Geok-lin Lim

Introduction

Many of the concepts deployed in this chapter – such as freewriting, workshops, prompts, and meditation – are familiar to teachers of creative writing. Many of these teachers tend to be creative writers themselves and thus embedded in the practices of their craft, drawing on histories of rhetoric and poetics for their classroom ideas, strategies, goals, and pedagogical philosophy. Aristotle's (2003) *Poetics*, Longinus' (2001) "On the Sublime," and Wordsworth and Coleridge's (1800; 1802/2001) "Preface to the *Lyrical Ballads*" offer some historical notions of what constitute good writing. But throughout the recent centuries, noted authors as diverse as Edgar Allen Poe (Poe, 1846/2004), Rainer Maria Rilke (Rilke, 1934/1993), Edith Wharton (Wharton, 1924/1998), E. M. Forster (Forster, 1927/1986), T. S. Eliot (Eliot, 1919/1975), Virginia Woolf (Woolf, 1929/2008), George Orwell (Orwell, 1946/2004), David Lodge (Lodge, 1994; 2011), John Gardner

(Gardner, 1991), Ursula Le Guin (Le Guin, 1998; 2004), Patricia Highsmith (Highsmith, 2001), and Margaret Atwood (Atwood, 2002), just to name a handful, continue to share their ideas and best practices on observing poetic form, producing narrative structure, the best choice of diction, the most engaging dramatic action, and so forth. These authorial concepts underlie much of contemporary teaching in the creative writing classroom; and the practical teacher–student exchanges that current creative writing textbooks so popular in college classes model repeat standard and usually un-interrogated maxims and dogma that have been generally valorized as "lore" (Lim, 2010).

Louis Menand in 2009, in fact, bluntly states that the "skepticism" that "creative writing is something that can be taught" is "widely shared" (Menand, 2009: 106), and notes that creative writing programs usually merely concede that point, citing the University of Iowa' Writers' Workshop official position: "our conviction that writing cannot be taught but that writers can be encouraged" (*ibid.*). That is, in contrast to the research on teaching composition, the theories that form the skeletal core in creative writing curricula and that animate their teaching exercises and strategies have yet to be tested against any empirically based research as to their efficacy. In contrast, composition research has proven its value in rigorously investigating students' writing processes in different social and psychological contexts, resulting in useful interventions in the writing classroom (Bazerman, 2008; MacArthur, Graham, and Fitzgerald, 2006: 222–234). The need for students to be tutored in the particular (even peculiar) genre, "academic writing," under which category falls a host of other writing genres – narrative, description, analysis, argument, exposition, summation and précis, etc. – remains undebated in universities. Indeed, teaching composition has been a robustly expanding industry, growing in complexity, reach and numbers to include teaching writing in the disciplines (Bazerman, Little, Chavkin, Fouquette, Bethel, and Garufis, 2005; McLeod, 2007).

It is therefore not surprising that, despite sporadic attempts to include rhetorical studies and the teaching of writing as process in creative writing courses (Moxley, 1989), there has been little interchange between creative writing and composition programs, nor between creative writing teachers (often poets, dramatists, essayists, and fictionists) and faculty teaching composition, that is, academic writing. The common understanding is that there is no common ground between the two teaching enterprises; in fact, a climate of indifference if not antipathy is often anecdotally recorded about the relationship between the two, sometimes housed in the same department although more and more institutionally separated and/or competing for the same diminishing resources. At the same time, scholars such as Rodney H. Jones, Vijay K. Bhatia, Stephen Bremner and Anne Peirson-Smith (Jones, Bhatia, Bremner, and Peirson-Smith, 2012) have been investigating the relationship between creativity and discursive forms in other domains, not only in writing on literature (which is a major academic writing activity), but also in professional communication, as in the public relations industry, advertising, the arts, and new media.

Background

The theories and concepts discoverable in the increasing numbers of texts and guidebooks on creative writing arguably have a long and venerable trajectory. Studies of what imaginative writing was, from the Greeks through the Roman writers such as Cicero and later to include the French, German, Italian, and English writers (to name only the most visible) – its multiple genres, typologies, historical models and exemplars, definitions, refinements, fine-grained analyses, and illustrations – served to establish, at least in the West, traditions of literary production. These traditions continue to resonate in modern and postmodern literary discourse, and in a more and more transnational and cosmopolitan global cultural matrix. When creative writing was first introduced in the

U.S. classroom in the late 19th and early 20th centuries, the schools and colleges called on elite classical scholarship to rationalize the implementation of these new curricula (Lim, 2003; Myers, 1996/2006).

My chapter argues that cross-talk between creative writing and composition teachers, despite the different pedagogical traditions they are located in, will prove helpful in composition teaching. Composition research and teaching enjoy the security of a social mission – the social work that composition teaching accomplishes for the individual student, for the university, and for the larger national society – that forms the core of its practices and that creative writing teaching struggles to articulate (Smagorinsky, 2006). As someone who has taught both academic and creative writing courses to two-year associate degree students, research university undergraduates, and graduate students, I have often answered the question, *Is academic writing instruction different from creative writing instruction?*, with the equivocation, *It all depends*.

For many years the teaching of critical reading and writing took as hard-wired the binary between "convergent" and "divergent" thinking. Drawing on J. P. Guilford's popular concepts of convergent and divergent production (Guilford, 1955), both academic and creative writing instruction have incorporated activities that allegedly enable a generative (prewriting) stage (e.g. brainstorming, mapping, journaling, deploying visuals and alternate forms of media, listing, meditation). The prewriting activities culminate in a freewriting activity and conclude with peer feedback, critique, and revision/rewriting that are usually associated with convergent thinking (i.e. with selection of standard observation of "correct" language forms, logical structuring of paragraphs, and clear development of argument). Some of the differences noted as distinguishing between the two classrooms are differences in the nature of the writing goals that dictate differences in approaches and processes to achieving these goals. Creative writing students, for example, are expected to find and select their own themes/subjects and encouraged to use life stories, to write in a personal and subjective voice, and to foreground narrative and dramatization. Pre-eminent attention is paid to dialogue, as a way to encourage a dialogical imagination, what M. M. Bakhtin had theorized as characteristics of fictional narrative, featuring heteroglossia, polyphony, and dialogism, referring to the complex expressivity in all forms of utterance as they draw upon a matrix of earlier utterances and dense socio-cultural associative networks.

In addition, creative writing privileges a stylistics that encourages the use of figurative language to produce affect, language play, and a self-reflexive consciousness of the performance of language itself. In academic writing, the major concern is with constructing an impersonal voice and "objective" point of view. The skills of précis, thesis-antithesis-synthesis structure, citation and documentation are required in a toolkit intrinsically related to the skills of research and the central role of researched materials/content in developing a persuasive argument. Academic writing deploys exposition, description, and narrative to further argument; and to maintain a dialectical structure chiefly for the sake of a coherent, unified thesis. Students also master the techniques of expansion, under-standing the power of multiple examples, development, explication, abstract reasoning, clarity of statement, linearity, and general versus particular statement in producing successful academic papers. In prose creative writing, whether fiction or creative non-fiction, the delineation of characters, action-driven plots, the dynamics of a dialogical imagination, language economy, contraction, suggestion, figurative language, the affective dimension of aurality/orality, and a non-linear (foreshadowing, flashbacks) structure – all are primary concerns that are less foregrounded in academic writing

Yet there are useful crossovers from creative writing features to academic writing practices. Some examples are the occasional deployment of a personal voice/subjective narrator; the use of different points of view and of narrative to dramatize an argument; and the appeal to human interest, in the portrayal of characters and particularities. Shared stylistic concerns include the function of economy and the judicious use of figurative language; and the deployment of narrative, description – setting – and dialogue for greater clarity and illumination. That is, academic writing is never without the resources that mark the creative writing text in vivifying the argument paper. My chapter's opening location is in the creative writing classroom; and it is from there that it addresses the divide between teaching academic writing and teaching creative writing. In fact, the chapter is premised on the concept that creativity as an aspirational feature and dynamic is common to both the creative and academic writing classroom.

What is *creativity?* Generally, it is the presence of the creation of "newness," whether in material, ideational, or abstract form. Modernity has endowed any identifiably new "thing" with qualitative and subjective value, and particularly in the era of the knowledge industry, creativity is associated with both thought/ idea and product. Mihaly Csikszentmihalyi, in *Creativity: Flow and the Psychology of Discovery and Invention* (Csikszentmihalyi, 1996), offers a brilliant mapping of characteristics of the creative psychology through an analysis of interviews with over ninety exceptional achievers in diverse fields – politics, the sciences, the arts, business, and so forth – basing his analysis on his original concept of flow to reflect on how creativity also impacts less exceptional individuals. The emergence of creative agents, according to Csikszentmihalyi, is not simply a result of individual genius but a matter of complex flowering fostered by a sociocultural and material support structure. While Csikszentmihalyi defines creativity as a systemic "process by which a symbolic domain in the culture is changed" (p. 8), that is, through the production of novel work, he argues that receptivity and recognition by others are important both to the work's production and to its visible contri-bution to the field and domain. My core conviction in teaching writing, both to creative writing and composition students, is that in the writing classroom, creativity is associated with features of discovery and innovation, and so marked by originality and freshness in the writing product. Insofar as we acknowledge that writing is heuristic, that the writer finds out what he or she knows chiefly through the process of writing itself, then every act of writing is inevitably related to the making of new knowledge (arguably with the exception of précis, summary, simple synthesis, and plagiarism, which are forms of repeated rather than new knowledge).

The workshop I led in the City University of Hong Kong Summer Institute in 2013 attempted to model for the teacher participants the kind of writing classroom strategies that I often deploy to generate writing that can then be revised/redrafted/shaped as poetry, fiction, and creative non-fiction narratives, and that, to my mind, would also prove effective in generating academic writing in straightforward composition classrooms. Of the self-selected group of 30 or so participants that June, only one had ever taught courses in creative writing. The majority had never attempted to write creatively (i.e. poems and stories), and none had taken creative writing courses. All of the participants were teaching English language writing classes in tertiary institutions, the majority working in Chinese contexts. In requesting participants to introduce themselves, I asked for name, institutional affiliation, a brief bio of teaching experiences, present professional and career goals, one narrative of successful classroom strategy, and one narrative of a teaching problem or failure. In sharing this information within small groups, the participants were able to arrive at their collective identity as teachers of writing while also communicating their individual stories.

Description of Activity and Strategies for Implementation

I began this workshop for teachers of writing as I always do for my creative writing courses by creating "a safe space" for participants' social and cultural production. I underlined that writing, while seemingly a solitary activity coming out of individual thought and motivation, is also always a social act, embedded in a community of readers and writers, contextualized in a set of previous or current readings and assignments, responding to specific shared prompts, energized by collective discussion, attentive to established criteria and models, and intended for an audience. That is, writing is both an individual private production and a public document. As such, it is beset by anxiety, compounded by the ambiguity of its status and the ambivalence writing students experience in negotiating between the intensely private and intensely public sentiments and features of the writing assignment. As many scholars have noted, the intrinsic inextricability of personal utterance and social context makes writing a more fraught project both to teach and undertake than is understood in writing pedagogy. Judith Harris argued:

> How can a student write as a self without first formulating a social context in which to express the personal? Even the most personal registry of utterance is implicitly a response to the social context determined by subjectivity.... Language has a deeply inherent value for us, loaded with affect, beginning with the resonance of what was heard and absorbed in our earliest interactions with other people, which the mind contains and associates with present events. (Harris, 2001: 177)

Creating a safe space is crucial to encouraging students to risk self-expression (sometimes viewed by the more timid as "self-exposure"), to engage in more probing and complicated questions, and to attempt innovative forms of linguistic communication, such as using dialogue, new varieties of English, and so forth. Without the shared sense of a safe space, student writers usually choose easy subjects, stay on conventional paths of thinking, and avoid stylistic challenges, including complex syntactical structures, time shifts, non-linear structures, and more.

What constitutes a safe space? It is a temporal consensual space in which specific group dynamics are clarified, agreed on, observed, and practiced. Some teachers have offered more elaborate descriptions of a "safe place" for writing (e.g. Megnin, 2013). The usual student introductions many courses begin with therefore have more significant psychological work to do in my creative writing class. When students offer name and background (major, year), they also tell one memorable thing about themselves. Subjective identity thus forms the links by which these writers mark themselves as singular, their singularity being the location from where they will address each other. In the Institute workshop, because of time constraints, the participants introduced themselves only in their small groups. In the usual semester-long course, students introduce themselves to the entire class, a process that may sometimes take up one-third of that first meeting, but which time is effectively spent in that it helps establish the supportive climate and familiarity essential for the constitution of a writing community. At the same time I ask students to write certain information on note cards that I consult through the semester. The information (name, major, year) also includes favorite authors, films, two positive character traits, one negative character trait, their goals in the course, career ambition, and other information that will help me understand that individual and his or her sensibility and writing process. The development of a writing community that provides the feedback, cheering squad, catalyst, models, and audience for the students has to be encouraged in every meeting; and the instructor's interventions, through overt comments, organizing small groups or pairs of students for exchange of feedback, and other similar strategies, are crucial to sustaining that community.

The ground rules I lay down are simple: always respect each other and the individual's work; and always first offer one comment on the success of a writing assignment before volunteering one concrete suggestion for revising/strengthening/tweaking that assignment. That is, the feedback must be positive and constructive, all comments must be concretely related to specific passages of writing, and every critique must be accompanied by specific suggestions for revision. That is, the whole goal of the workshop and peer review process is to improve individuals' work; as a not-too-minor point, to raise the individual's course grades; and to strengthen sentiments of communal identity that frequently are maintained outside of the classroom, particularly fostered through assignments for the small groups to deliver collective oral presentations (e.g. an analysis of a short story, political speech, newspaper article, essay, etc.), activities that require working together outside of class time.

To further create a communal and collaborative *habitus* – a term the sociologist Pierre Bourdieu theorized to mean embodied dispositions that relate to an individual's primary habits and skills, that result in her/his social power (Bourdieu, 1977), and that signifies in this chapter values and expectation of specific social groups arrived at through everyday life experiences – I have developed multiple safe space practices. These include the option for students to submit their writing to the class anonymously; to use pseudonyms to disguise their authorship; to request that their works *not* be shared with either small or whole-class groups; and to fold their submissions over to a blank page with the request that the instructor not read the submission (this option is to encourage the writing and submission of texts, even if not to be read or shared). I also rely heavily on one-to-one office conferences, when the individual writer's writing challenges – freighted as they are with anxiety, embarrassment, fear of failure, risk-aversion, resistance to specific assignments, and more severe psychological dynamics – may be calmly discussed with concrete reference to particular individual writing submissions.

English language writing teachers in Asia particularly face cultural issues in getting their students to write expressively, personally, openly, and emotionally and then to share such writing publicly, as the social inhibitions against exactly such values and behavior are fairly strong. The development of a writing community identity helps to mitigate against these cultural injunctions. Another safe space strategy I always deploy is to break up the public domain of the large classroom, to place students in smaller groups or paired with a partner whose initial introductory information promises a sympathetic bond. Indeed, after the first class introductions, I re-organize students into smaller groups of four to five participants each. The small groups enable a greater sense of intimacy and camaraderie, and they are more time-efficient in ensuring that attention gets paid to every writer in the class. Student writers read their in-class or take-home writing to the members of their small groups, listen to their comments and suggestions, and re-write in response to this discussion. Each group will select one or two writing assignments to be read to and critiqued by the entire class. Over the course of the weeks of instruction, each student will be able to have her/his work critiqued by the entire class multiple times, an important feature that prevents excessive attention being paid to more assertive students or the neglect of more subdued participants.

Equally important are writing models that offer the beginning writer sanctioned, even valorized, examples of such self-expressive, personal, and emotional texts. Reading and writing strategies are inseparably linked mental acts. The English composition teacher, especially in second language classrooms, must serve effectively as a reading instructor in order to lead students to a discursive comfort with talk on rhetorical strategies, stylistics, thematic analysis, and other matters usually related to critical interpretation and evaluation (reading) rather than production (writing) of texts. Charles Bernstein notes that he "tend(s) to teach reading rather than creative writing classes…. I call my classes creative reading workshops, meaning you write creatively in response to reading" (Bernstein, 1996: 63). The selection of such models is key to students' growth as readers, thinkers and writers. Numerous composition textbooks include carefully selected essays, memoir texts, and other genres of narrative and argument intended to formulate coherent and sequential patterns for students' rhetorical mastery. Local instructors in Hong Kong and China believe they must task themselves with discovering reading materials that are regionally and culturally relevant (that is, not wholly Euro or Western-centric), and also curriculum-topical (for example, models of business, legal, or sociological writing of interest to students in business, law and social sciences departments).

Other pre-writing preparatory activities that may usefully be deployed for both creative and academic writing classes are the use of prompts and of meditation/mindfulness exercises. These prewriting features serve to enable successful freewriting activities that will then be closely reviewed in workshops. The academic writing teachers in my Summer Institute session reported that they had never attempted these two classroom activities that are key to my own teaching of creative writing and that have been practiced as central to creative writing pedagogy. While strategies such as prompts, reading assignments, directed writing, peer and instructor feedback, group and collaborative work, online collective feedback, and scaffolding are common in both academic writing and creative writing classes, freewriting and workshopping proved new, yet excitingly promising and fruitful, for these teacher participants. All of the session evaluations ranked the in-class freewriting as the most valuable takeaway, together with the preparatory meditation and prompt exercises.

In fact, I first introduced imaging prompts and deep breathing relaxation (meditation) exercises as prewriting activities in my very first forays into teaching creative writing, as part of a determination to encourage community college students to be more receptive to reading and discussing poetry in literature classes. I believed that under-prepared students would become more receptive to poetry if they were to write poems themselves (Lim, 1996). These chiefly part-time, commuting students who were required to register for a two-semester course on composition and literature were resistant to reading, and particularly reading texts whose stylistics presented challenging decoding skills that they believed they were not prepared to learn. In assigning them to write their own poems using these prompts (e.g. to recall a very early memory or to evoke the sensory experience of a smell associated with strong emotion or a disturbing experience) for imaging/mediation/freewriting/ workshop classroom practices, I was able to generate their interest in the patterns of poetic form and the affective power in figurative language. I first elaborated on the meditation process in "Make it New: Introducing Poetry through Writing Poetry" (Lim, 1983).

In the thirty years since that article was published, I have gone on to teach academic and creative writing at research universities, to graduate students, teachers, young children, and seniors; and in a recent article (Lim, 2010), I offered an expanded discussion of these strategies. Indeed, my pedagogical goal – to mute the outside distractions (noise) for the writer, to establish a writing environment that best encourages an internal condition for individuals to experience what Csikszentmihalyi in his theories of positive psychology has conceptualized as the temporal space for "flow" – has been discussed and practiced by other creative writing teachers. In my interview with Maxine Hong Kingston (Lim, 2008), for example, she elaborates on her strategy of establishing silence, conscious breathing, and "tuning…for your writer's ear," and her use of "the bell of mindfulness" as a prewriting strategy. Kingston's description closely matches my deep breathing, relaxation, imaging exercises, without the Buddhist context in which Kingston places her practice: "In Buddhism, when you hear the bell. Then you are mindful and you place yourself in the present moment; you are not flying off into the past or the future" (Lim, 2008, p.169). It is intriguing how closely matched the goals of the prewriting exercises are to the components that Csikszentmihalyi (1996) had theorized as present in his concept of "flow," the dimension in which creativity, he argues, is possible. For Csikszentmihalyi, these include clear, challenging but attainable goals; strong concentration and focused attention; intrinsically rewarding activity; accompanied by positive feelings of serenity with a loss of self-consciousness; and time as timeless, with a feedback loop that posits the work as achievable and thus producing a sense of personal control over the situation. The ideal classroom climate for freewriting embodies these components, and whether it is Kingston's practice of silent tuning to the writer's ear with the bell of mindfulness or my own triple strategy of meditation, imaging, and freewriting, the end goal is to enable the experience of "flow" in the individual writers.

The deep breathing, relaxation exercise usually takes no more than a few minutes, during which time the room is darkened, and students close their eyes and make themselves comfortable. They are then guided through slow deep breathing to the count of eight for each inhalation and each exhalation, and are walked through relaxing various parts of their body. Beginning with their scalps and foreheads, they are told to relax (untense) muscles around their eyes, their mouths, their jaws, the back of their necks, their upper shoulders, and so on, till the tension is released from the entire body to fall past thighs, calves, feet, and toes to the floor. The exercise leads immediately to a prompt; the instructor repeats and elaborates on the day's writing assignment – providing a detailed litany of possible topics, time frames, characters, settings, narrative voices, and so forth. In the Summer Institute, the participants were prompted to write of a vivid memory having to do with the sense of smell, a story from early childhood or of more recent vintage, to recall characters associated with the sensory memory, to describe the smell in all its complex features, to include the setting for that storied memory, the narrator's feelings then, and other relevant context or feelings. While the selection of topic is important – it must appeal and be accessible, ready for mental development, and familiar rather than alien and arcane – the instructor's assistance in guiding the writers to imagine and vivify, using the rhetorical tools of description – for character, place and time, setting, and so forth – and narration – for narrator's voice, dialogue, chronological structure, etc. – is crucial for beginning writers who have not yet internalized these skill sets in their repertoire for freewriting. That is, while the core activity of the writing session is freewriting itself, "freewriting" in the classroom is of course a term open to shading, as I argue below.

Peter Elbow's many treatises on writing pedagogy, beginning with his first book, *Writing without Teachers* (Elbow, 1973), have made a near-fetish of the freewriting activity as the major exercise for academic and creative writing. Natalie Goldberg's later text, *Writing Down the Bones: Freeing the Writer Within*

(Goldberg, 1986/2006), extended Elbow's pedagogy of freewriting to encompass more activities that as a fictionist she has practiced and that have succeeded in moving her out of self-critical inhibitory writing blocks. Freewriting has been incorrectly categorized as a prewriting exercise, but I find that freewriting is itself a writing performance albeit with looser constraints. The workshop participant is set the task of continuous writing for a prescribed period – usually ten or fifteen minutes – denying any impulse to pause in this continuous writing to check on spelling, grammar, and vocabulary or to revise idea, as is the wont in the normal writing process. The goal of freewriting is to produce material – ideas, images, expressive language, stories, language – if not in a stream of consciousness at least in a stream of written text. The assumption is that writing with no attention to the self-critical inner voice and with the noise of the world turned off, individuals should be able to tap into their emotional and intellectual resources in more spontaneous, unfettered manner. Resources once materialized as text, rough, even inchoate and incoherent, nonetheless can be reshaped and rewritten using the tools of rhetoric that form the conscious core of writing instruction.

The writing produced through these strategies, however, is still in process. That is, the workshop following after the freewriting is the conclusive practice, encompassing audience sharing, peer review, and rewriting – from major revision of themes, ideas, stories, characters, structure, and language to copyediting and minor tweaks – leading to the production of a successful creative writing or academic writing text. I structure my classroom workshops alternatively as small group work, paired collaboration, and whole-class audience critique. As described earlier, a major strategy to encouraging more risk-taking, open and expressive writing is the construction of a safe space for individual writers, and the small group work and paired collaboration are aimed at equalizing the attention given to every student.

At the same time, however, small groups need their own internal structure. I assign different roles to group members (two group facilitators who are responsible for keeping discussion on track and relevant; a note-taker who writes down the points raised; a presenter who will share these points and summarize the discussion with the entire class; and if there is a fifth member, to serve as a second note-taker). These roles both underline the dynamic of personal responsibility in even the "freest" of group interactions and provide a means by which quieter individuals are required to more actively participate in their groups. As Jones et al. (2012) observe in their chapter on research findings on creative collaboration in the public relations industry about the processes for teamwork, observations that are relevant also to creative collaboration in the writing classroom:

> [P]articipants often find it necessary to negotiate different kinds of face to face relationships at different stages in the creative process. Brainstorming sessions, for example, were seen to work best when everyone felt they had an equal right and equal responsibility to contribute, whereas in the stage of drafting documents more rigid and hierarchical role differentiation was favored.
>
> Ironically, however, it was often the underlying hierarchy which seemed to foster more creative participation. In brainstorming sessions, for example, team leaders and other more powerful participants saw it as part of their job to create the space for less powerful people to contribute, and also to ensure that more aggressive or talkative members did not dominate the discussion. (p. 101)

The line in the workshop between divergent and convergent production is arguably more marked in the academic than the creative writing classroom, for with academic writing the individual work must successfully incorporate research on the assigned topic. The paper is intrinsically a collective document in that it draws on, summarizes, synthesizes, interprets, analyzes, critiques, and valorizes other documents, clearly citing at each point the writer's reference and intellectual debt to and direct borrowing/reproduction of these other authors' texts. In short, every piece of academic writing is already intertextual, and intertextual productions demand convergent practices of research and its discursive forms of précis, indirect and direct quotations, citations, bibliographical recording, and other inscription skills. To arrive at these convergent academic writing skill sets, however, via workshop strategies, instructors must articulate clear and accessible principles, guidelines and criteria that are established in handouts (e.g. questionnaires, evaluation grids, and comment categories) that students observe when revising their own work and that they complete for their peer reviews of others' work, and whose rhetorical features are thus internalized through regular consultation.

The Summer Institute participants, all teaching in tertiary institutions, uniformly expressed frustration with the English-language writing course: students whose command of English is weak, who will not engage with the materials, whose critical and analytical skills are inadequate, who read at a low level, and other critical evaluations. As with all college teaching, one cannot expect students to be capable of helpful, not to say insightful, peer reviews without guidance and a great deal of practice. Colin Irvine notes:

> Because 'writing' is historically determined and situationally constrained…, because it often occurs in diverse discourse communities, with representatives of many educational and cultural backgrounds [an apt description of the tertiary second language or multilingual classroom (my comment)], and because it is – despite educational trends that might suggest otherwise – paralogic and nonlinear, it should come as no surprise that the peer review activity so central to the workshop model proves less than productive. (Irvine, 2010: 142)

Irvine explains, "Nearly all instructors trained in teaching composition according to the workshop model carefully, deliberately set up the peer-review activity by explaining to the students that the first time they read their peer's paper they need to focus their feedback on essay-level strengths and areas for improvement" (p. 136); but this instruction is often ignored as studies show that students despite their best intentions focus on error-hunting, as evident in the results of the empirical research on eye-tracking that Irvine cites (see Paulson, Alexander, and Armstrong, 2007). As Irvine further notes, "Some of the reasons peer review fails have to do with how well-prepared the students are to do this sophisticated, challenging type of work with and for each other; and others have to do with the overlapping contexts in which the work occurs, contexts that include the group itself, the classroom, the course, the college, and the society in which all of these social constructs take place" (p. 134).

In creative writing courses, which are elective rather than mandatory and where students are usually motivated, have already completed some contextual readings, and are cued in to some of the craft features covered in the curriculum, the workshop peer review structure may be more easily implemented. But even with creative writing students, workshops based on peer reviews and where students revise according to these reviews may be similarly challenging. Bizzaro (2010: 43) has noted earlier complaints that creative writing students, like composition students, may be unfamiliar with writing as a process. Mary Ann Cain (Cain, 2010: 218) cites Joseph Moxley's (1989) point that creative writing students may have "little experience with invention, critical reading, revision, and editing, as well as overall understandings of composing processes," and agrees with Moxley (1989) when she notes that "revision is often not taught, and…it needs to be taught" (Cain, 2010: 223). I have found the workshop structure one of the best methods for modeling and teaching the revision process, provided that the workshop is revised from its "standard approach…the teacher leading a critique of a work while the author remained silent and the alpha students fought for the class' attention or the teacher's approval" (Moxley, 2010: 230). In importing the workshop structure (reading aloud to an audience, group discussion, peer review) to the academic classroom, students need some kind of scaffolding that helps contain, structure, and offer substance to their analysis of their peers' texts – usually disorganized, error-riddled, digressive, undeveloped rough first drafts. I offer a number of scaffolding directions for group discussion and take-home peer reviews. For the discussion activity:

1. Each peer reviewer must always begin with a positive statement that focuses on the big picture that the draft is communicating.
2. Then the peer reviewer may proceed to offer one helpful and concrete point for revision, which may be as minor as a noting a misspelling or suggesting a syntactical shift or as major as a change in chronology, point of view, narrative voice, etc.

For the take-home peer review, when students read their peer's draft and submit their review in the next class:

3. The peer reviewer uses the evaluative grid provided by the instructor and demonstrates a full understanding of the features of good academic writing that the grid/checklist articulates, as in some of the following items:

For Introduction and Thesis
- Introduces topic and provides background to establish relevance of the issue
- Thesis demonstrates clear purpose, complexity, and originality
- Raises issues to be discussed
- Previews the structure of the essay

For Development and Support
- Clearly demonstrates complexity of thought
- Argument and analysis are logically and sophisticatedly thought through
- Primary and secondary sources:
  a. included to demonstrate and develop main points
  b. used in effective and balanced ways
  c. included in appropriate and interesting ways
  d. have specific & integral quotations to be included in paper

- Quotations from text(s):
  a. are introduced and contextualized
  b. relate to central argument
  c. are cited
  d. are closely read and analyzed
- Close reading (literary analysis) and use of passages:
  a. Primarily from your main text(s) which must be one or two piece(s) of literature (short story, novel, poem, etc.)
  b. integral quotations analyzed to build upon and support thesis
  c. looks closely at the author's word, stylistic, and/or thematic choices
  d. analyzed with a specificity that makes the reading *yours*
- Counterarguments are presented and addressed
- Overarching generalizations such as "Asians today have…" should be avoided. In other words, be as specific as possible.
- Paragraph length summarization of book/short story should be avoided
- Relevant engagement with social, historical, cultural contexts/data/facts which are cited

For Structure and Organization
- Paper is organized in a way that fully supports thesis and purpose
- Paragraphs follow logically to build to a conclusion or claim about the research topic/thesis
- Effective and explicitly detailed sequence of ideas
- Clear transitions which support your thesis

4. The peer reviewer completes the comments page on the paper s/he is reviewing.

5. These comments themselves are given a grade point by the instructor; that is, the writing teacher also evaluates the review assignment submitted by the peer reviewers, signaling an appreciation that peer reviews themselves exhibit conscientious work and skills.

To my mind, there is no reason to repress students' tendency to discover writing errors, a trait that is useful for copyediting, although not the central function or goal of peer reviews, and copyediting notations are acceptable as part of the peer review work.

It is here, however, with the full relocation of the workshop practice (what I call Workshop 1) to the academic writing classroom (Workshop 2) that the highway of nurturing individual writers' creative divergent productions may well collapse into a sinkhole of incoherent, unformed or ill-formed, uninformed badly written morass of opinions, feelings, and irrelevant digressions. The workshop model for academic writing (Workshop 2) must be grounded on preliminary instruction on what is good academic writing; for example, what constitutes a clear thesis, how arguments are organized and developed, how sequential paragraphs work through related topic sentences and transitions, what are good and adequate numbers of examples, including all the features that a respected writing guide such as William Strunk, Jr., and E. B. White's *Elements of Style* (Strunk and White, 1959/2008) addresses.

The major difference between having students review their peers' writing in Workshop 2 classroom activity and the teacher sitting alone marking every paper with comments and grades is that with the former, students' learning is continuous; there is no pause between their production and the authoritative reader/teacher's critique. Instead, immediately after the freewriting exercise, students read their work aloud to the members of their small group, who respond following specific guidelines. When the work is enlarged, revised, and submitted to their peers, their immediate audience, in the next writing session, the feedback is tracked in written evaluations and not carelessly offered. Examples of instructional materials for students to refer to include handouts on drafting, revising, and submitting a research paper; notes on how to produce a topic suitable to a specific course; what is involved in generating an annotated bibliography; models of abstracts of the assigned paper's content; and a grid of rhetorical features that mark a successful academic paper.

In this Workshop 2 ecology for academic writing, where the goal is convergent production, the conventions-bound regime of accurate citation and research-based expository writing and coherent persuasive argument; the regulating scrutiny of spelling and grammar checks; and the muting of self-expression, subjective opinion, and the ludic that gets in the way of the lucid – all these features of "correct" academic writing must be respected. The grid that guides peer reviews must also change from an evaluation of divergent features (what is fresh, new, an arresting image, a memorable character, strong phrasing; versus cliché, undeveloped, confusing, or otherwise problematical) to one that evaluates the aspects of a solid argument paper. By then, the hope is that students will have already formed a sense of a supportive intimate writing community, willing to share their drafts with their constructed audience, and willing to serve as first reviewers whose critiques will be thoughtful and informed, fair, and useful.

Reflections and Recommendations

The Institute workshop participants' reflections expressed enthusiasm for the concepts, practices, and strategies concerning a safe space, group work, and a writing community; meditation and imaging; and peer review and audience sharing, including the prospect of student publication – to assign a final whole class project to publish an anthology of selected best class writing as self-publication, or with institutional support, including online publication. We discussed the thorny issue of assessing student work produced through freewriting and workshops (an entire chapter is needed for this subject). The teachers who come from two-year colleges and comprehensive and research universities and who teach in writing centers and in regular composition and second language/multilingual courses found the strategies used in creative writing classes productive as they submitted to these strategies themselves during the session. The pleasure and success the participants experienced in this session re-affirm that when it comes to writing, purposeful assignments that allow participants to take control of their composition processes, the discovery process that makes something new out of internal and external resources, and the sharing of these new creations with a supportive, like-minded community are as valuable in academic writing as in creative writing classrooms.

References

Aristotle (2003) *Poetics*. London: Penguin.

Atwood, Margaret (2002) *Negotiating with the Dead: A Writer on Writing*. Cambridge: Cambridge University Press.

Bakhtin, Mikhail M. (1981) *The Dialogic Imagination: Four Essays* (ed. Michael Holquist; trans. Caryl Emerson and Michael Holquist). Austin: University of Texas Press.

Bazerman, Charles (2008) *Handbook of Research on Writing: History, Society, School, Individual, Text*. New York: Erlbaum.

Bazerman, Charles, Little, Joseph, Chavkin, Teri, Fouquette, Danielle, Bethel, Lisa and Garufis, Janet (2005) *Writing Across the Curriculum*. Reference Guides to Rhetoric and Composition. South Carolina: Parlor Press and WAC Clearinghouse. Available at http://wac.colostate.edu/books/bazerman_wac/.

Bernstein, Charles (1996) On poetry, language, and teaching: A conversation with Charles Bernstein. *Boundary 2* 23(3): 45–66. http://dx.doi.org/10.2307/303637.

Bourdieu, Pierre (1977) *Outline of a Theory of Practice*. Cambridge University Press.

Cain, Mary Ann (2010) 'A space for radical openness': Re-visioning the creative writing workshop. In Dianne Donnelly (ed.) *Does the Writing Workshop Still Work?* 216–229. Bristol: Multilingual Matters.

Csikszentmihalyi, Mihaly (1996) *Creativity: Flow and the Psychology of Discovery and Invention*. Harper Collins: New York.

Guilford, Joy Paul (1956) The structure of intellect. *Psychological Bulletin* 53(4): 267–293. http://dx.doi.org/10.1037/h0040755.

Elbow, Peter (1973/1998) *Writing Without Teachers*. Oxford: Oxford University Press.

Eliot, T. S. (1919/1975) Tradition and the individual talent. In Frank Kermode (ed.) *Selected Prose of T. S. Eliot* 37–44. New York: Farrer, Straus and Giroux.

Forster, E. M. (1927/1986) *Aspects of the Novel*. London: Penguin.

Gardner, John (1991) *The Art of Fiction: Notes on Craft for Young Writers*. New York: Vintage.

Goldberg, Natalie (1986/2006) *Writing Down the Bones: Freeing the Writer Within*. Boston: Shambhala.

Harris, Judith (2001) Re-writing the subject: Psychoanalytic approaches to creative writing and composition pedagogy. *College English* 64(2): 175–204. http://dx.doi.org/10.2307/1350116.

Highsmith, Patricia (2001) *Plotting and Writing Suspense Fiction*. New York: St. Martin's Press.

Irvine, Colin (2010) 'It's fine, I gess': Problems with the workshop model in college composition courses. In Dianne Donnelly (ed.) *Does the Writing Workshop Still Work?* 130–145. Bristol: Multilingual Matters.

Jones, Rodney H. (ed.) (2012) *Discourse and Creativity*. Essex: Pearson.

Jones, Rodney H., Bhatia, Vijay K., Bremner, Stephen and Peirson-Smith, Anne (2012) Creative collaboration in the public relations industry. In Rodney H. Jones (ed.) *Discourse and Creativity* 93–108. Essex: Pearson. http://doi.org/10.1111/j.1467-971X.2010.01675.x.

Le Guin, Ursula K. (1998) *Steering the Craft*. Portland: The Eighth Mountain Press.

Le Guin, Ursula K. (2004) *The Wave in the Mind: Talks and Essays on the Writer, the Reader, and the Imagination*. Boston: Shambhala.

Lim, Shirley Geok-lin (1983) Make it new: Introducing poetry through writing poetry. *Insight* (Spring): 21–25.

Lim, Shirley Geok-lin (1996) *Among the White Moon Faces: An Asian American Memoir of Homelands*. New York: Feminist Press.

Lim, Shirley Geok-lin (2003) The strangeness of creative writing. *Pedagogy* 3(2): 151–169. http://doi.org/10.1215/15314200-3-2-151.

Lim, Shirley Geok-lin (2008) Reading back, looking forward: A retrospective interview with Maxine Hong Kingston. *MELUS* 33(1): 157–170. http://doi.org/10.1093/melus/33.1.157.

Lim, Shirley Geok-lin (2010) Lore, practice, and social identity in creative writing pedagogy: Speaking with a yellow voice. *Pedagogy* 10(1): 79–93. http://doi.org/10.1215/15314200-2009-022.

Lodge, David (1994) *The Art of Fiction*. London: Penguin.

Lodge, David (2011) *The Practice of Writing*. London: Vintage.

Longinus (2001) On Sublimity. In Vincent B. Leitch et al. (eds.) *The Norton Anthology of Theory and Criticism* 138–154. London: W.W. Norton & Co.

MacArthur, Charles A., Graham, Steve and Fitzgerald, Jill (eds.) (2006) *Handbook of Writing Research*. New York: Guilford Press.

McLeod, Susan H. (2007) *Writing Program Administration*. South Carolina: Parlor Press and WAC Clearinghouse. Retrieved on 15 December 2013 from http://wac.colostate.edu/books/mcleod_wpa/.

Megnin, Ria (2013) Compassionate communication – Class 2: Creating safe space. Retrieved on 15 December 2013 from http://riamegnin.com/cc/cc2/.

Menand, Louis (2009) Show and tell – Should creative writing be taught? *The New Yorker Magazine* (June 8, 2009): 106–112. Retrieved on 15 December 2013 from http://www.newyorker.com/arts/critics/atlarge/2009/06/08/090608crat_atlarge_menand?currentPage=all.

Moxley, Joseph (ed.) (1989) *Creative Writing in America: Theory and Pedagogy*. Urbana: National Council of Teachers of English.

Moxley, Joseph (2010) Afterword: Disciplinarity and the future of creative writing studies. In Dianne Donnelly (ed.) *Does the Writing Workshop Still Work?* 230–238. Bristol: Multilingual Matters.

Myers, David Gershom (1996/2006) *The Elephants Teach: Creative Writing Since 1880*. Chicago: University of Chicago Press.

Orwell, George (1946/2004) *Why I Write*. London: Penguin.

Paulson, Eric J., Alexander, Jonathan and Armstrong, Sonya (February 2007) Peer review re-viewed: Investigating the juxtaposition of composition students' eye movements and peer review processes. *Research in the Teaching of English* 41: 304–335. Retrieved on 15 December 2013 from http://www.ncte.org/library/NCTEFiles/Resources/Journals/RTE/0414-may07/RT0414Subject.pdf.

Poe, Edgar Allan (1846/2004) The philosophy of composition. In G. R. Thompson (ed.) *The Selected Writings of Edgar Allan Poe* 675–684. London: W.W. Norton & Co.

Rilke, Rainer Maria (1934/1993) *Letters to a Young Poet*. London: W.W. Norton & Co.

Smagorinsky, Peter (2006) *Research on Composition: Multiple Perspectives on Two Decades of Change*. New York: Teachers College Press.

Strunk, William, Jr., and White, E. B. (1959/2008) *The Elements of Style*. London: Longman.

Wharton, Edith (1924/1998) *The Writing of Fiction*. New York: Touchstone

Woolf, Virginia (1929/2008) *A Room of One's Own*. Oxford: Oxford University Press.

Wordsworth, William and Coleridge, Samuel Taylor (1800, 1802/1991) Wordsworth's Prefaces of 1800 and 1802. *Lyrical Ballads* (eds. R. L. Brett and A. R. Jones, 2nd edition) 241–272. Edinburgh: T. & A. Constable Ltd.

Part 4
Supporting Creativity and Discovery in Composing Multimedia Texts

14 Watching/Reading
Graphic Narratives and University Writing

Jeffrey Mather

Introduction

This chapter comes out of experience teaching graphic novels in the contexts of Hong Kong and Mainland China and conducting a workshop on using the graphic novel as a foundation for critical thinking at the Summer Institute for Creativity and Discovery in University Writing that was held at the City University of Hong Kong in the summer of 2013. In the first part of this chapter I discuss the potential strengths of using graphic novels in university writing classes. In the second part, I discuss activities and strategies for implementing graphic narratives into the classroom by referring to two texts: Guy Delisle's *Burma Chronicles* (Delise, 2007) and Joe Sacco's *Not in my Country* (Sacco, 2010). I close with some brief reflections and recommendations.

Changing Perceptions about Comics

In the past, published material on the pedagogical uses of the graphic novel has focused primarily on literacy and reading in primary and secondary education (Hammond, 2013; Hughes and King, 2010). The argument has often been made, in some form or another, that the graphic novel can be an effective stepping-stone for young, challenged, and reluctant readers into conventional text-only novels and books (in other words, the world of adult literacy). Increasingly, however, scholars and teachers have examined the potential uses of the graphic novel at the post-secondary level, a movement that has challenged some of the underlying perceptions about graphic novels, and to some extent the notion of literacy as a whole. In some cases, critics have attempted to raise the cultural profile of graphic novels (Versaci, 2007), arguing that they need to be brought into a closer discussion with more recognized forms of literature, while in other cases scholars have shown that graphic novels have a place in various other postsecondary teaching contexts like geography, women's studies, history, and philosophy.

In composition studies, there have been similar efforts to incorporate graphic narratives into classroom practices and to consider how graphic narratives can inform and provoke alternative ways of understanding the nature of composition. For example, in her insightful article, "Batman Returns (to Class): Graphic Narratives and the Syncretic Classroom" (MacDonald, 2012), Katharine Polak MacDonald describes how graphic novels are particularly useful for encouraging students to see the relationships between different genre forms. She writes:

> It is particularly important to use graphic narratives and comics in the composition classroom for this reason – they represent a basic formulation of rhetoric at play between genres, and how those genres combine to create a new mode of communication. (MacDonald, 2012: 226)

Furthermore, graphic novels allow students to see that texts are not only complex in terms of the generic features (for example, a graphic novel like *Watchmen* (Moore and Gibbons,1995) can subvert a reader's expectations of a "superhero" text as it incorporates elements of realism and horror), but also mediated within different social and cultural contexts:

> [M]ultimodality as it is deployed in comics develops the way in which students recognize milieu, and gestures to the way in which they encounter the world in terms of multiple literacies which must be simultaneously read for subtextual elements, as well as for their interrelations. (MacDonald, 2012: 223)

Similarly, in "Comics as Sponsors of Multimodal Literacy," Dale Jacobs has argued that "...comics are a rhetorical genre, comics are multimodal texts, and comics are both an order of discourse and discrete discursive events" (Jacobs, 2007: 182).

While such academic discussions address the theoretical value of graphic novels in composition instruction, many practicing teachers remain unaware of the pedagogical potentials of graphic novels. When I had a chance to discuss the possible uses of graphic novels with local teachers who attended my workshop at the Summer Institute, most people confessed that they had never read a "graphic novel" before. When I asked if they would consider using comics in the class, they responded positively, but also expressed some concerns. As teachers who work at improving language skills, it seemed counterintuitive to require students to read texts that contain less written language. When prompted, people voiced concerns, quite rightly, about the declining attention span of our students, who are constantly fiddling with their phones; the length of the average text communication may be no larger than a status update or, at best, a post about last night's karaoke on Facebook. Others suggested that students should be reading longer texts in order to build up their mental and intellectual stamina, and that comic books are just another example of consumer culture that encourages quick and easy, disposable reading. Somebody raised the point that people don't need to think as much when the pictures are there to make it clear, and that they don't need to use their imagination when the artist has already done the work for them. Another objection that was raised was that many graphic novels that young people are reading these days are gratuitously violent, reinforce negative gender stereotypes in their renderings of the "ideal" body type, or even propagandistic in terms of how they celebrate and idealize heroes.

While these concerns are certainly valid, the teacher comments revealed a lack of awareness among educators that graphic novels and comics are not just about superheroes and science fiction (and it can be argued that even those that are can deal with social issues in intelligent ways). It is not my aim here to defend graphic novels as a whole – since there are so many different types of graphic novels in public circulation – but instead to show that educators in Hong Kong and Greater China carried a number of preconceptions that hindered them from exploring the genre further. The confusion over terminology does not help matters since even classifying "graphic novels" is problematic, and the terminology we use does not always seem clear or appropriate. Authors, publishers, audiences, and critics have been unsure how to describe works that blur the lines between fiction and non-fiction, challenge the boundaries between "suitable" content for adults and children, and suggest to readers different ways to read and enjoy narrative texts. We come across various terms such as "cartoons," "graphic narratives," "comic art," "sequential art," and, sometimes, just "comics." I should mention that for practical reasons I use the terms comics, graphic novels, and graphic narratives interchangeably, although one can certainly elaborate on their differences. Whatever term we use, we need to keep an open mind about what kinds of texts we are talking about. In Scott McCloud's *Understanding Comics* (McCloud, 1993) – an academic book that is about the history of comics and is written in the form of a comic book – McCloud prefers the term "comics" and describes such texts as "Juxtaposed pictorial and other images in deliberate sequence, intended to convey information and/or to produce an aesthetic response in the viewer" (p. 9). This may seem like an unnecessarily long definition, but there is some value in taking a moment to consider comics as a development in a long historical trajectory. McCloud points to works of art such as the Bayeux Tapestry, Max Ernst's surrealist "Collage Novel", or Egyptian hieroglyphics: nobody would normally call such cultural artifacts "comics" – although that is actually what they are if we can agree that comics are essentially visual/verbal texts read in narrative sequence.

With a broad and inclusive view of "graphic narratives" we can consider how using comics and other verbal/visual texts promote visual literacy.[1] Like it or not, increasingly, we are navigating through digital media forms where information is framed and structured in spatial and visual terms. In their book, *Infographics: the Power of Visual Storytelling* (Lankow, Richie, and Crooks, 2012), Jason Lankow, Josh Richie, Ross Crooks discuss how infographics (charts, graphs, maps, and other creative renderings used to convey information) have become essential in areas such as media discourse, financial news, and business communication. The prevalence of infographics, according to Lankow, Richie, and Crooks, has to do with the way our brains function: a good visual rendering of information not only aids in the retention of that information, it evokes a sense of pleasure and aesthetic appeal. When entering the workforce after graduation, many of our current students will likely confront writing tasks that involve combining the verbal and the visual; it behooves us as writing teachers to consider how our classes can prepare students for those challenges and give them skills to be more critically aware of how text and images can relate to each other.

I used the term "Watching/Reading" in the chapter title to emphasize the difference and play between these modes and to highlight the need for teachers to consider the interface between the visual and the verbal in our approach to teaching critical thinking and composition. I summarize my points about the pedagogical value of the graphic novel as follows. Graphic novels can:

- Promote reading (especially *but not only* for lower level, "reluctant readers" or English language learners);
- Activate student interest and motivation;
- Provide an alternative and accessible way into exploring social and ethical issues;
- Promote visual literacy by raising attention to the ways that words and images relate to each other;
- Stimulate writing: conventional text responses, collaborative, and multimodal projects;
- Stimulate other creative projects. Even non-artistically inclined students can create their own comics using free software like Comic Life (www.comiclife.com.)

What follows are two activities that could be used in different teaching contexts.

Classroom Activity: Using Comics to Inspire and Guide Narrative Writing

Composition teachers sometimes dedicate part of the course to narrative writing, but in many cases it is an area that is overlooked or passed over quickly. This could be due to the perception that narrative writing is the most instinctual and natural form of composition since "telling a story of what happened" is a highly familiar type of communicative act. Yet producing successful narrative writing is deceptively difficult. Students need to make decisions about how to represent the passing of time and how and when to fill out their narratives with descriptive details. In successful narrative writing, time is rarely represented in consistent chronological sequence, and writers need to manage the level of detail and temporal focus of the narrative, a process that can lead to difficulties.

This activity can provide an entertaining way for students to engage with narrative writing and become better writers. Since travel is a universal experience, using graphic travel narratives in class provides an effective way to inspire students to share personal experiences, use their creativity, and free up their voices in writing. In the following lesson I will refer to short selections of Delisle's *Burma Chronicles* (Delisle, 2007), a humorous work that portrays the author, his wife, and their baby boy as they travel to Burma. This activity is appropriate for any level. The aims of the activity are to:

- Foster an interactive classroom where students reflect and discuss personal experiences;
- Expand global awareness by reading a text about travel to a foreign country;
- Convey basic terminology for discussing and understanding comics;
- Draw attention to the processes of narrative writing by mimicking and modeling;
- Build an awareness of how narratives are structured and how speed is controlled in both visual and verbal forms.

The following is a step-by-step approach to teaching Delisle's graphic novel. Ideally, this activity could be used in a composition course but teachers may find it useful in other classes or contexts.

Pre-reading: Introduce the Text

It is highly recommended that students purchase Delisle's novel, but given that this graphic novel is black and white, selections of the novel can easily be photocopied. The sections that I suggest for this activity are "Departure" and "Guest House." In total, a handout would consist of three pages. If you don't have access to Delisle's book, find an action sequence in another graphic narrative, preferably one that relies primarily on images and where written text is kept to a minimum.

For this activity you need to explain to the class that Delisle's book is a work of graphic nonfiction, or you might also call it an autobiographical comic since it seeks to represent real personal experiences. The Canadian author is travelling with his French wife, who works for the humanitarian organization Médecins Sans Frontières (MSF) or Doctors Without Borders. They are traveling to the country of Myanmar (or Burma). You might provide some background information about the political history of Burma/ Myanmar, and the troubled history of the country (Aung San Suu Kyi's recent release from a long period of house arrest, the history of global sanctions, the transition from the authoritarian rule of the Junta, ethnic tensions between Muslims and Buddhists, etc.).

Read and Discuss the Text

There are very few words in the opening sequence, and so the images tell the story of the dizzying excitement and increasing fatigue that the family experienced traveling from their previous assignment in Guatemala to their guesthouse in Burma. The first frame depicts the three travellers standing next to their luggage, with the diminutive figure of the baby boy comically depicted in front of the largest stack of luggage. The narrative continues with the family moving from car to train to plane to taxi, and finally arriving at their destination.

After they read the text, students can be asked to consider what is most striking, parts they liked, and how they felt as they read. For lower or intermediate level English language learners, this may be an opportunity to elicit some oral practice. Since there are no words on the page, have the students describe to each other in pairs the sequence of events, paying particular attention to the connecting phrases and transitions (a variation here would be to ask them to repeat their versions of the story a few times, a little faster each time to increase fluency). This would also help to prepare lower level students for the last step in this activity.

After reading the section, ask the students to discuss in pairs or small groups how meaning is communicated in visual terms and how the arrangement and organization of images relate to the content. Students will likely comment on the organization of frames, which are jumbled together (in describing comics "frames" are the small boxes and "panes" refers to the whole page). Some may confess that they were confused about which frame to read next. This could make for a good opportunity to mention an idea that Scott McCloud describes as "eye time" (McCloud, 1994). According to McCloud, time in comics is controlled through the content within the images (which may contain images of movement and depict transition from place to place) as well as through the arrangement of frames on the page. The "gutter" (which is the space between the frames) is not often consciously noticed by the reader but also plays an important role in controlling the speed of the reader's eye over the page and communicating the sense of time passing.

Students can hopefully recognize that the intended effect of the jumbled frames is to make the reader share in the travel experience. Readers should experience the eyes scanning the page back and forth, up and down, and perhaps even feel a sense of anxiety when reading because it is not always clear which frame to follow next. This sense of disorientation is, of course, appropriate to the subject matter, which depicts an exasperating travel experience.

The "Guest House" sequence provides a contrast to "Departure" as Delisle describes his family's arrival in Burma and his experience taking care of Louis in their Guest House room. Ask students to consider how the mood of the narrative changes and how those changes are communicated visually. Students should notice that there is a sense of relief as the family arrives safely, although there is still some tension as Delisle works to keep his son out of danger. They should point out that the frames are bigger and more proportionate, there is more white space, the lines are straight, and there is less clutter within each frame.

Another point of discussion could be how humor is effectively communicated. In this case, you can point out to the students that comic art often relies on exaggeration. McCloud (1994: 30) describes the act of cartooning as

> a form of *amplification through simplification*. When we *abstract* an image through cartooning, we are not so much *eliminating* details as we are focusing on specific *details*. By stripping down an image to its essential "meaning," an artist can *amplify* that meaning in a way that realistic art *can't*. (emphasis in original)

As they consider this definition, students can identify and discuss how such amplification functions in the text. Which parts are exaggerated and why?

Rewrite the Narrative

Ask the students to rewrite the story from the perspective of Delisle *without directly copying words* from the original. As with any narrative writing assignment, the difficulty is in making judgments about what to select and what to omit. Tell students that they need to make some choices and not describe events frame by frame. Before the students start writing, ask them to consider what events are most important.

This activity can also raise awareness about style and form, especially of how sentence and paragraph structure can affect the feeling of the narrative. This assignment can be done in class, but it may be necessary for students to take it home and work on it.

Variations and Possible Follow-Up Activities

Use of comics can motivate and set the stage for many other kinds of activities. A few possibilities are given below.

- **Travel Narrative**
  Students write their own travel narrative (perhaps a family trip), focusing on the hardships and annoyances experienced along the way. As in Delisle's narrative, students should pay

attention to details and individual actions and may consider amplifying their experience in way to make it more humorous.

- ***Multimodal Blog***
  Students create a multimodal travel blog, documenting a trip with pictures, maps, and charts. Students should be attentive to the semantic function of visual organization.

- ***Comicstrip***
  Students create their own "comicstrip." Introduce students to Comic Life, free software that allows users to insert their own photographs and then transform the work into a comic book. Limit the assignment to one or two panels, and tell students to be particularly attentive to the layout and the "eye time." This assignment can be done individually or as a collaborative writing assignment.

Classroom Activity: Documenting Local Issues and Comics Journalism

As writing instructors, we often strive to get our students outside of the classroom and promote interaction with the local community. Teachers may ask their students to perform ethnographic research, or in other cases the focus may be on journalistic style reporting. Either way, students can encounter difficulties when it comes to understanding methods of reporting, interviewing, and dealing with their own "insider" or "outsider" status. The emerging genre of comics journalism provides a highly motivating way for students to discuss critical issues to do with ethnographic and journalistic methods. There are several works of comics journalism that can be used for this type of activity. For this activity, I recommend Joe Sacco's graphic narrative "The Unwanted," which is a piece in his collection of short journalistic graphic narratives entitled *Journalism* (Sacco, 2012). Conveniently, this work is also available online in *The Guardian* (see References below for the URL). It is preferable that students bring copies of the graphic narrative to class, but the activity can also be done in a computer lab.

The aims of the activity are to:

- Foster global perspectives as students learn about social and human rights issues;
- Promote critical thinking as students consider and compare the effectiveness of different forms of media;
- Strengthen visual literacy skills as students consider how visual forms and structures affect meaning;
- Stimulate interest in local social issues and raise awareness of ethnographic and journalistic methods;
- Inspire students to create their own multimodal documentary texts.

The following steps can be followed in order to facilitate student interaction and set-up original and stimulating writing tasks.

Pre-reading: Introduce the Text

Readers of contemporary graphic novels will likely already have some familiarity with the works of Joe Sacco. His *Palestine* comics document the author's two months in the Occupied Territories in the winter of 1991–92 and were published in serial form between 1993 and 1996, and then released in a collected volume in 2001 (Sacco, 2001a). This volume, with its preface written by the renowned scholar and Palestinian activist Edward Said, demonstrated the capacity for graphic novels to carry serious political documentary content and established Sacco as the progenitor of the "comics journalism" genre. Since *Palestine* Sacco has documented conflict in other areas of the world: *Safe Area Goražde* (Sacco, 2001b) was published in 2001, depicting the Bosnian Serb conflict and the faltering international presence in the isolated and so-called "safe area" of Goražde. Another work that explores the Balkan conflict is *The Fixer: A Story from Sarajevo* (Sacco, 2003). More recently

Sacco returned to Palestine, and in 2009 *Footnotes in Gaza: A Graphic Novel* (Sacco, 2009) was released, depicting the author's 2003 investigation of a largely forgotten massacre that took place in the towns of Khan Younis and Rafah in 1956 – events that were formative in the development of the current Israeli-Palestinian crisis. In an interview (Pollie, 2010), Sacco described his frustrations working as a "normal" journalist and his early interest in the story that eventually became *Footnotes in Gaza*.

Sacco's graphic novels can be incorporated into a composition class as an effective way to provoke critical thinking about media, journalism and ethnographic writing generally. In their discussion of teaching Sacco's *Palestine*, Alla Gadassik and Sarah Henstra write: "Reading and discussing *Palestine* became a process through which our students grew aware of the rhetorical construction of mainstream news, including strategies that underlie their own work" (Gadassik and Henstra, 2012: 243). As an activity for undergraduate students, Gadassik and Henstra gave students the opportunity to produce images of themselves in their current or future media roles, "done through drawing, pasting together collages, or working with digital imaging tools" (p. 250). By having students imagine their own image as embodied reporters, the activity allowed students to better understand their own "journalistic personae" and the so-called "ethos" that surrounds a particular reporter.

If teachers do not wish to commit to an analysis of a full graphic novel like *Palestine*, similar aims can be achieved by examining Sacco's (2010) *"Not in My Country: A Tale of Unwanted Immigrants,"* which is short enough to be read in class. When introducing this work, teachers should provide some background information about Sacco's successful career as a comics journalist. Sacco is Maltese-American, and in this particular short graphic narrative he visits his home country of Malta to report on the local issue of African immigration, a complex topic that has created social and political tensions. Depending on the class, providing some background information about the country of Malta would help students to visualize and make connections with the narrative.

Read and Discuss the Text

One might start by addressing the issue that Sacco's text raises: the problem of African migration to Malta. How are we to feel about the predicament of the Maltese people? How are we to feel about the predicament of the African refugees? You might ask students to weigh both sides and consider possible solutions.

Next, ask the class to describe and consider the effectiveness of Sacco's drawing style. Students can hopefully recognize that Sacco's visual style helps to convey meaning: the frames are cluttered and the characters are rendered in more detail (compared to Delisle's *ligne claire* style, which is a cleaner and bolder way of drawing comics). As the frames are slightly askew and seem thrown together, and as the text boxes crowd the images, Sacco effectively creates a noisy and claustrophobic atmosphere – which is of course highly appropriate to the densely populated and socially tumultuous context of Malta. Students might recognize that the arrangement of some frames resemble photographs on a table, giving the work a more journalistic feel. Students might discuss the relationship between the photographic image and the hand-drawn form.

Students can also discuss the strengths and weaknesses of using the graphic narrative form as a way to communicate serious social issues. Why not just write the story the traditional way? What is gained and lost by rendering the story in a graphic narrative form? You can point out to students the effectiveness of using illustrated maps to succinctly convey information. Another related topic can be to do with Sacco's self-reflexivity as a reporter. Students can discuss the effect of the author portraying himself as a character in the story. Should reporters or ethnographers reveal their own identity? Are Sacco's personal feelings relevant or do they mask the issue and disrupt the sense of objectivity that should be present in journalistic work?

Writing Activities

The above discussion can hopefully bring out a number of possible writing topics, and so you might allow students to generate their own writing topics from the discussion. Here are some possible directions:

- Write a research paper that investigates "unwanted" people in the local community. As in Sacco's graphic narratives, students should explore the issue from multiple perspectives and consider how these people are made both visible and invisible by society. This assignment could also be completed as a blog that contains photographs or graphics.
- Create a work of comics journalism that explores a problem in the school or community using Comic Life, other software, or by using hand-drawn images (for those artistically inclined).

Reflections and Recommendations

Reading, and even creating, comics can stimulate interdisciplinary work across different subject areas. In their discussion of interdisciplinary approaches to teaching comics, Alison Mandaville and J. P. Avila point out that teachers should not be afraid of taking a hands-on approach and giving students opportunities to use their creative talents, which may in some cases be latent and undiscovered (Mandaville and Avila, 2009). They write:

> The issue of creativity in the literary classroom is sometimes vexed, but in our experience it is often more vexed for instructors than for their students. English professors worry because they can't draw. Design professors worry because they can't write. So both shy away from asking their students to draw or write creatively. Students don't seem to worry so much since they still see themselves as learners, not experts. (Mandaville and Avila, 2009: 250)

Composing graphic narratives (and other types of visual/verbal hybrid texts) not only pushes students into new directions, it is also inherently a collaborative process, something that requires students to successfully engage with a range of social and communication skills.

Despite such potential for creative and collaborative work and despite the fact that there is an explosion of popular interest in graphic novels and a growing body of academic work on the pedagogical uses of comics in promoting visual and verbal literacies, many teachers are unaware of the possibilities for using graphic narratives in class. It is hoped that teachers can explore the uses of graphic novels since, as the workshop at the Summer Institute demonstrated, graphic novels can at the very least function as excellent conversation starters and writing prompts, and they can provide a great way to motivate the creative thinking and writing of people with different backgrounds and interests. The aim of the Summer Institute was to go beyond teaching writing primarily in terms of structure, grammar, and language proficiency, and instead to promote creativity in teaching, learning, and the acquisition of knowledge of all kinds. Teachers who attended the workshop, most of whom were English language instructors, commented on the potential for using comics for development of English language proficiency, but perhaps more importantly, recognized that reading, interpreting, and creating graphic narratives often requires strong cognitive abilities and creative skills. In a context where published ELT materials are often sanitized and are intentionally written to be politically neutral (therefore securing a wide global distribution), graphic novels can provide an accessible and exciting way into discussing and writing about contemporary, and sometimes controversial, issues. While the onus is still on the teacher to select works that are appropriate for their particular needs, I hope this discussion offers some practical tips as well as some useful insights into the main pedagogical goals and issues at stake.

Note

1   By visual literacy, I mean the ability to negotiate, make meaning from, and otherwise "read" pictures and other visual images. Readers who wish to explore visual literacy in more depth can refer to Gunther Kress and Theo van Leeuwen's *Reading Images: The Grammar of Visual Design* (Kress and van Leeuwen, 2006).

References

Delisle, Guy (2007) *Burma Chronicles*. Montreal: Drawn and Quarterly.

Jacobs, Dale (2007) Marveling at *The Man Called Nova*: Comics as sponsors of multimodal literacy. College Composition and Communication 59(2): 180–205. Retrieved on 15 December 2013 from /library/NCTEFiles/Resources/Journals/CCC/0592-dec07/CO0592Marveling.pdf.

Gadassik, Alla and Henstra, Sarah (2012) Comics (as) journalism: Teaching Joe Sacco's *Palestine* to media students. In Lan Dong (ed.) *Teaching Comics and Graphic Narratives: Essays on Theory, Strategy and Practice* 243–259. Jefferson, North Carolina: McFarland & Company.

Hammond, Heidi (2013) Graphic novels and multimodal literacy: A high school study with American born Chinese. *Bookbird: A Journal of International Children's Literature* 50(4): 22–32. http://dx.doi.org/10.1353/bkb.2012.0131.

Hughes, Janette and King, Alyson E. (2010) Dual pathways to expression and understanding: Canadian coming-of-age graphic novels. *Children's Literature in Education: An International Quarterly* 41(1): 64–84. http://dx.doi.org/10.1007/s10583-009-9098-8.

Kress, Gunther and van Leeuwen, Theo (2006) *Reading Images: The Grammar of Visual Design*. New York: Routledge.

Lankow, Jason, Richie, Josh and Crooks, Ross (2012) *Infographics: the Power of Visual Storytelling* Hoboken, New Jersey: Wiley.

MacDonald, Katherine Polak (2012) Batman Returns (to class): Graphic narratives and the syncretic classroom. In Lan Dong (ed.) *Teaching Comics and Graphic Narratives: Essays on Theory, Strategy and Practice* 221–231. Jefferson, North Carolina: McFarland & Company.

Mandaville, Alison and Avila, J. P. (2009) It's a word! It's a picture! It's comics! Interdisciplinary approaches to teaching comics. In Stephen E.

Tabachnick (ed.) *Teaching the Graphic Novel* 245–253. New York: The Modern Language Association of America.

McCloud, Scott (1994) *Understanding Comics*. New York: HarperCollins.

Moore, Alan and Gibbons, Dave (1995) *Watchmen*. New York: DC Comics.

Pollie, Robert (2010) Joe Sacco: Wide-Eyed In Gaza. *The Seventh Avenue Project*, Jan. 2010. Retrieved on 9 August 3013 from http://7thavenueproject.com/post/13528995922/joe-sacco-gaza7thavenueproject.com/post/13528995922/joe-sacco-gaza.

Sacco, Joe (2001a) *Palestine*. Seattle: Fantagraphics Books.

Sacco, Joe (2001b) *Safe Area Goražde: The War in Eastern Bosnia 1992–1995*. Seattle: Fantagraphics Books.

Sacco, Joe (2003) *The Fixer: A Story from Sarajevo* Montreal: Drawn and Quarterly.

Sacco, Joe (2009) *Footnotes in Gaza*. London: Jonathan Cape.

Sacco, Joe (2010) Not in My Country: A Tale of Unwanted Immigrants. *The Guardian*, 17 July 2010. Retrieved on 9 August 2013 from http://www.theguardian.com/world/interactive/2010/jul/17/joe-sacco-unwanted-immigrants.

Sacco, Joe (2012) *Journalism*. New York: Metropolitan Books.

Versaci, Rocco (2007) *This Book Contains Graphic Language: Comics as Literature*. New York: Continuum.

15 Re-Presenting Academic Writing to Popular Audiences
Using Digital Infographics and Timelines

David R. Gruber

Introduction

In academic writing, there is a seemingly inextricable tie between scholarly value and field-specific writing practices. To people outside a field of study, writing practices can seem idiosyncratic, excessively technical, or simply odd. The field of Group Psychotherapy, for instance, dramatizes patient-therapist narratives in first-person language, while the field of Biology extracts the voice of the writer by using passive constructions. The field of Cognitive Neuroscience considers participant studies of thirty people to be acceptable, while the field of Marketing would demand elaborate justifications for such a small sample size. There are, of course, reasons why scholarly value is tied to these different practices and expectations.

The intended audience for a traditional academic text is, more often than not, scholars in the immediate field who are invested in specialty language and quickly able to fill any logical gaps left by the writer who reproduces disciplinary assumptions. To address a broader audience, to drop the specialty language, or to spell out each step in the logical process of developing conclusions can mean that the audience or the contribution are unclear. Promotion and tenure procedures ensure certain genres – and certain inaccessibilities – and, to a large extent, guide the amount of time we, as scholars, are willing to spend on other genres of writing, even if those genres appeal more readily to people who need, or would like to know about, our work. The question is whether the academic writing situation is flexible. I believe that it is and that it allows for some creative choices in expression.

In agreement with Psychology Professor Gail Hornstein, I would, first, like to suggest that most academic writers deeply desire their ideas to be widely accessible as well as "sharply defined, vivid, and pleasurable" (Hornstein, 2007: para 3). But producing this kind of prose may require some serious adjustments. As Hornstein notes, all too often the word "'academic' is shorthand for lifeless prose, cumbersome to read, filled with unnecessary complication" (para 5). If this situation implies the need for change, and I believe that it does, then Hornstein argues, first and foremost, that scholars need to "start caring about their [audience's] interests" (para 9). Of course, this raises the central dilemma: who is the scholar's audience anyway? The difficulty in the answer is that the audience is divided.

On the one hand, the scholar's audience is the handful of individuals working in her/his field. On the other hand, the scholar's research, probably intended for the public good, demands a public audience, and this audience can be expansive and varied. Consequently, the scholar works for a large number of people but writes only for a few, aspires to change the world but encounters a world where, according to some estimates, only around 10% of academic articles are cited (Swartz, 1997). Writing scholar Alex Reid puts the situation bluntly when he says, "It would seem to me that the average academic (or academic journal) seeks to avoid exposure" (Reid, 2011: para 3).

This chapter is one small attempt to find ways to reduce the gap between the so-called academic and the popular styles of writing, to undo the perception that scholars avoid exposure by using prosaic and technical prose, and to find ways to re-think academic writing so that we might communicate "academically" and at the same time comprehensibly to wider audiences.

There is good reason to pursue such a goal at this moment. Recently, growing numbers of scholars are arguing for open access to journal publications and rebelling against a pay system of publication, rooting their argument in calls for democratic access to academic work (Alberti, 2010; Jha, 2012). This is an argument about systems of knowledge, but it is also one inherently tied to writing. To be brief, there is a danger in fooling ourselves into believing that eliminating a payment system solves a problem of public accessibility to academic texts. In all likelihood, it does not. The practices of writing are much too local, contextual, disciplinary, and convoluted for that. As professional writers and scholars, we must find ways to reach wide and varied audiences *through our writing*. Is it enough to make academic texts freely available online? I believe we must also try to make research compelling to and interactive with those people outside our fields who consider it valuable. In so doing, we bring our discoveries to a wider public and experiment with other means of discovery. Being invested in such a project, however, may require us to re-think our attitude toward language.

If we hold what Richard Lanham calls the "Western attitude toward language" that "only ideas matter, not the words that convey them" (Lanham, 2003: 1), then we may be prone to be satisfied to let individuals unfamiliar with our fields figure out academic texts for themselves – a "sink or swim" attitude. However, if we hold a rhetorical attitude toward language, then we may see the writing process and the text itself as intimately involved with our ideas. As Lanham (2003) shows in his landmark work *Analyzing Prose*, looking *at* text is inextricable from looking *through* it. Put another way, rhetoric is not what we "should get rid of in prose" (p. 2), but rather, it is prose itself. There is no a-rhetorical, a-contextual, value-free language that presents ideas clearly independent of audience and historical situatedness. Taking this lesson to heart means paying attention to words, where they are placed, and in relation to what and to whom in order to see how meaning is constructed and audiences are addressed (or ignored or displaced). A rhetorical view toward language, in other words, does not presume that academic writing, in its traditional conception and mode of production, will accomplish the democratic job. In fact, a rhetorical view suggests exactly the opposite.

Because a rhetorical view always considers audience, purpose, and arrangement together – and seeks persuasion, as Aristotle said, by "any available means" (Rhet 1.2) – traditional academic writing will likely never resemble anything "open" even if it is available and, in that sense, democratized. It seeks to persuade too few. It is too mired in its institutional prerequisites, disciplinary conventions, and theoretical jargon. Of course, many people *can* wade through rigorous, field-specific academic work, if they choose to do so. But how many want to do so, are compelled to do so, or find the time to read the necessary background texts in order to do so? In brief, we must stop looking *through* our text and stop expecting others, who stare *at* it as part of the process of looking *through* it, to not view it with dissatisfaction, distraction, or disdain. By adopting some visual strategies of new media texts, thinking about the role of design in composing, and reflecting on the value of online genres, the academic writer has the potential bridge traditional disciplinary audiences and with popular ones.

In the following pages, I therefore try to re-present academic writing and what it might achieve. I do this – and offer practical ways to move forward – by examining how new genres of digital communication can help us to re-position academic writing as "writing-as-new-media-composing" (Haas, 2011; Wysoki, 2004) or as "writing-as-building" (Ramsay, 2011), exposing how academic writing can become something more visual, accessible, and open if it engages digital media. I aim to show how re-presenting academic writing to popular audiences by composing variations of digital genres might be embraced. It is not something to be conceptualized as a distraction to rigorous academic work, but it can, instead, be part and parcel of it. In fact, I go further and argue that new genres can express academic values in new ways, that they can prove valuable to our careers and institutions, and that they can help to dissolve/resolve the divide between the scholar's field-specific audience and her/his inherently public one.

In this chapter, I discuss and demonstrate "digital infographics" and "digital timelines" as a first step in complicating the categories of the "academic" and the "popular."[1] Examining the benefits and uses of these digital communications, I hope, will challenge academic writers to build/compose new texts that are "sharply defined, vivid, and pleasurable" (Hornstein, 2009; para 3) fit for citation, compatible with research expectations, but also accessible to wider, varied audiences. This does not mean that these specific digital genres will or should be the only genres in use. Additionally, this does not mean that these genres are a solution to a problem of divided audiences for scholars. These genres alone cannot do all of that heavy lifting. They are, instead, intended as starting points for readers' own explorations and re-imaginings for the future of academic writing. They are also intended as pedagogical tools and can be tied directly to courses in Academic Writing and English for Specific Purposes, as I will later demonstrate.

Taking the Argument Further: Three Assertions

Before looking specifically at two digital genres useful to academic writing and then outlining how I have used them in my own scholarship and classes, I would like to put forward three additional, perhaps more daring, assertions. They are:

(1) As teachers and scholars, we should actively and regularly experiment with alternate forms of composing texts;

(2) We can and should blur the lines between popular and academic texts;

(3) Digital compositions are valuable to our institutions because they present information in compact forms and supplement and complement other textual genres such as essays or research papers. However, these new genres will be recognized as valuable only when we can competently and comprehensively make use of them.

The first assertion is not new; it is commonly made on appeals to communicating to the public the value of our "in-house" scholarly work (Perry, 2013; Rankins-Robertson, Cahill, Roen, and Glau, 2012), or it is made in an effort to reach a student population conceptualized as disinterested in long passages of texts but savvy with flashy new media technologies (Palfrey and Gasser, 2008). However, I hope to show that new digital tools make experimentation with popular forms of composing – like infographics – practical and compelling as a way to think through our own research questions, as a way to reveal our data, and as a way to teach students how to research. Indeed, new forms may even be more compelling than "older" digital forms like blogging, which to my mind remain hyper-personalized, potentially idiosyncratic, and less readily distributed by masses of social media users.

The second assertion – about the need to blur lines between academic and popular texts – is also not new. It has been made to support arguments insisting on the postmodern erasure of hierarchical orders (Dunn, 1991; McRobbie, 1986) or, alternately, made through arguments suggesting that integration across genres becomes inevitable in an era of socio-technological change (Kang, 2006; Miller, 2007). I add to these arguments in this chapter by showing that blurring popular and academic genres of writing holds potential to improve both and to make something new. Popular forms can change by becoming invested with scholarly practices

– such as source checking and source recognition – and scholarly forms can change by becoming invested with popular practices – such as increased brevity and visual attractiveness. These changes, in themselves, are worth the effort.

Finally, the third assertion – that new digital forms should be valuable to our academic institutions and to us – is commonly supported through arguments for a technologically mindful system of promotion that accounts for digital works (Kahn, 2013; Mandell, 2013). I add to these arguments by showing that the publicity obtained from oft-circulated new media genres inherently holds value because it offers the chance for invention and for crowd-sourced feedback on the meaning and value of scholarly work. It also, of course, advertises our work and institutions in ways traditional academic articles do not. Accordingly, the following discussion about digital infographics and digital timelines aims to reveal how teachers and students can do more with digital forms of composing.

Infographics

What Are They?

Infographics are visual representations of information sets. As the popular online magazine *Mashable* explains it, they are designed to "present complex information quickly and clearly…. They illustrate information that would be unwieldy in text form" (http://mashable. com/category/infographics/). Communication researcher Ellen Coomber suggests that infographics usually contain (1) a catchy title, (2) a visual technique – such as a pyramid or a flow-chart – to condense a lot of numerical information into an easily readable and defined set of claims, (3) images or charts to act as visual support, and (4) a defined message (Coomber, 2008). Images 1 and 2 are examples. Accordingly, mass media researchers Sandra Utt and Steve Pasternack have called infographics "qualitative devices to

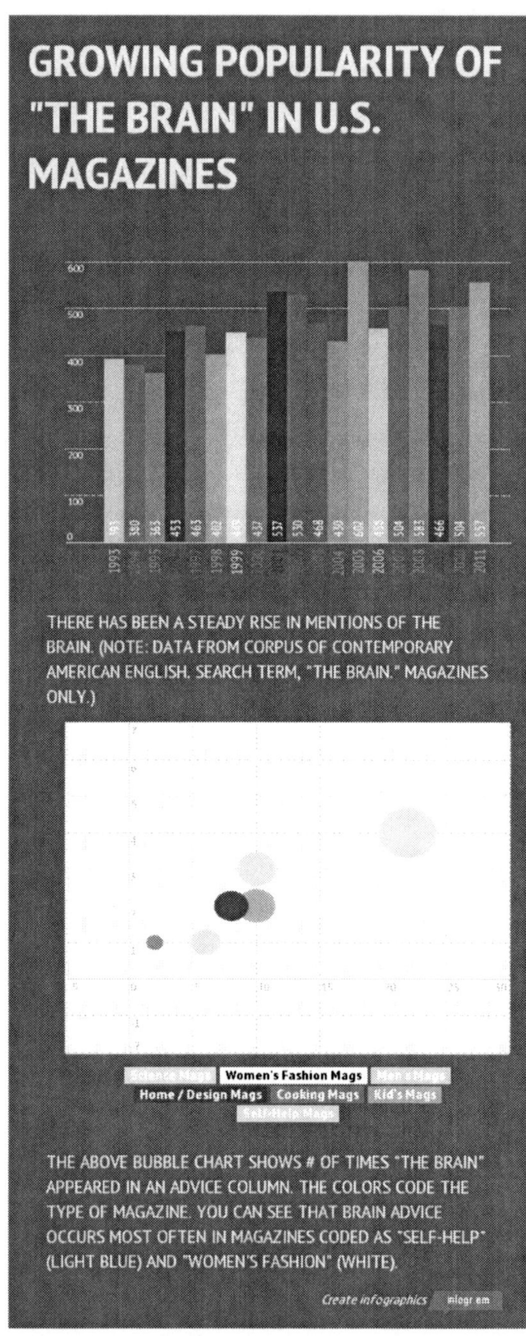

Image 1. Brain Infographic, Example of Data-Driven Infographic (created by David R. Gruber using Info.gram)

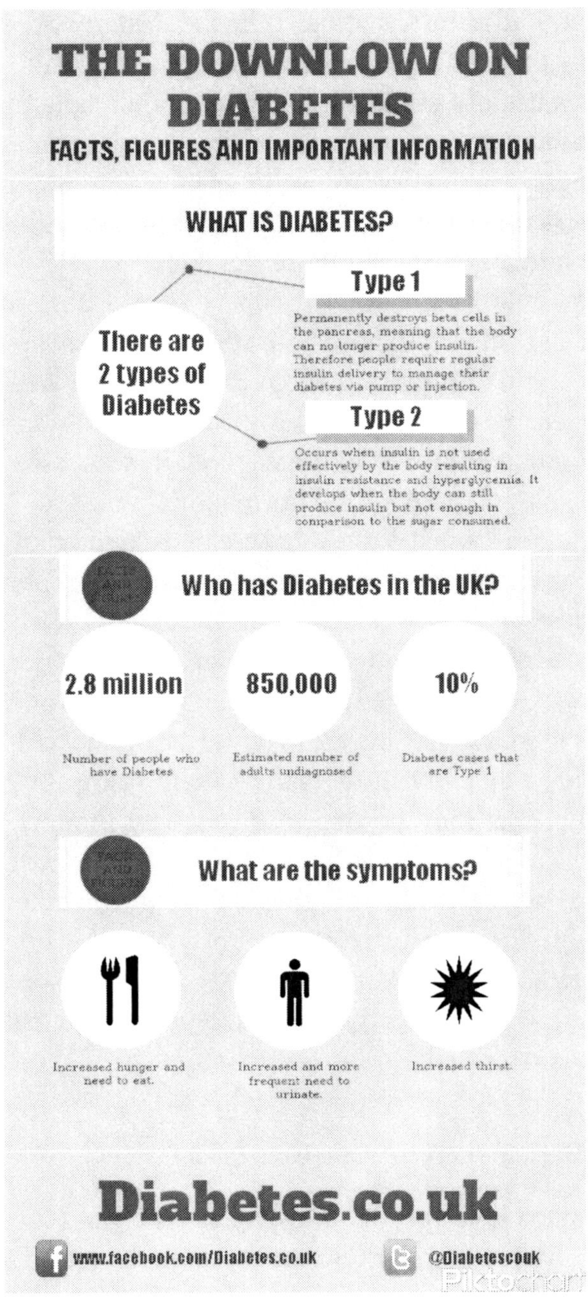

Image 2. Diabetes Infographic, Example of Visual Strategy Combined with textual Information (created by Diabetes.co.uk) [Used by permission of Diabetes Digital Media, Ltd and Diabetes.co.uk]

display quantitative information" (Utt and Pasternack, 1993: 146). Although this overall characterization is generally true – insofar as infographics usually contain a lot of numerical data in digestible form and contain messages that researchers want to convey – new digital infographics may also use images and quotations without much numerical data. That is, the possibilities of digital creations now make infographics a bit more flexible.

Infographics are not new to mass media communicators. Pasternack and Utt (1990) have noted their use in newspapers going back to the 1980s. In writing about the topic for *Communication World*, Angelo Fernando (2012) even traces infographics to 18th Century Scottish engineer William Playfair, who uses charts and graphs to display technological information (Fernando, 2012). Prior to that, however, Leonardo da Vinci created elaborate sketches and drawings for engineering purposes as well as to explore his own artistic endeavors.

Many scholars have commented on the recent increase in digital infographics (Angelo, 2012; Bekhit, 2009; Rubel and Wheaton, 2011). This increase may be due to new, free online tools that allow people to create their own infographics fairly easily (Angelo, 2012). Additionally, this may be due to a renewed interest in "telling stories with data" (Visual.ly) as a way to make encounters with massive amounts of available digitized information more accessible and digestible for a mainstream audience. When everything from home prices to the number of diabetes patients is available for viewing, people need effective ways to organize and make relevant that information.

What Are Digital Infographics Good For?

On the simplest level, digital infographics are good for drumming up interest. Marketing agencies now routinely comment on their popularity and discuss how social media users excitedly pass them around (Hartsfield, 2013; WebsitePulse.com). Stew Langille, the self-proclaimed "infographic guru," argues that infographics greatly improve online traffic to websites (Langille, 2011). Infographics also seem to be good for communicating effectively.

Newspaper editors suggest that infographics are helpful to readers, making articles more attractive and comprehensible (Utt and Pasternack, 2000). Communication researchers Barbara Miller and Brooke Barnett argue that infographics raise interest and prove especially effective when paired with a written text about a topic (Miller and Barnett, 2010). Their study involved 138 undergraduates responding to risk information, and they found that a "textual explanation offered additional insight into the risk situation" such that risk perceptions became more balanced when an infographic was paired with textual explanations (pp. 61–62). In addition, in a study using eye-tracking technology, visual communication researcher Peter Schumacher found that "visuals like photos and infographics and short text formats like additional text boxes or short news get high attention rates" (Schumacher, 2007: 3). This insight, paired with other research findings highlighting the importance of grids, maps, and images, led to the conclusion that "reception of newspapers was driven by design" (p. 4).

The implications of design for composing can hardly be understated. As Gunther Kress and Theo van Leeuwen have famously commented in their book on the grammar of visual design, good visual design holds immense social purchase because certain visual 'rules' have developed in a semiotic system, making good design persuasive (Kress and van Leeuwen, 2006: 2–3). Kress and van Leeuwen go further, stating, "'Visual literacy' will begin to be a matter of survival" as visual communication is becoming, through new media, "less and less the domain of specialists" (p. 3). Put simply, for academics, infographics are one productive place to investigate changes in a text's persuasive power through thinking about scope and design. Taking design in texts seriously will likely affect the work of producing scholarship and the work of getting others to pay attention. In brief, infographics may help researchers communicate anew and reach new audiences. The same is true for our student's work as well as for teaching our students good composing practices. Indeed, there seems to be a burgeoning opportunity for teachers and writers to take advantage of the social purchase of compelling design and to adapt new forms, like infographics, to classroom projects and academic production.

How Can I Make Infographics?

There are several good websites for creating infographics freely and easily. One that I have used is http://Infogr.am. I am not supported by this company, so I have no particular interest in promoting them. In fact, it seems likely that new infographic-making websites will emerge even during the process of publishing this chapter. Others include: http://visual.ly and http:www.piktochart.com. The main point here is that many websites provide the following features: the ability to add images, generate text, make graphs, arrange maps, and do it all in a visually compelling, unified way. In fact, infographics look like infographics precisely because of the unified templates designed to organize information and be visually pleasing. Infographic-making websites offer these pre-designed templates, and they are available without much need for design skills.

Websites for making infographics are not without their pitfalls. Pre-formatted infographics may look pre-formatted as users become accustomed to seeing the same automatically generated formats over and over again. With that said, I have not yet found this to be the case; the options are wide-ranging enough at the present moment. Further, it is worth mentioning that infographics websites might require an email address or use your own (or your students') email to sell products, so be sure to read the terms of agreement. Many companies specify that they do not sell your email address, but it is important to decide what is acceptable for you and your students.

Classroom Assignments with Infographics

There are two infographic assignments that I have found to be useful in teaching rhetorical sensitivity and digital composing. The first involves asking students to make an infographic, and the second involves asking students to analyze two infographics visualizing the same topic. Each assignment has a slightly different learning goal, but overall, instructors can, in my view, use infographics as a way to help students think rhetorically about choices of evidence and arrangement and to make good composing decisions as they pair text and graphical images. Put somewhat differently, these assignments engage students in multiple modes, offer multiple routes of discovery, and teach multi-literacies in so far as they ask for critical engagement with textual-visual forms online.

Assignment Option #1 – Composing Information for Multiple Audiences

For this assignment, I ask students to adapt an academic research paper into an infographic. The goal is to help students develop greater rhetorical awareness and to consider how textual-visual presentation and audience are inextricable.

The first step is for students to choose an academic paper on a topic of interest to them. This assignment might be paired with an argumentative essay for which students already have a paper or have previously collected data to support an argument. At City University of Hong Kong, for instance, I designed an "information visualization" assignment for the first-year writing course in which students created an infographic as part of the process of writing an argumentative essay. The goal was to use the infographic to help students think about the best available resources and to identify the evidence most convincing to an audience unfamiliar with their topic. Students had to display that information/evidence in an infographic form and follow certain "rules." Those rules were as follows:

(1) Develop a compelling title, which does not repel an audience, seem threatening, or appear too strong-headed.

(2) Incorporate graphs or maps to display data that seems compelling to an audience unfamiliar with the topic.

(3) Use one of the images or charts in the infographic to offer the reader a wide view of the topic, and use another to offer a more personalized or small view. For instance, if arguing against building a nuclear power station in Hong Kong, one image should show negative effects of nuclear power on a global or national scale, while another should show the effects on a personalized scale.

(4) Intersperse alphabetic text strategically and sparingly to communicate needed details and qualitative claims.

(5) Cite all sources.

As an additional component to this assignment, instructors might request a short reflection essay on the process of developing the infographic. The essay might explain how the chosen graphs and images contribute to the argument and appeal to the target audience. In it, students could also explain their arrangement or detail the information discarded, justifying composing decisions.

Alternatively, instructors might ask students to annotate each item in the infographic, explaining their reasons for choosing each. This might be a way to compel students to reflect on how audience and purpose led their presentation. As another option, students might compare the infographic to the traditional argumentative essay and discuss differences.

Assignment Option #2 – Comparative Analysis of Two Infographics

This assignment asks students to compare two infographics on the same topic and then discuss how the infographics frame the issue differently through textual-visual choices and arrangements.

This assignment is a good fit for an introductory rhetoric and composition course or for an argument and logic course. I recommend that students be allowed to find two infographics on their own. Instructors can assess whether the infographics address the same topic and ensure that students are invested in the topic.

Although I have only completed this assignment as an in-class activity in cooperation with my students, I believe that it will also function as an assessed task. In my classroom, students chose two infographics and were required to comment on the title, the overall visual design technique employed, the images or graphics used, the placement of those graphics, the textual content and the amount of text, as well as the use or abuse of source citations. Doing so amounted to an assessment about which infographic proved more persuasive to which kind of audience. My students and I quickly learned that some infographics address a hostile audience more effectively than others, while some provide too little information or prove overbearing. Whatever the case, students can make the assessment and write up the reasons and results of the comparison.

Reflections On Making Infographics

Infographics have helped me to see visual design as a crucial aspect of communicating my research. They have aided in the process of collecting relevant information by improving my awareness of what would appear convincing and pleasing to an audience unfamiliar with the topic at hand. Further, making infographics has aided in the process of summarizing and condensing by forcing me to say what I am studying without much theoretical or specialized language. They have also pushed me to see new areas of research by visualizing my data and revealing gaps, allowing me to see my data and allowing others outside my field to ask questions.

As one example, I was recently writing a paper on the use of brain research in advice columns appearing in popular magazines. I decided to code the number of advice segments in each magazine and then color code the magazine based on its marketing orientation – whether it was primarily about fashion, sports, etc. This second decision, however, arose only after I created the infographic about how often brain research is used in advice segments in magazines. The insight happened as the infographics website offered to display my data as a bubble chart wherein an additional variable could be considered. In this particular case, the bubbles could be automatically colored, and the colors could show how placement on the chart related to some new factor. Thus, my data could not only show how many advice segments using brain research appeared in each magazine, but it could also display, visually through color coding, the type of magazine. This raised new questions about how men's and women's magazines treated neuroscience research in relationship to advice as well as how that advice itself was gendered (See Infographic Example 1 above).

Although I may have started to explore these additional factors on my own, the infographic became part of my composing process. In fact, writing alongside of making visual displays typifies, in my view, writing-as-building in multi-modal, new media environments. Text and image are able to come together for communication – and do. But more than this, showing the infographic to friends and family opened up the possibility for interesting questions about my work in ways that an academic paper never would – because academic journal articles can be too dense or take too long to engage many people for notes and comments. My colleague, who could scan the infographic with little time commitment, asked about the appearance of technology magazines in the data, and my wife asked about the meaning of "advice." These questions enabled further development. I now aim to include additional textual descriptions as pop-up boxes attached to the various parts of the infographic. Likewise, I also aim to re-write my formal academic publication on the topic to include these new insights and to incorporate more compelling visual charts. In brief, thinking about multi-modal creations cannot but influence, in my experience, the process of generating so-called academic texts.

Digital Timelines

What Are They?

Timelines are visual representations of changes over time. Digital timelines use online resources – such as maps or photographs – to show a series of events or changes across people, places, institutions, laws, etc. One exciting aspect of timelines is in how "temporal and topical interrelationships are highlighted" (Ruggles, 2011). Showing an ecology of factors and their relations – and thinking about what is and is not included in the timeline – proves to be a compelling lesson in whose voices are heard and how history is shaped and understood.

Of course, timelines have been around for some time. Old methods of creating timelines have included using posters or pen and paper. Such timelines have been used in classrooms for years; students might have, for example, cut out magazine images or drawn pictures and attached them to a line representing the history of their lives (http://www.homeschoolinthewoods.com). Digital timelines, however, provide new kinds of affordances.

What Can I Do With Digital Timelines?

Digital timelines, like digital infographics, are now easy to make and are also able to be customized. The Massachusetts Institute of Technology's Educational Consultant, Molly Ruggles, sees digital timelines as "a vehicle for understanding complex events in history as well as a structure to which students can contribute materials and scholarship" (Ruggles, 2011: 1). She suggests using digital timelines as a way to help students feel included in the process of gathering scholarly resources and in the process of engaging in scholarly investigations (p. 1). This can be accomplished because resources are available online and able to be shared and arranged by multiple people. Working in this way allows multiple people to engage in the process of discovery and builds partnerships between students and teachers as they locate and use timeline software to visualize compelling sources.

Timelines may also, in some sense, feel intuitive and can, therefore, be used as an entry point to a research topic. According to language researcher Cristóbal Pagán Cánovas, the idea of timelines as poetic devices is common – such as life is like a river – and these "create powerful affective meanings" (Pagán Cánovas, 2013: 45). Since the idea of timelines is already embedded in our language, timelines may be useful for communication. Additionally, because history is commonly imagined as a linear process, timelines might seem to provide a natural way to show the historical development of, for instance, a technology or a court case. They can help people come to better understandings about how social changes, institutional rules, human actors, natural ecological events, and new inventions can all work together to produce change.

Yet, timelines risk presenting simplistic views of history as singular, linear, and univocal. Consequently, digital timelines may also be used to undermine simplistic renderings. Digital timelines allow for multiple voices and multiple contributors, producing a space for contestation and for different perspectives and different resources to interact.

How Can I Make Digital Timelines?

Like infographics, digital timelines can be made easily through online tools and resources. In particular, I have used two websites dedicated to creating timelines. The first is called TimelineJS (http://timeline.verite.co). Another website is called Neatline (Neatline.org) which was created by the University of Virginia's library. These websites have tutorials and walk users through the process of making timelines. They are both free, educational websites.

The process of making a timeline works like this: visitors to the websites first download a template, presented as an Excel document or a Google doc. Visitors then enter their own customized information into the template and "publish" that information through the website. The website uses its own computer code to translate the information which visitors have entered – such as URL addresses with image locations, titles, descriptions, citation information, etc. – and the website displays that template as a timeline. The final timeline format often looks quite professional, and it mirrors what is commonly created by the world's leading news organizations when they, for example, display a story through images or produce image-based articles about the most interesting news stories from the past week. The British Broadcasting Network's "Week in Pictures" segment is an excellent example (http://www.bbc.co.uk/news/in_pictures/). In addition, each new timeline can have multiple editors, and each timeline can have its own URL address and/or have its viewing restricted by its creator. The specific details of creation and dissemination vary according to each website, so it is always a good idea to read the tutorials.

Classroom Assignments With Digital Timelines

There are numerous assignments that use digital timelines. Here are two that I find especially interesting and useful.

Assignment Option #1 – Working Together to Build a Visual History

This is an assignment in which students form groups and build a documented visual history of a technological device. Each element included in the timeline should be cited and documented with a description, and the final product – the timeline – should be group work and available for public viewing and discussion online. I often frame this assignment as writing an autobiography for a technology by connecting online resources and documenting images (including images of people, scanned documents, maps, etc.). This assignment has worked well in my Science and Technology Studies course and could be effective in a Rhetoric of Science course or a course where science and engineering students seek to improve their writing skills, such as in an English for Specific Purposes course. The assignment could easily be transformed into writing the history of a court case or the history of an important social event.

During my recent presentation on digital timelines, one of the attendees to my workshop suggested that two groups could work on the same topic, could avoid consulting each other during the composing process, and could then compare timelines after completion. I found this to be a valuable idea because the learning goal would then be enhanced insofar as class members and the instructor could critically engage each group's different research strategies, discuss history as a social construct made by interested people, and reveal how multiple perspectives present history in alternate, sometimes compatible and sometimes competing ways.

Assignment Option #2 – Reflecting on Timelines as a Research Tool

This is an assignment in which students conduct online research for an argumentative or research paper on a topic and visualize what they found in the timeline format. The assignment requires students to organize their information temporally and to document that information, writing a short description of each document's place in time and relevance to the research question. In many ways, this assignment functions like an annotated bibliography. Instructors might, additionally, ask for a reflection on the process of organizing the information temporally to explore how such a design/pattern exposed new insights about the subject.

I have found this assignment, or some variation of it, productive in courses on writing for science and engineering. Students in those courses frequently need to understand why some engineering problem occurred, and answering that question involves under-standing the development of the problem. Likewise, students writing within the discipline of law might need to explore problems and precedents underlying legal findings in court cases. Students could effectively connect multiple online resources to show the history leading to a more recent judicial decision.

Reflections On Making Timelines

My first digital timeline documented the history of the x-ray. I started making it as an example for my students, and in the process, I was testing the viability of the first assignment that I described above. That particular x-ray timeline turned out to be much more than an exercise in demonstration for my students. It taught me just how many questions remained about the history of this well-known technology, and it helped me to realize how testing new modes of writing can fuel further inquiry and discovery and thus more and better academic work.

While researching images and documents that could visualize the history of the x-ray in a timeline format, I was able to uncover a letter sent from Wilhelm Röntgen to Nikola Tesla about the invention of the x-ray. I learned that Tesla made claim to discovering the x-ray months before Röntgen, but nothing of this rivalry appeared in the very cordial letter. In addition, I read many news articles available in the New York Times newspaper database documenting a rivalry between Tesla and Röntgen and, likewise, between Tesla and Thomas Edison. Being beaten out by Röntgen both Tesla and Edison desired to capture the first x-ray image of a human head, the newspapers claimed. These subsequent discoveries raised all kinds of research questions for me about how the newspaper industry hyped the x-ray and created rivalries to dramatize the story of the x-ray, which led to investigations about the role of the news in hiding the severe health effects of the technology. In other words, what the timeline made clear was not only how long it took for any mention of health effects to occur but how quickly mentions of competition and showmanship entered public discourse. In my view, this is what timelines should do – expose the speed or the slowness of events, visualize interconnections and disconnections, and allow for the interrogation of a specialized version of history by the way events are strung in a series. Organizing researched resources in this way should allow us, as researchers, to uncover gaps by engaging the design of the timeline as an interconnected and often overly simplistic series that hides as much as it reveals.

Re-Presenting Academic Writing / Inventing with Digital Media

Rhetoric and writing professor David Rieder makes a potent argument for learning how to teach and use digital media, including platforms for digital writing. He begins with the claim, "programming is the new ground of writing" (Rieder, 2012: 1). What he means is summed up in the statement, "In computational media, writing wants to take a walk, not sit on the couch and be analyzed" (p. 2). That is, in his view, writing in digital environments creates a situation in which writing can move and change. As a result, being "a writer" today is about being a digital composer, and knowing about digital media and how to use digital tools is fast becoming "*the* new ground of writing" – both the place where writing takes place and the means through which it is accomplished. As such, writing becomes more cooperative and participatory. Making dynamic timelines, for example, displaces the stability of writing a traditional essay and makes writing more about the act of invention, combination, and contact with the user who can add to it or interact with it. In putting forward these comments, Rieder builds from Richard Lanham's observation that "all our attention [usually] goes to the meaning of text" (Lanham, 2006: 81) while computational media puts increasing attention on "ways in which it [text] can move and be transformed" (Rieder, 2012: 2). It is my hope that, in the future, academic writing will move and be transformed so that larger audiences can be also.

In an effort to transform scholarly attitudes and practices toward academic writing and teaching, I have tried to convince the reader of three propositions:

(1) As teachers and scholars, we should actively and regularly experiment with alternate forms of composing texts;
(2) We can and should blur the lines between popular and academic texts;
(3) Digital compositions are valuable to our institutions because they present information in compact forms and supplement and complement other textual genres such as essays or research papers. However, as noted, these new genres will be recognized as valuable only when we can competently and comprehensively make use of them.

Whether the reader is convinced or not, I hope that the discussion of digital infographics and timelines encourages exploration with different forms and means of composing texts. Indeed, changing our composing and making a practice of new media composing will likely, and certainly should, change how scholarly value is generated.

As a researcher and writer myself, infographics have allowed me to make evident the kind of narrative I am constructing with my data, have prompted me to learn how that narrative might be visualized using graphics, and have taught me to share my research in more accessible ways with audiences outside my field that I want to reach. Likewise, timelines have forced me to question my own understanding of history and to explore new digital ways to present information.

Note

1   I specify "digital" timelines and "digital" infographics because each has an older, analogue iteration.

References

Alberti, Fay Bound (2010, June 23) Democratic access to academic knowledge. *OpenDemocracy*. Retrieved on 10 October 2013 from http://www.opendemocracy.net/cite/form/website.

Angelo, Fernando (2012) Killer infographic! But does it solve TMI? Tech Talk. *Communication World* 29(2):10–12. Retrieved on 10 October 2013 from http://discovery.iabc.com/view.php?cid=3183.

Aristotle (1954) *Rhetoric* (trans. W. Rhys Roberts, Ingram Bywater; intro. Friedrich Solmsen). New York: Modern Library.

Bekhit, Elsayed (2009) Infographics in the United Arab Emirates newspapers. *Journalism* 10(4): 492–508. http://dx.doi.org/10.1177/1464884909104952.

Coomber, Ellen (2008) The visual advantage. *Communication World* 25(5): 36–38. Retrieved on 10 October 2013 from http://discovery.iabc.com/view.php?cid=853.

Dunn, R. (1991) Postmodernism: Populism, mass culture, and avant-garde. *Theory, Culture & Society* 8(1): 111–135. http://dx.doi.org/10.1177/026327691008001006.

Haas, Christina (2011) Building and maintaining contexts in interactive networked writing: An examination of deixis and intertextuality in instant messaging. *Journal of Business and Technical Communication* 25: 276–298. http://dx.doi.org/10.1177/1050651911401248

Hartsfield, Brett (2013, May 6) Infographics are so hot right now. *R+M Agency*. Retrieved on 10 October 2013 from http://www.rmagency.com/2013/05/06/infographics-are-so-hot-right-now/.

Hornstein, Gail (2009, September 7) Prune that prose: Learning to write for readers beyond academe. The Chronicle Review. *The Chronicle of Higher Education*. Retrieved on 10 October 2013 from http://chronicle.com/article/Prune-That-Prose/48273/.

Infographics & Data Visualization (2013) *Visually*. Retrieved on 10 October 2013 from http://visual.ly/.

Infographics (2013) *Mashable*. Retrieved on 10 October 2013 from http://mashable.com/category/infographics/.

Infographics' Growing Popularity (2013, May 29) *Website Pulse*. Retrieved on 10 October 2013 from http://www.websitepulse.com/blog/infographics-growing-popularity.

Jha, Alok (2012, April 9) Scientists boycott academic journals to protest the high cost of paywalls. *Raw Story*. Retrieved on 10 October 2013 from http://www.rawstory.com/rs/2012/04/09/scientists-boycott-academic-journals-to-protest-the-high-cost-of-paywalls/.

Kahn, Rebecca (2013) Debates in the digital humanities. *Information, Communication & Society*, 16(6): 1017–1018. http://dx.doi.org/10.1080/1369118X.2012.750680.

Kang, Yoonhee (2006) "Staged" rituals and "veiled" spells: Multiple language ideologies and transformations in Petalangan verbal magic. *Journal of Linguistic Anthropology* 16(1): 1–22. http://dx.doi.org/10.1525/jlin.2006.16.1.001.

Kress, Gunther and van Leeuwen, Theo (2006) *Reading Images: The Grammar of Visual Design*. New York: Routledge.

Langille, Stew (2011, July 28) Infographic guru. *Modern Men in Numbers*. Retrieved on 10 October 2013 from http://www.greatmalesurvey.com/stew-langille-infograph-guru/.

Lanham, Richard A. (2003) *Analyzing prose* (2nd edition). London: Continuum.

Lanham, Richard A. (2006) *The Economics of Attention: Style and Substance in the Age of Information*. Chicago: University of Chicago Press.

Mandell, Laura (2013) Promotion and tenure for digital scholarship. *IDHMC*. Retrieved on 15 December 2013 from http://idhmc.tamu.edu/commentpress/promotion-and-tenure/.

McRobbie, Angela (1986) Postmodernism and popular culture. *The Journal of Communication Inquiry* 10(2): 108. http://dx.doi.org/10.1177/019685998601000209.

Miller, Barbara M. and Barnett, Brooke (2010) Understanding of health risks aided by graphics with text. *Newspaper Research Journal* 31(1): 52–68. Retrieved on 15 December 2013 from http://connection.ebscohost.com/c/articles/48376794/understanding-health-risks-aided-by-graphics-text.

Miller, Carolyn R. (2007) Book review - Tracing genres through organizations: A sociocultural approach to information design by Clay Spinuzzi (MIT Press, 2003). *Technical Communication Quarterly* 16(4): 476–480. http://dx.doi.org/10.1080/10572250701551432.

Pagán Cánovas, Cristóbal (2013) Anchoring time-space mappings and their emotions: The timeline blend in poetic metaphors. *Language & Literature* 22(1): 45–59. http://dx.doi.org/10.1177/0963947012469751.

Palfrey, John G. and Gasser, Urs (2008) *Born Digital: Understanding the First Generation of Digital Natives*. New York: Basic Books.

Perry, David M. (2013, July 22) My initial public offering. *Chronicle of Higher Ed*. Retrieved on 10 October 2013 from http://chronicle.com/article/My-Initial-Public-Offering/140407/.

Ramsay, Stephen (2011, January 11) On building. *Stephen Ramsay Personal Website*. Retrieved on 10 October 2013 from http://stephenramsay.us/text/2011/01/11/on-building/.

Rankins-Robertson, Sherry, Cahill, Lisa, Roen, Duane and Glau, Gregory (2010) Expanding definitions of academic writing: Family history writing. *Journal of Basic Writing* 29(1): 56–77. Retrieved on 15 December 2013 from http://files.eric.ed.gov/fulltext/EJ898358.pdf.

Reid, Alex (2011, March 5) On the value of academic blogging. *Digital Digs*. Retrieved on 10 October 2013 from http://alex-reid.net/2011/03/on-the-value-of-academic-blogging.html.

Rieder, David (2012) Programming is the new ground of writing. *Enculturation* 15. Retrieved on 15 December 2013 from http://www.enculturation.net/node/5267.

Rubel, Steve and Wheaton, Ken (2011, Nov 14) The infographic is suddenly the Uzi of choice in the Great Attention War. *Advertising Age* 82(41): 18. Retrieved on 15 December 2013 from http://adage.com/article/steve-rubel/infographic-suddenly-media-uzi-choice/230919/

Ruggles, Molly (2011, October 19) Timelines as a nexus for pedagogy and research? *ThatCamp: The humanities technology camp*. October. Blog. Retrieved on 15 December 2013 from http://newengland2011.thatcamp.org/10/19/timelines-as-a-nexus-for-pedagogy-and-research/.

Schumacher, Peter (2007) Size matters: Comparing the reception of design and visual language of newspapers in tabloid and broadsheet format. *Conference Papers – International Communication Association*. Retrieved on 15 December 2013 from http://citation.allacademic.com//meta/p_mla_apa_research_citation/1/7/0/6/6/pages170662/p170662-1.php.

Swartz, Charles (1997) The rise and fall of uncitedness. *College & Research Libraries* 58(1): 19–29. Retrieved on 15 December 2013 from http://crl.acrl.org/content/58/1/19.full.pdf+html.

Utt, Sandra H. and Pasternack, Steve (1993) Infographics today: Using qualitative devices to display quantitative information. *Newspaper Research Journal* 14(3/4): 146. Retrieved on 15 December 2013 from http://connection.ebscohost.com/c/articles/18050890/infographics-today-using-qualitative-devices-display-quantitative-information.

Utt, Sandra H. and Pasternack, Steve (2000) Update on infographics in American newspapers. *Newspaper Research Journal* 21(2): 55–66. Retrieved on 15 December 2013 from http://www.questia.com/library/journal/1G1-65863603/update-on-infographics-to-in-american-newspapers.

Week in Pictures (2013, October 23) *BBC News*. Retrieved on 15 October 2013 from http://www.bbc.co.uk/news/in_pictures/.

Wysocki, Anne F. (2004) *Writing New Media: Theory and Applications for Expanding the Teaching of Composition*. Logan: Utah State University Press.

16 Online Writing as a Discovery Process
Synchronous Collaboration

Brian W. King

Computer-Supported Collaborative Writing in Education

Repeatedly since at least the 1980s it has been predicted by some, often in a climate of utopian/dystopian fever (Florida, 2013; Howcroft and Fitzgerald, 1998), that computers would revolutionize learning to the degree that it would be unrecognizable, and perhaps even make teachers themselves obsolete (for early critiques, see Becker, 1984; Hativa and Lesgold, 1991). For the most part, such predictions have (also repeatedly) proved to be unfounded (see Barbour and Reeves, 2009; Bigum, 2012; Cuban, Kirkpatrick, and Peck, 2001; Loveless, 1996). Perhaps the resiliency of this (now timeless) gestalt suggests that such predictions are manifestations of "technological solutionism" – a deterministic stance in which technologies, particularly Internet-based technologies, are framed as a present day form of a "snake-oil" cure-all, perhaps seeing problems where nothing is in fact "problematic" (Morozov, 2013: 6). Far from endorsing technological solutionism, I would instead like to position this chapter as resistant to the idea that the use of the Internet in the teaching and learning of writing is *inherently* beneficial. Rather, this study aims to conduct a preliminary exploration of the use of online collaborative writing software in the classroom, asking not what this software *does* but rather what informed writing teachers and learners might be able to *do with* it to develop resourceful, confident, and creative writers. It will also consider the possibility that it might in fact be better sometimes to *do without* it.

Collaborative Writing – What Is It?

Building upon the idea that collaboration is about jointly addressing a problem, it follows that truly collaborative online writing occurs in an environment where the central questions or problems driving the writing task are to be addressed by all members in common. Johann Ari Larusson and Richard Alterman have theorized such an environment in terms of a joint problem space in which students "[share] a joint focus on important material" (Larusson and Alterman, 2009: 398). They also argue that a common focus is not to be taken for granted, and requires that the students share a common view of their joint endeavor. In other words, the group members all realize that they are expected to *write* together, and this leads them to treat the online space they are working in as a place of convergence in which they remain (at least periodically) aware of the contributions, alterations, and deletions of others and, crucially, maintain their common view of the enterprise via communication.

Clearly, the development of such a joint problem space will unfold somewhat differently based on the varied nature of tasks, but what is perhaps less obvious is that the challenges involved will differ quite sharply depending upon whether it is a *synchronous* or *asynchronous* writing task. In synchronous writing, the participants all write simultaneously whereas asynchronous writing is done by the group members at times which are convenient for their own individual timetables. In both cases, writers depend upon communication along various channels in order to coordinate their efforts. Google Drive for example (which has subsumed the writing software formerly marketed separately as Google Docs) provides an online chat window for communication with other writers who are logged in at the same time, and it is possible to leave comments/ notes for others to read, explaining changes or additions. These types of "awareness mechanisms" (Larusson and Alterman, 2009) and communication tools are helpful to keep the group focused, and good collaboration has been found to depend greatly upon two-way communication (Anandarajan and Anandarajan, 2010; Lee and Wang, 2013) and a sense of the "social presence" of writers (Nippard and Murphy, 2007), defined as "the degree to which participants are able to project themselves affectively within [a] medium" (Garrison, 1997: 6), coming across as "real people" and achieving a sense of immediacy in interaction. However, the question arises as to whether the simple *provision* of a communication *facility* is enough to enable coordination. That is, do writers actually make use of such facilities? Research into asynchronous collaborative writing in educational contexts has suggested that they sometimes do not, and so collaboration scripts (guides which lead writers through drafting and revision steps) and other forms of instructional and technical "scaffolding" have proved helpful (see also Erkens, Jaspers, Prangsma, and Kanselaar, 2005; Kobbe et al., 2007; Kollar, Fischer, and Hesse, 2006; Larusson and Alterman, 2009; Wichmann and Rummel, 2013). These guides seem to assist writers to overcome the communication barrier that sometimes arises during asynchronous writing, breaking the sense of isolation that can develop between writers whose individual contributions are made at random times.

The circumstances of synchronous writing are different from asynchronous in many ways, and not least of these is the provision of support or scaffolding. The fact that drafting and revision tend to become intertwined in synchronous writing makes the separation of activities into a useful script difficult (see Wichmann and Rummel, 2013). Consequently, it is more difficult for teachers to provide effective scaffolding. As a result, Astrid Wichmann and Nikol Rummel have called for more research into characteristics of synchronous collaborative writing (Wichmann and Rummel, 2013: 269). In response to this call, the workshop which is the focus of this chapter explored synchronous collaborative writing in Google Drive in an attempt to encourage teachers to explore these technologies as well as to shed some light on this under-researched area.

One argument in favor of familiarizing students with online collaborative writing software (e.g. Google Drive) is that its use has become more frequently expected in workplaces as it has become more sophisticated and more readily available via the Internet. Even seven years previous to the publication of this volume, which is a lengthy passage of time in the evolutionary rhythms of the Web 2.0 software industry, Stéphane Weiss, Pascal Urso, and Pascal Molli argued that collaborative writing was at that time becoming more and more common in the workplace (Weiss, Urso, and Molli, 2007; see also Lowry, Curtis, and Lowry, 2004). Still more recently, we have learned that engineers spend 20–40 percent of their workday writing and much of it is collaborative; furthermore, 85 percent of office and university documents are produced collaboratively (Calvo, O'Rourke, Jones, Yacef, and Reimann, 2011). Thus, students who intend to join the office-based sector of the workforce would be well served by a highly developed critical awareness of collaborative online writing processes and tools. There are numerous tools available, including wikis (i.e. websites developed collaboratively by a community of users, allowing any user to add and edit content) and cloud-based software (i.e. various kinds of applications, services, or resources which users can access on demand via the Internet) such as Google Drive, which is one resource that has been developed specifically for the centralized writing of shared documents online (other examples include Office365, Xaitporter, Titanpad, Draft, Primarypad, and

My Simple Surface). Google Drive was selected for this workshop because its interface is of a style very familiar to most internet users (thus facilitating the "flow" of our workshop), and this choice was also partly based on the assumption that it is currently a widely used program in the workplace. These types of online tools have proved to be very useful for collaborative writing because their "superior collaborative functionality" often permits students to work on the document simultaneously if necessary while still making it clear which contribution belongs to whom even in the case of synchronous writing (Calvo et al., 2011, p. 10). This is a twofold benefit, for without this functionality writers are forced to do one of two things:

(a) work on separate versions offline and subsequently merge the multiple versions into one document, which is potentially a very confusing and self-defeating process; or
(b) work on the same central document but take turns individually in the writing/editing process in a predetermined sequence of authorship, which tends to be an inefficient and inconvenient option.

Another interesting finding of the Calvo et al. study was that teams who engaged more frequently in *sustained* collaborative writing sessions with their group received higher grades on the course than those who engaged in team revisions only a few times and did so in "bursts" rather than over long periods or those who mainly edited the document rather than participating in the collaborative writing sessions. This suggests that collaborating by synchronously writing together is likely to have pedagogical benefits. What, then, has research revealed thus far?

Research on Collaborative Online Writing

Of the online tools which can be used for collaborative writing, Wikis have been studied most extensively (e.g. Judd, Kennedy, and

Cropper, 2010; Larusson and Alterman, 2009; Lee and Wang, 2013; Wei, Maust, Barrick, Cuddihy, and Spyridakis, 2005; Wichmann and Rummel, 2013; Witney and Smallbone, 2011). Wikis provide a platform of "bundled" features that are used in teaching programs for a number of collaborative tasks, including (but not limited to) online discussion, collaborative problem-solving, and collaborative writing. When used extensively in a course, students become familiar with the particular wiki's interface and tools. Cloud-based applications for collaborative writing, on the other hand, are specialized for writing, and some, like Google Drive, deploy a word-processor-based interface that is already familiar to most "computer literate" people. In contrast to wikis, cloud-based technologies are only in the early stages of investigation as tools for collaborative writing and learning. However, when the affordances and constraints of wikis are spelled out, cloud sites such as Google Drive have largely the same benefits, and the limitations of wikis either do not apply to tools like Google Drive or they become less relevant in a professional environment.[1] For instance, Table 1 below is a summary of the affordances and constraints of Wikis for collaborative writing, in which we see that there is only one strength that does not apply to Google Drive, and that is the ability to style one's profile in a dynamic fashion, altering its appearance and functionality to better suit one's purposes and aesthetic preferences. However, I would assert that for most people writing in a professional context this is a minor consideration, particularly if a group's primary goal is to collaboratively write a document, a task which Google Drive, for example, is designed to support.

Although Google Drive shares one or two constraints with wikis (see Table 1), there are several other serious constraints which simply do not apply to Google Drive. Foremost is that, writers familiar with other widely used word processing applications will find the Google Drive environment instantly familiar; therefore, they will be able to begin writing immediately with no learning burden. This benefit is important because collaborative writing in professional contexts has long been driven by desktop-based

Table 1. Affordances and constraints of Wikis (based on Wei et al., 2005: 205–206)

Affordance	Wikis	G. Dr.	Constraint	Wikis	G. Dr.
A lived space where all writers can have equal privileges	✓	✓	Editing wars can develop, rendering the "version history" function useless	✓	✓
Centralized platform which is easy to access	✓	✓	Basic design can be quite primitive looking	✓	✓
Easy to make small and spontaneous edits	✓	✓	Users have to learn the syntax of the wiki to maximize use	✓	✗
Eliminates need to continually redistribute documents	✓	✓	Editing can be intimidating to those accustomed to word processing software	✓	✗
Account home pages increase social presence of contributors	✓	✓	One or two users can change the wiki structure until it is useful only to themselves	✓	✗
One's web presence can be tailored to feel "alive and dynamic"	✓	✗	Can consume a great deal of storage space on a server, leading to crashes	✓	✗

tools such as Microsoft Word (Calvo et al., 2011). In contrast, the inability to master the less familiar tools of a wiki – or even the perception of one's own inability – can be a significant barrier to success (see Lee and Wang, 2013). Additionally, because the software is cloud-based, it is not possible for the interface to be altered by users, and so there is no danger of more experienced users "blinding" others with their innovations of the basic interface (something which is possible with wikis). The cloud-based aspect also means that server storage space ceases to be a serious issue. Finally, I would also like to suggest that workplaces are more likely to adopt a ready-made "cloud-based" program for collaborative writing than to use wikis for this purpose because of the growing awareness of the advantages of cloud platforms (Leavitt, 2009) as well as the familiar desktop-based interfaces of these tools. This means that teachers can help students in professional degree programs develop critical awareness of the specific affordances and constraints of such software in a wide range of scenarios.

Thus, it seems that Google Drive (and likely other similar cloud-based software) offers an easily accessible, intuitive and relevant platform with which students can begin to learn about collaborative writing. However, much research remains to be done in terms of the skills required for success and how teachers can support learners in this process. For example, there is a dearth of research into the processes of student revision of shared documents (Judd et al., 2010), leading to a shortage of knowledge about the forces which enable and constrain peer editing in this context. Some researchers have also oriented to a long-held distinction between collaboration and cooperation, pointing out that student participants tend to "divide and conquer," splitting up group writing tasks in a way that might very well facilitate completion but prevents them from *jointly* solving the core problems of an assignment (often the primary rationale of collaborative group work). In other words, although working cooperatively in one sense, the only problems they work on *together* are: (a) how to divide up the work into sub-tasks, and then (b) how to synthesize the results (Lee and Wang, 2013). Tasks must be designed to be truly collaborative in nature, with the task regulated so that each student's contribution to writing can be traced and evaluated, something Google Drive is well set up to facilitate, as will be outlined later in this chapter. This channeling of students into truly collaborative writing is crucial because in professional contexts, responsibilities of co-authorship rarely permit the type of "free riding" (Witney and Smallbone, 2011: 107) or "social loafing" (Lee and Wang, 2013: 236) which can often arise during student group work. Rather, in terms of the actual drafting and development of the written product, one is expected to make a contribution that is proportional to the credit one is to receive.

Purpose and Desired Results

This activity is designed to give writers a hands-on experience with synchronous collaborative writing in Google Drive, and the intended result is to awaken writers to the possible creative and analytical benefits of writing together simultaneously while also giving them a realistic impression of the limitations. Additionally, by experiencing a type of writing in which the writing *process* is publicized among their peers, the hope is that writers will gain some insight into how others approach various acts of writing and editing.

Intended Audience

It could be adjusted for any age group, but the workshop described here was targeted at teachers of undergraduate university students. Adjusting for younger writers would obviously involve changing the writing task to better reflect the ability of the writers (more on this below).

Processes

This activity can be broken down into a series of 4 steps:

1. Getting Started (invite the students to their shared documents)
2. Practice Stage (assign a simple writing task for familiarization)
3. Post-Practice (group discussion of impressions)
4. Collaborative Writing

Getting Started – Decisions and Procedures

Well before the lesson is to begin, the shared documents must be set up and writers will need to be invited to the corresponding shared document for their group. There are some choices to be made at this initial stage, and your choices will be guided by what you hope to be able to do with the students' writing (e.g. subsequently trace who wrote what, observe the writing process in real time, or simply get them to submit it as a finished product).

First of all, in order to be able to monitor the students' work without difficulty (should you desire this level of teacher surveillance for whatever reason), the document must be set up in the instructor's *own* Google Drive account or she/he will not be able to view it later. The instructor will then prompt each group to complete the whole writing task on that centralized document. This orientation will allow you to open each document at will and observe the progress of each group as well as view the document history later on. Of course this activity can also be run as a completely student controlled exercise with no teacher surveillance, and in that case each student group can set up its own document. Should you choose this option it will be difficult to observe in real time what the group is writing or to later observe who wrote what within each group.

There are three options for the type of document employed, and these are based on the mode by which writers are given access:

- *Private*
- *Anyone with the link*
- *Public on the web*

If the "who is doing what" question is important to you, then you will also have to make sure that you setup a *private* document, That is, you must specifically *invite* each student to the document using Google Mail (gmail) addresses, which you will first have to gather from them.[2] If the students access the document via their invitation, each person's contribution will be linked to her/his personal Google ID. In this way it is possible to see exactly what each writer contributed.

If this extra level of scrutiny (i.e. knowing who wrote what) is not important to you, then another option is to set up an *Anyone with the link* document. This changes the settings so that anyone who has been provided with the URL link can write on the document, but it cannot be discovered by the general public (as it can with

Public on the web documents). Under this mode, you, as instructor, can see the central document unfold but contributions will not be attributed to a specific user account. This means that you cannot identify exactly who contributed what unless the writers inform you of their identities. This approach can be set up more rapidly than *private* because you will not have to go through the process of gathering gmail addresses and inviting each participant separately. You simply notify the group members of which URL to access (see numbered steps below for more detailed information).

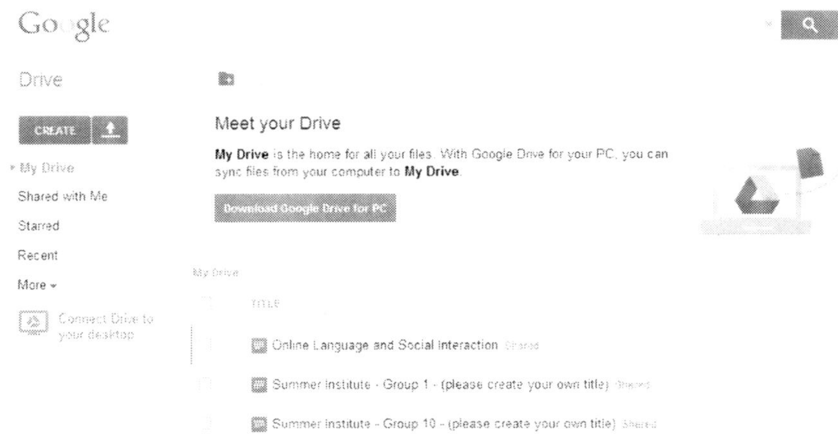

Figure 1. Google Drive Home Screen

Setting up the document is quite easy once you have made the decisions outlined previously.[3] Figure 1 is a screen capture of the home screen for Google Drive, which appears after you log on. In order to create a new document, simply go through the following steps:

(a) Click the red *Create* button (positioned on the left just under the Google logo).
(b) Select *document* from the consequent drop-down menu, and you will be presented with a blank Google document (Figure 2).
(c) In the top right corner of this document screen you will find a blue button inscribed with an image of a padlock and the

word, *share*. Click this button, and you will be prompted to give the new document a title (e.g. Group One's Document).

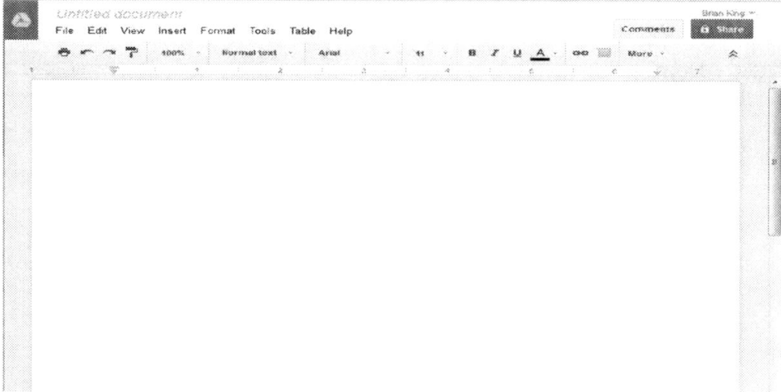

Figure 2. Blank Google Document

(d) After you have entered a title, you will be presented with the *Shared settings* window (see Figure 3). This is where you can decide exactly how to provide access.

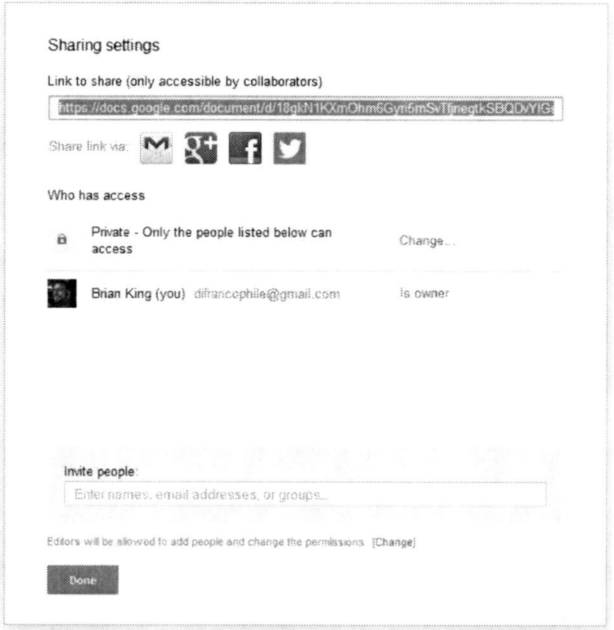

Figure 3. Shared Settings

Invite people:

Enter names, email addresses, or groups...

Can edit ▾

Notify people via email - Add message

Send a copy to myself
Paste the item itself into the email

Share & save   Cancel

Editors will be allowed to add people and change the permissions. [Change]

Figure 4. Invite People

Further Steps for *private* Documents

(e) If you are inviting writers using individual Google accounts (i.e. to a *private* document, which permits you to identify who writes what), then you simply type the gmail address of each person in the *Invite people* typing field near the bottom. Once you've clicked on the typing field, further options will open (Figure 4).

(f) Make sure that the setting to the right of the typing field is set to *Can edit* (which should be the default setting) so that those whom you invite will be permitted to actually type on the shared document.

(g) Make sure the *Notify people via email* box is ticked, and you can choose to include a message with the invitation email if you like, by clicking on *Add message*.

(h) Next, simply enter all of the gmail addresses for that group, separated by commas, and click the green *Share and Save* button at the bottom left. The group members will now be able to access the document via the email in their gmail inboxes.

Should you wish to dispense with individual invitations (thus relinquishing the ability to know who wrote what), you must find your way to the *Shared Settings* window (Figure 3) by following steps a-d above, and then proceed to the following steps:

Further Steps for *Anyone with the link* Documents

(i) Find the *Who has access* caption and click on the word *Change*, which is on the right.

(j) You can then change the *Visibility options* to *Anyone with the link*, and the document can then obviously be accessed and contributed to by anyone who joins the document via the link.[4]

(k) The URL link is displayed at the top of the *Shared settings* window, and you can share it with the group's members in one of two ways. You can provide them with it manually, or you can click one of the choices beside the caption *Share link via*. This selection will prompt Google to send the URL for you electronically via email, Google +, Facebook, or Twitter.

Regardless of whether you choose to create *private* documents or *Anyone with the link* documents, there is one more setting in the *Shared settings* window (Figure 3) that offers you alternatives. At the very bottom of the *Shared settings* screen, there is a message that reads *Editors will be allowed to add people and change the permissions* (the default setting). This setting means that the writers themselves can invite others and perhaps even block you, or some of their groupmates, from having access to the document by changing the permissions. If you anticipate that this option could lead to problems, simply change this setting so that only you, the "owner" of the document, can make such changes. Once the document is set up and the groups have been informed of how to access it, then the writing can begin.

Practice Stage

Group members should be given a chance to get acquainted with the software's tools and gain a bit of experience with what it feels like to write together synchronously. This could take place in a previous lesson, or, if time permits, at the start of the activity. In practical terms, a computer lab is useful but not essential, provided that every single student can bring a laptop or other suitable device to class. The possible topics are many but could include writing about a famous person whom everyone in the group knows something about, or perhaps writing an essay that introduces everyone in the group. Encourage them to edit each other's writing along the way. Also encourage them to experiment with the various communication modes that are available such as side comments in the document itself, the online chatting window, and face-to-face conversation.

Post-Practice Discussion

After everyone has finished, ask them to reflect together on how they felt about the experience. Subsequently, they must agree as a group about some guidelines or ground rules for the writing activity to follow the practice round. For example, one group in the workshop agreed to resist editing the work of other writers without first checking that the writer has finished drafting the identified section. This point arose out of a discussion in which one member felt "violated" when another member was editing his sentences before he had finished them. Once these basic guidelines have been agreed upon, then the primary writing task can begin.

Collaborative Writing Stage

In the Summer Institute workshop, the groups chose their topic from a list of options to avoid delays in getting started. This was expedient because advance preparation was impossible in this case. Some of the examples involved interpreting very simple graphs or tables of information while others were focused on answering a question (e.g. *Travelling in group with a tour guide is the best way to travel. Agree or disagree, giving reasons for your answer and providing examples*). To be truthful, the topic was treated as somewhat inconsequential in the workshop because of the imperative of getting finished in a narrow timeframe. Groups were encouraged to just choose a topic and "go with it," focusing on the writing experience rather than the product. Because the participants were adults and teachers, I felt I could rely on them to be tolerant of this approach. With your students, you might take a similar approach, or alternatively the writers could conduct some research about their topic in previous lessons or outside of class time. Making this choice is significant because writers must be well armed with ideas for synchronous writing to work effectively.

The amount of time given for writing will depend upon the level of "polish" required for the final document. In the workshop, participants were given about an hour to write together. For most groups, this will not be enough time to finish completely, but it was enough time for the workshop participants to thoroughly experience the processes of synchronous writing and editing in Google Drive. Closing the lesson with a reflection session will provide students with an opportunity to realize the affordances and constraints of synchronous writing and carry some of these ideas forward with them. The results of our workshop's reflection are summarized in the next section.

Findings and Thoughts

Communication

In accord with Hsiao-chien Lee and Pei-ling Wang (Lee and Wang, 2013), the workshop group found that real-time communication is the key to successful synchronous collaborative writing. An interesting development was that even though (multiple times) I encouraged the groups to meet face to face if necessary, only one group out of eight actually chose to do so. Instead, most of the communication took place in the online chatting window, which appears on their screen immediately beside their document. This could have been partly a result of their dispersed seating around the computer laboratory; however, there was plenty of room to congregate elsewhere for a meeting if needed. The participants generally agreed that they found the text chatting window to be highly appropriate and useful because the communication appeared in close proximity to the document itself. Participants were already typing, so it was easy to type messages to one another and negotiate the writing process "on the fly" instead of breaking out of their writing space and meeting face to face. However, it must be said that some participants found the "popping up" of messages to be an unwelcome distraction at times. Topics in the chat window included decision-making about what to include in the paper, reminders to one another, queries for permission to edit sections of work, and mutual encouragement to complete the task. That is why, in spite of the group members' dispersal around the computer laboratory and a lack of face-to-face discussion, the communication enabled a sense of "social presence." This is nearly impossible in asynchronous collaborative writing, but social presence is an important component of successful online collaborative learning (Nippard and Murphy, 2007).

Publicizing the Writing Process

Additionally, in synchronous collaborative writing, as a result of this sense of social presence of co-writers, the writing *process* is publicized instead of just the product. In other words, other writers see your words appear and disappear from the page as you turn your thoughts into words. As teachers, participants in our workshop could see pedagogical potential in this unique opportunity. In terms of writing processes, there is potential for peer monitoring of each other's habits. For example, one writer might notice that a groupmate tends to free write whole paragraphs and then backtrack to edit, whereas she herself tends to work on one sentence at a time. This noticing could be valuable in and of itself by raising the writer's awareness of other possible approaches to drafting. It is of course also possible that some writers might find this type of peer monitoring of the drafting process intimidating or unhelpful (see more about affective responses below). Another opportunity lies in the stimulation that the writers felt from their groupmates. Being able to see what the others were writing provided a stimulus for their own ideas, serving perhaps as a replacement for free writing, which is a commonly suggested antidote for writer's block (i.e. just starting to write what comes into your mind).

Editing processes are also publicized in synchronous writing, and this is where communication becomes so crucial. Without the ability to converse, participants might feel hesitant about editing one another's work, and this has been identified as a real problem in asynchronous online collaborative writing (Wichmann and Rummel, 2013). However, the ease of instantaneous text communication in the synchronous mode provided the necessary space for politeness and immediate negotiation. Rather than editing the work of others directly, participants could first suggest alterations that the original writer could then implement or reject; failing that, the writer could give the editor permission to alter her/his work. In the absence of facial expressions and tone of voice, this text-only medium does require special attention to politeness; the "smiley" emoticons available in the chatting software were found to be useful for softening messages and requests.

Affective Responses

The synchronous writing process is likely to be a new experience for many and so could prompt affective responses from participants. For example, in the workshop some expressed frustration with it (cf. Caspi and Blau, 2011), even finding the interference of others in the drafting process to be unwelcome and a "violation." This observation stimulated a discussion about the importance of giving students an opportunity for preliminary, relatively casual, "low-stakes," experimentation so that groups could agree on their preferences before proceeding to write more formally in this mode (should that be the goal). This observation about feelings of violation also re-emphasized the crucial importance of two-way communication and politeness. Consideration of these affective responses prompted discussion of whether synchronous writing is best suited to low-stakes experimentation or whether it could also be used for higher stakes tasks such as assessment.

To Assess or Not to Assess?

The answer to this question depends on the instructor's pedagogical goals. If the goal is to stimulate noticing and reflection in relation to writing and editing processes and strategies, then perhaps it is best to frame it as a non-assessed classroom task in order to encourage experimentation, under the assumption that being assessed is likely to prevent students from taking productive and necessary risks. For example, the task could be a groupwork exercise in which each individual student is delegated to be the observer of a specific process during collaborative writing, reporting their observations back to their group. One person could pay attention to how (and whether or not) the writers build on each other's ideas, another person tracking how much editing takes place and what type, and another taking note of who edits whose work.

A different or separate goal might be to encourage creativity, and again the assumption is that a low-stakes environment would be more likely to stimulate fruitful risk-taking. For example, the task could be framed as a contest between groups to see which group can collaboratively write the most creative introduction to an essay in which the original introductory paragraph has been obscured. The results would be evaluated by the class as a whole, perhaps through a ballot, finally leading to a discussion about ways to creatively enter a topic in a genre-appropriate way. This creative experimentation could ultimately be applied to their later writing, online or otherwise, and perhaps assessed at that later time if the teacher wishes.

Alternatively, if the pedagogical goal is for students to actually master synchronous writing *per se*, then assessing their performance is ultimately more tenable because risk- taking is not imperative for success. For example, groups could write together to produce a coherent and cohesive document and be assessed by the teacher on those two outcomes provided that they have had adequate instruction and opportunities for practice. In these ways, the pedagogical goals are likely to be served by assessment rather than "derailed" by it.

Synergies and Distractions

There were also mixed reactions concerning the experience of "juggling" quite a broad array of tasks at once: formulating ideas, putting them into words, monitoring the queries of groupmates, responding to these queries, attending to the face needs of groupmates, and editing the text. This regime can be a bit demanding of one's cognitive faculties (although the workshop format, a short one-off session, likely exacerbated this effect). One affordance of *asynchronous* collaborative writing (i.e. not writing simultaneously) is that everyone has more time to consider their ideas and use them to draft cogent contributions. Our workshop members did find that writing together was inspiring because of a *synergy* of ideas, but this was somewhat balanced by the constraint of having less time to be thoughtful.

Conclusion

In summary, the teachers who attended the Summer Institute workshop agreed with Evgeny Morozov that technology is not the solution to everything (Mozorov, 2013). They could see a place for synchronous online writing in classrooms, but agreed that it would not be suitable for all people and all types of writing. It is perhaps a very valuable way to get students noticing many things about writing and editing. It also has an intriguing role to play as a stimulant for rapid group inspiration and consensus, while some time for writing alone (and thinking deeply) could also be fruitfully integrated. Synchronous online writing also has creative potential, stimulating writers to be more experimental by moving out of their comfort zone and creating new kinds of work. Although it is quite a busy and demanding task, participants in the workshop felt inspired by the ideas of others as they unfolded on the page. This type of "riffing" off of each other's spontaneous contributions could be harnessed for productive pedagogical ends. Furthermore, our teacher groups' observations about the affordances and constraints of synchronous collaborative writing raise questions for further research, such as the following:

- What specific impacts do text chat discussions have on the writing and editing processes?

In other words,

- Which kinds of discussions result in changes to the text, and which do not?
- What kinds of changes are produced in this type of collaborative online writing context?
- How often do group members consult one another and how does this frequency relate to the unfolding of the text?
- To what extent do writers type their sentences directly into the shared document? Or do they craft their sentences separately and paste them in later? What are the writers' reasons for their decisions?
- How is creativity encouraged or discouraged by collaborative writing? What are the exact processes which influence creativity for better or worse?

It is hoped that research will soon address these many potentially revealing uncertainties.

Notes

1 However, Charlotte Robidoux and Beth L. Hewett ran into some challenges with Google Docs in terms of forgotten passwords and other access issues and emphasize that this software is not useful for all intended purposes of collaborative writing teams (Robidoux and Hewett, 2010).

2 Experience has revealed that it is best to insist on gmail addresses because although many other email providers are indeed compatible with Google Drive, some are not. At the time of writing, I was unable to determine any useful patterns in the incompatible addresses, so in order to avoid a last minute scramble on writing day, make sure each student provides you with a gmail address well in advance.

3 The description of screens is based on the Google Drive interface at the time of writing. It could potentially change in its details over time, but the basic principles will likely remain the same.

4 Note that this setting is different from the *Public on the web* setting, which makes the document accessible to all and sundry via search engines like Explorer, Safari, Chrome, and Firefox.

References

Anandarajan, Murugan and Anandarajan, Asokan (2010) *E-Research Collaboration: Theory, Techniques and Challenges*. New York: Springer. http://dx.doi.org/10.1007/978-3-642-12257-6.

Barbour, Michael A. and Reeves, Thomas C. (2009) The reality of virtual schools: A review of the literature. *Computers & Education* 52: 402–16. http://dx.doi.org/10.1016/ j.compedu.2008.09.009.

Becker, Henry Jay (1984) Computers in schools today: Some basic considerations. *American Journal of Education* 93: 22–39. http://dx.doi. org/10.3102/000283120038004813.

Bigum, Chris (2012) Schools and computers: Tales of a digital romance. In Leonie Rowan and Chris Bigum (eds.) *Transformative Approaches to New Technologies and Student Diversity in Futures Oriented Classrooms: Future Proofing Education* 15–28. London & New York: Springer. http:// dx.doi.org/10.1007/978-94-007-2642-0_2.

Calvo, Rafael A., O'Rourke, Stephen T., Jones, Janet, Yacef, Kalina and Reimann, Peter (2011) Collaborative writing support tools on the cloud. *IEEE Transactions on Learning Technologies* 4: 88–97. http://doi. ieeecomputersociety.org/ 10.1109/TLT.2010.43.

Caspi, Avner and Blau, Ina (2011) Collaboration and psychological ownership: how does the tension between the two influence perceived learning? *Social Psychology of Education* 14:283–298. http://dx.doi. org/10.1007/s11218-010-9141-z.

Cuban, Larry, Kirkpatrick, Heather and Peck, Craig (2001) High access and low use of technologies in high school classrooms: Explaining an apparent paradox. *American Educational Research Journal* 38: 813–34. http://aer. sagepub.com/cgi/doi/ 10.3102/00028312038004813.

Erkens, Gijsbert, Jaspers, Jos, Prangsma, Maaike and Kanselaar, Gellof (2005) Coordination processes in computer supported collaborative writing. *Computers in Human Behavior* 21: 463–86. http://dx.doi. org/10.1016/j.chb.2004.10.038.

Florida, Richard (2013) Robots aren't the problem: It's us. *The Chronicle of Higher Education* March: http://chronicle.com/article/ Robots-Arent-the-Problem-/138007.

Garrison, D. Randy (1997) Computer conferencing: The post industrial age of distance education. *Open Learning* 12: 3-11. http://dx.doi. org/10.1080/0268051970120202.

Hativa, Nira and Lesgold, Alan (1991) The computer as a tutor - Can it adapt to the individual learner? *Instructional Science* 20: 49–78. http://dx.doi. org/10.1007/BF00119686.

Howcroft, Debra and Fitzgerald, Brian (1998) From utopia to dystopia: The twin faces of the Internet. *Proceedings, International Federation for Information Processing, Working Groups 8.2 and 8.6 Joint Working Conference on Information Systems: Current Issues and Future Changes*. Retrieved on 27 November 2013 from http://swcta.net/ moore/ files/2012/04/dystopia.pdf.

Judd, Terry, Kennedy, Gregor and Cropper, Simon (2010) Using wikis for collaborative learning: Assessing collaboration through contribution. *Australasian Journal of Educational Technology* 26: 341–54.

Kobbe, Lars, Weinberger, Armin, Dillenbourg, Pierre, Harrer, Andreas, Hämäläinen, Raija, Häkkinen, Päivi and Fischer, Frank (2007) Specifying computer-supported collaboration scripts. *International Journal of Computer-Supported Collaborative Learning* 2: 211–24. http://dx.doi. org/10.1007/s11412-007-9014-4.

Kollar, Ingo, Fischer, Frank and Hesse, Friedrich W. (2006) Collaboration scripts – A conceptual analysis. *Educational Psychology Review* 18: 159–85. http://dx.doi.org/ 10.1007/s10648-006-9007-2.

Larusson, Johann Ari and Alterman, Richard (2009) Wikis to support the 'collaborative' part of collaborative learning. *International Journal of Computer-Supported Collaborative Learning* 4: 371–402. http://dx.doi.org/10.1007/s11412-009-9076-6.

Leavitt, Neal (2009) Is cloud computing really ready for prime time? *Computer* 42: 15–20. http://dx.doi.org/10.1109/MC.2009.20.

Lee, Hsiao-chien and Wang, Pei-ling (2013) Discussing the factors contributing to students' involvement in an EFL collaborative wiki project. *ReCALL* 25: 233–49. http://dx.doi.org/10.1017/S0958344013000025.

Loveless, Tom (1996) Why aren't computers used more in schools? *Education & Educational Research* 10: 448–67. http://dx.doi.org/10.11 77/0895904896010004002.

Lowry, Paul Benjamin, Curtis, Aaron and Lowry, Michelle René (2004) Building a taxonomy and nomenclature of collaborative writing to improve interdisciplinary research and practice. *Journal of Business Communication* 41: 66–99. http://dx.doi.org/ 10.1177/0021943603259363.

Morozov, Evgeny (2013) *To Save Everything, Click Here: The Folly of Technological Solutionism*. New York: Public Affairs.

Nippard, Eric C. and Murphy, Elizabeth (2007) Social presence in the web-based synchronous secondary classroom. *Canadian Journal of Learning and Technology* 33. Retrieved on 27 November 2013 from http://cjlt.csj.ualberta.ca/index.php/cjlt/article/view/24/22.

Robidoux, Charlotte and Hewett, Beth L. (2010) Collaborating virtually to develop this book. In Beth L. Hewett and Charlotte Robidoux (eds.) *Virtual Collaborative Writing in the Workplace: Computer-Mediated Communication Technologies and Processes* 400–432. Hershey, Pennsylvania: IGI Global. http://dx.doi.org/10.4018/978-1-60566-994-6.ch022.

Wei, Carolyn, Maust, Brandon, Barrick, Jennifer, Cuddihy, Elisabeth and Spyridakis, Jan H. (2005) Wikis for supporting distributed collaborative writing. *Proceedings of the Society for Technical Communication 52nd Annual Conference*, Seattle. Retrieved on 27 November 2013 from http://depts.washington.edu/ibuxl/docs/STC_Wiki_2005 _STC_Attribution.pdf.

Weiss, Stéphane; Urso, Pascal; and Molli, Pascal (2007) Wooki: a P2P Wiki-based collaborative writing tool. *Proceedings of the Web Information Systems Engineering-WISE Conference* 503–12. Nancy, France. Retrieved on 27 November 2013 from http://hal.archives-ouvertes.fr/docs/00/15/61/90/PDF/main.pdf.

Wichmann, Astrid and Rummel, Nikol (2013) Improving revision in wiki-based writing: Coordination pays off. *Computers & Education* 62: 262–70. http://dx.doi.org/ 10.1016/j.compedu.2012.10.017.

Witney, Debbie and Smallbone, Teresa (2011) Wiki work: Can using wikis enhance student collaboration for group assignment tasks? *Innovations in Education and Teaching International* 48: 101–10. http://dx.doi.org/1 0.1080/14703297.2010.543765.

17 Mashing, Modding, and Memeing
Writing for a New Generation of University Students

Rodney H. Jones

Introduction

There has been considerable interest in – and, in some quarters, alarm at – the ways digital media are affecting students' writing practices. Many educators are convinced that the internet has led to an epidemic of plagiarism and a shallow "cut and paste" approach to writing which works against the development of either creativity or criticality (Duggan, 2006; Schur, 2012). Studies conducted at major US universities (see for example McCabe, Butterfield, and Trevino, 2012) have found that large numbers of students regularly copy from online sources, and the popular press is awash with headlines announcing a "cheating crisis" (ABC News, 2013) and a "plagiarism plague" (Campbell, 2006). Teachers and educational institutions have mostly responded to these developments with a morally charged, "take no prisoners" attitude towards plagiarism, often accompanied by strict penalties and supported by the use of plagiarism detection software.

Students, on the other hand, are sometimes confused when the practices of "sharing," "curating" (Potter, 2012), and re-using content that are central to their everyday writing practices out of school are so frowned upon in the composition classroom. As Martine C. Rife and Nicole, D. DeVoss put it, "Attempting to convince today's digital writers that writing practices that are seamless and may seem 'natural' in and across digital spaces are actually suspect and perhaps dishonest is difficult" (Rife and DeVoss, 2012: 92). Adding to this difficulty is the fact that much of the writing students will engage in in workplaces after they graduate more closely resembles their everyday "cut and paste" practices than the practices that they learn in school. For example, in a recent study of writing practices which I carried out in public relations firms with collaborators Vijay Bhatia, Stephen Bremner, and Anne Peirson-Smith, we found that proposals, reports, and press releases were typically prepared using templates and recycled "boilerplate" text, as well as by recombining content taken from internet websites without attribution (Jones, Bhatia, Bremner, and Peirson-Smith, 2012; see also Rife and DeVoss, 2012).

Unfortunately, many contemporary discussions of plagiarism in educational institutions effectively short-circuit opportunities to engage students in fruitful discussions about issues like the ethics of sharing and borrowing, the origin and purpose of intellectual property laws, and the different conventions for citation and attribution associated with different writing contexts. They also represent a missed opportunity to get students to reflect upon more fundamental aspects of the writing process associated with what Mikhail Bakhtin calls "heteroglossia" (Bakhtin, 1981) – the borrowing and mixing of multiple "voices" which is an inevitable part of all writing. Understanding how to effectively borrow the ideas of others, to curate them and combine them, and to make something new out of them, are important literacy practices necessary for successful participation in a whole range of online practices such as blogging, social networking, and online gaming (Jones and Hafner, 2012). They are, however, also important skills for successful academic writing, albeit involving very different conventions of borrowing and citation.

One problem with the way issues of textual ownership are addressed in both composition classrooms and in discussions of internet piracy is that they often focus more on what cannot or should not be borrowed, than they do on the creative possibilities that ethical borrowing open up. Another problem is that discussions of plagiarism and intellectual property are often oversimplified to the degree that all copying is treated equally as theft. The widespread use of metaphors related to *property* and *theft* is perhaps one of the most insidious features of contemporary discourse about plagiarism, belying a lack of understanding among many administrators and faculty (not to mention students) of the fundamental difference between copyright law (which is meant to protect the economic interests of copyright holders) and conventions of academic citation, which are meant to facilitate the creation of knowledge by giving people ways to ethically borrow and build upon the ideas of others.

There are major differences between copyright law and conventions of academic honesty. The first is that copyright law has nothing to do with attribution. Even if one clearly cites the source of a copyrighted text, if it is copied in ways that are not considered *fair use* (see below), it can constitute an offense. So it is possible to violate copyright law and *not* commit plagiarism. At the same time, copyright law generally only applies to the expression of ideas, not the ideas themselves, and so it is possible to commit plagiarism by using someone else's ideas without attribution and *not* violate their copyright.

Students in contemporary composition classes need to understand *both* copyright law *and* conventions of academic honesty (especially since most contemporary composing practices involve both copying and reusing existing materials and the necessity to attribute those materials to their sources). At the same time, they need to know the difference between the two, and to understand when and where it is appropriate to apply these different rules of "textual ownership" (Spigelman, 2000). Finally, they need to be given the opportunity to explore how both copyright laws and conventions of academic writing are the products of certain historical conditions and relationships of power and the opportunity to engage in critical debates regarding their aims and principles and their contemporary manifestations in things like corporate prosecutions of people who share content online and the use by universities of computerized tools that purport to be able to "analyze" the "originality" of student writing.

In this chapter, I will introduce a series of activities designed to engage students in exploring how their everyday literacies associated with sharing and reusing the content of others can actually contribute to rather than detract from the development of creativity and sound academic writing skills and to foster the conditions in the composition classroom for more open, non-judgmental discussions about intellectual property.

I will be focusing primarily on three different but related literacy practices, which I call *mashing* – the ability to borrow and effectively combine ideas and content from others, *modding* – the ability to alter borrowed ideas or content in a way that makes it "new," and *memeing* – the ability to promote one's "new" idea in a way that encourages other people to borrow it and to further alter it or combine it with other ideas or content. These activities aim both to sensitize students about the different conventions around borrowing and remixing associated with different kinds of writing, and to open up space for them to participate in larger debates about the economic, legal and cultural implications of copyright and intellectual property legislation and conventions (Lankshear and Knobel, 2003; Lessig, 2004).

Mashing

I use the term "mashing" to refer to the practice of "remixing" or "mashing up" different content to produce some kind of new textual product. Contemporary notions of remixing are usually traced back to the music industry and, in particular, hip-hop, whose artists regularly "sample" segments of previously recorded music in producing their songs (Arewa, 2006). More recently, however, the term "remix" has been used to refer to nearly any instance where people use digital technologies to copy and combine the work of others. Critics like Bakhtin (1981) and Roland Barthes (e.g. Barthes, 1978), of course, would be quick to remind us that the practice of remixing is as old as communication itself. One reason for the increased prominence of this practice in recent years has to do with the fact that digital technologies, by their very nature, make remixing so much easier: processes which before required laboriously copying text, recording and re-recording on analog tape, or operating complicated professional film editing equipment can now be accomplished by anyone with a few clicks of a mouse.

Scholars in literacy studies (see e.g. Jones and Hafner, 2012; Lankshear and Knobel, 2003) have identified remixing as a core practice associated with "digital literacies." Examples they have given of this practice include remixing clips from movies to create "faux" movie trailers, superimposing new music or soundtracks onto video clips, making videos from captures of online gameplay (*machinima*), recombining or photoshopping images found on the web, and recombining plots and characters from novels, movies, or television shows (*fan fiction*). The simplest kind of remixing can be found on social networking sites like *Facebook* and *Pinterest* where users simply collect and "curate" different kinds of content from a wide variety of websites (as well as their own photos and texts) to create online albums, timelines, or "boards." Even the simple process of collecting different content in one place requires a certain understanding of audience and of *intertextuality* – how the different texts one has brought together interact with one another.

Such skills, of course, are also important for academic writers. Lessig (2005), in fact, uses academic writing as a classic example of remixing. The essence of the teaching of writing (in a traditional sense), he argues, is teaching students to take material from different sources and to combine it to create something new. Part of this process is teaching students certain conventions of attribution. The basic principles governing academic writing and electronic remixing, however, are not very different, and by helping students to see this, the process of weaving the voice of different scholars together in academic writing can be made to seem more familiar and more manageable to students.

Modding

"Modding," or modifying, is a term that is usually associated with a practice commonly engaged in by video-gamers of modifying in some way the software of the games they play to alter graphics and other aspects of gameplay. This practice has become so widespread that sometimes game companies even encourage it, and some of the most popular games on the market today are actually the result of such acts of unauthorized customization by players. Here I am using the term in a broader sense, to refer to the practice of altering an idea or a piece of content (such as an image or a video) in a way that transforms it into something new. Whereas mashing involves combining content from different sources, modding involves taking content from a single source and adding something of your own to it.

Like mashing, modding is a literacy practice which is central to both new forms of digital creativity and to more traditional forms of writing, including academic writing. In his book *Borrowing Brilliance* (Murray, 2010), business writer David Kord Murray argues that nearly all good ideas in business are, to some degree, simply creative "mods" of old ideas. The processes he discusses by which old ideas are made new are processes which are also central to more academic forms of reasoning and creativity, processes of selecting, incubating (including discussing and debating), judging (or critiquing), and enhancing (altering or expanding). To some degree, modding can be seen as a higher level skill than mashing. Whereas mashing simply involves mixing different ideas or texts in an inventive way, modding takes invention to a new level, building on old ideas to make something new. This process is not just an important part of academic writing – it can be argued that it is the very basis of scholarship itself.

Memeing

Of course, not all old ideas are good enough to borrow and transform, and not all transformed ideas catch on (Berger, 2013) as really significant contributions to a particular field. "Memeing" refers to ways that writers and other creators shape new ideas in ways that are able to attract the attention of others.

The term "meme" was introduced by evolutionary biologist Richard Dawkins to refer to a "contagious idea" (Dawkins, 2006; see also Berger, 2013; Jenkins, 2013). "Examples of memes," he writes,

> are tunes, ideas, catch-phrases, clothes fashions, ways of making pots or of building arches. Just as genes propagate themselves in the gene pool by leaping from body to body via sperms or eggs, so memes propagate themselves in the meme pool by leaping from brain to brain via a process which, in the broad sense, can be called imitation. (Dawkins, 2006: 192)

The notion that ideas or content can have a kind of "viral" quality is, of course, especially associated with the Internet, where, because of the high speed at which information travels, the ease with which it is borrowed and reproduced, and the way the medium's network structure facilitates the exponential growth of audiences, people often speak of Internet content (such as images, blog posts, and YouTube videos) as "going viral."

Colin Lankshear and Michelle Knobel argue that the literacy practice of "meming" is central to successful human communication, both online and off (Lankshear and Knobel, 2003). "Memes," they write, "highlight the profoundly social dimension of language and literacy. In a nutshell, memes require networked human hosts in order to get established, to grow, and to survive" (p. 233). Although teachers regularly caution student writers to consider their audience, students are seldom invited to consider their ideas as having a life beyond the page, as things that can potentially be taken up by others, spread, remixed, and modded. Along with learning how to appropriately borrow, combine, and build upon the ideas of others, students of writing need to be given a chance to reflect on the qualities that make ideas and texts worth borrowing in the first place, the features which make a piece of writing potentially "contagious."

Description of Activity and Strategies for Implementation

The following activities draw on students' understandings of their everyday digital literacies and aim to: (1) engage them in meaningful discussions about intertextuality, intellectual property, and the ethics of borrowing; and (2) help them to understand how they can transfer skills associated with these everyday literacies to their academic writing. The activities are suitable for upper secondary or beginning university students who are involved in learning the basics of academic writing.

Warmup Exercises

These exercises serve to focus students' attention and sensitize them to the concept of "mashing" through getting them to do short, imaginative writing tasks.

Task 1: Parisian Love

(a) Play the following video for students:

http://www.youtube.com/watch?v=rS4Lb-ie4Lc

The video consists of a series of Google search terms combined with different sound effects. The search terms are as follows:

> study abroad paris france
> cafes near the louvre
> translate tu est très mignon
> how to impress a french girl
> chocolate shops paris
> what are truffles?
> who is truffaut?
> long distance relationship advice
> jobs in paris
> AA120
> churches in paris
> how to assemble a crib

(b) Ask students to explain the story and to retell it as a conventional narrative.

(c) Discuss how the video is a combination of two different "genres": Internet search and a love story. Ask students what the benefits are of mashing these two genres together.

(d) Ask students to write their own "story" using only search terms. Have selected students read their list of terms aloud and ask their classmates to guess what the story is.

NOTE: This activity has many benefits beyond its aim to get students to start thinking about what happens when two very different genres are mashed up. It also helps students who are likely engaged in Internet research understand that searching for information is a kind of journey or narrative during which external events and results from previous searches inform the choice of future search terms.

Task 2: Mini Mashups

(a) Ask students to produce a short text which mashes up one text from column A and one text from column B.

Column A	Column B
• "Dear John" Letter	• License plate
• Complaint Letter	• SMS message
• Job Application	• Birthday card
• Political Speech	• Advertisement
• Lab Report	• Facebook Update

(b) After students have shared their texts with one another, engage them in a discussion about: (i) the difficulties of fitting together two disparate text types, and (ii) what their mash-ups reveal about the nature of the different kinds of texts they used.

NOTE: The key point to emphasize to students is that combining different kinds of texts nearly always results in a product that is more that the "sum of its parts," that it usually results in a product that produces some kind of new insights or knowledge.

Task 3: Critically Evaluating an Internet Mash-up

(a) Choose a mash-up from the Internet. Some examples of what you might choose are:
   (i) A faux movie trailer that mashes up the plots of two different movies (see for example "Brokeback to the Future," which combines the plots of *Brokeback Mountain* and *Back to the Future* http://www.youtube.com/watch?v=8uwuLxrv8jY)
   (ii) A piece of fan fiction (for examples see http://www.fanfiction.net)
   (iii) A popular internet "meme" which involves the combination of content from multiple sources (for example, video clips, audio soundtracks) (see below).

The example chosen to illustrate this exercise is the You Tube video "Ain't Nobody Got Time for That" featuring "Sweet Brown" (Kimberley Wilkens). The video is based on a segment of a Baltimore news report featuring an interview with a woman ("Sweet Brown") whose home caught on fire. The interview is remixed and edited with numerous clips from movies and a musical soundtrack that samples Brown's words in the interview. This video is an excellent example of the kind of creative product that can be produced through practices of remixing (mashing and modding), as well as of the ethical and legal issues associated with this practice. In fact, this video led to a lawsuit in which Wilkens sued Apple Corporation for offering a version of this remix for purchase on iTunes.

(b) Play the original source material for students (for "Ain't Nobody Got Time for That" see http://youtu.be/zGxwbhkDjZM). Then play the remixed version (for "Ain't Nobody Got Time for That" see http://youtu.be/bFEoMO0pc7k). Ask students to try to identify the different sources that were drawn upon in the remix, the degree to which a "new creation" was produced through remixing, and how the new text differs from the original texts in terms of message, purpose, and tone/style.

(c) Ask the students to discuss in small groups whether or not they think the remix constitutes a violation of copyright. To make this determination, they will need to decide whether or not the use of the original source material can be considered "fair use" (or, "fair dealing" in U.K. terminology). Go over with students the criteria for "fair use" set out in Section 107 of the US Copyright Law (Title 17, U. S. Code) (U.S. Copyright Office, 2013). They are:

(1)   The purpose and character of the use, including whether such use is of commercial nature or is for nonprofit educational purposes;

(2)   The nature of the copyrighted work;

(3)   The amount and substantiality of the portion used in relation to the copyrighted work as a whole;

(4)   The effect of the use upon the potential market for, or value of, the copyrighted work.

NOTE: You may use instead the criteria for fair use relevant to whatever jurisdiction you are in.

(d) Ask the student groups to pretend to be a jury and to render a verdict in a court case in which the creator or distributor of the remix is being sued for copyright violation. (For information on the case in which "Sweet Brown" sued Apple Corporation for copyright violation, see http://www.businessinsider.com/sweet-brown-apple-lawsuit-2013-3.)

NOTE: For an interesting interpretation of the "Sweet Brown" case, see the blog *Above the Law* (http://abovethelaw.com/2013/03/sweet-brown-has-her-voice-autotuned-sues-itunes-and-others-for-15-million/)

(e) Go over with students the criteria for plagiarism in your school or university. (You may be able to find documents explicitly stating these criteria on your university website). Ask students to discuss in small groups whether or not they think the remix constitutes a case of plagiarism. Have two students from each group role-play a teacher accusing the creator of the remix of plagiarism and the creator (in the role of a student) defending him or herself.

(f) Based on the discussions above, ask students to formulate a clear list of differences between the criteria for plagiarism and for copyright violation. Ask them how these criteria might be relevant for the kinds of assignments they produce at their school or university.

(g) Ask students to consider if and how the remix they analyzed became a popular Internet meme. The main criteria for determining whether or not a cultural product has become a meme is the extent to which other people refer to it, link to it, and borrow from it to create other remixes. Examples of this for the "Ain't Nobody Got Time for That" meme include the large number of references to it in popular culture, its appropriation by other remixers, including advertisers (see e.g. http://youtu.be/oSTy4qVw9yQ), and its widespread adoption for "picture caption memes" (see for example http://memegenerator.net/AinT-Nobody-Got-Time-Fo-That).

(h) Ask students to make a list of the qualities of the remix that they think contributed to it becoming a meme (possible qualities might include humor, relevance, timeliness, etc.). Introduce to the students the following features of "contagious ideas" suggested by business guru, John Berger, in his book *Contagious: Why Things Catch On* (Berger, 2013). Ask them to discuss the degree to which the remix they analyzed demonstrates these features:

   (1) *Social currency* – People like to share this idea because it makes them look good, that is, it makes them seem interesting, clever, intelligent, hip, or funny;

   (2) *Triggers* – The idea is easy to remember because of things like memorable wordings, music, or images;

   (3) *Emotion* – The idea evokes in people some kind of strong emotion such as joy, amusement, anger, or sadness;

   (4) *Practical value or relevance* – People think the idea has something to do with them or that it is useful;

   (5) *Stories* – The idea "tells a story;" in other words, people can imagine an interesting group of characters and series of events associated with the idea.

Task 4: Academic Mash-ups

(a) Choose a piece of academic writing from a student or from the Internet. The example used here is from the blog, *a moment in the life of paul* (http://paulburns8616.blogspot.hk/2009/01/different-views-on-copyright-laws.html).

Different Views on Copyright Laws

I just read two very interesting articles with contrasting views on the laws of copyright. Both articles were very interesting and produced valid reasoning for their points of view. After I had finished reading the articles I could not take a side for either one because I felt like both of them were sound arguments.

The first one I read was about was from the point of view that copyright laws are essential to protect the producers of the information. He brought up a great viewpoint and talked about an animated Disney film that had taken four years to produce because so much new technology and been invented just for the one film to be produced. He also went into depth about how when the film was being created massive amounts of information had to be compacted and condensed on many separate computers just so that all the time and effort could be saved. He said all this to say that even though millions of dollars had been put into the project along with countless man hours it could all be undone if just one copy of the movie was prematurely copied and put on the internet. Not only would the Disney company lose money because people would be able to access the movie for free via the internet the anticipation and eagerness for people to see the movie would be dimmed because it could be freely accessed through the internet. This argument had many valid points and showed how copyright laws were essential to protect peoples ideas, money, and work.

The second article did not completely disagree with the fact that copyright was needed but rather put a different spin on the subject. The man point of view from the writer of the second article was that for people to continue to invent and develop new ideas they would need free access to works from the past. One quote the author repeated multiple times was, "Creativity and innovation always build on the past." I thought that this quote put a lot of things in perspective; one thing I think you can get out of it is that in order for people to evolve and come up with new ideas they would need access to prior works so that they could learn from previous works and ideas. In some ways this outlook is good because one can not truly know where he are going until they have seen where they have been.

To conclude I think it is fair to say that copyright laws are essential to society but can sometimes hinder creativity because information is not always easily accessible to people.

(From http://paulburns8616.blogspot.hk/2009/01/different-views-on-copyright-laws.html)

(b) Explain to students that a lot of academic writing involves remixing the ideas of different scholars in a way that creates some kind of new product. Ask them to read the sample of academic writing that you have chosen and have them discuss the following questions:

(i) What are the original sources that are mashed-up in this piece of writing? Has the author clearly identified these sources? How does the identification of the sources affect its effectiveness as a remix?

(ii) What strategies does the author use to remix the ideas from the different sources (e.g. direct quotation or paraphrase)? How does he or she structure the material? Do the ideas *interact* in interesting ways? Can you think of a more interesting way to remix these ideas?

(iii) Does the remixing of these ideas result in a *new* idea? If not, can you think of a way the author could create a new idea through the integration of these borrowed ideas?

(iv) Does the author commit either plagiarism or copyright infringement? What steps can he or she take to avoid this?

NOTE: Perhaps the most interesting point that can be made from the example above is that the piece would be much better if the writer had borrowed *more* from the original sources rather than less, that is, if he had directly quoted key passages or phrases from the two texts so that the reader could learn more about what each one said and get a sense of the "voices" of the two writers. Another interesting point is that, while the author does not technically commit plagiarism since he does not try to pass off the ideas of the writers he refers to as his own, by failing to reveal who the writers are, he makes the passage much less effective, and much less useful for readers who may want to seek out and read the articles he refers to.

(c) The website Goodreads (https://www.goodreads.com/) has a function that allows users to generate a list of quotes about a particular keyword (https://www.goodreads.com/quotes). Ask students to use this tool to generate a list of quotes about the topic of their choice. Then ask students to choose 3–5 quotes and remix them in a paragraph in a way that avoids plagiarism and results in some kind of interesting, original product. Ask the students to discuss their remixing strategies (such as their choice of either paraphrase or direct quotation) with their classmates.

(d) Ask students to apply the criteria they discussed for Internet memes to either the piece of writing they analyzed in (b) or the piece of writing they produced in (c). Ask them to make suggestions about how the "meme potential" of these pieces of writing could be increased (in other words, how they could be made more memorable, relevant, useful, and emotionally evocative for readers).

Reflections and Recommendations

The activities described above are meant to introduce students to the processes of intertextual borrowing that are central to most academic writing by relating these processes to the digital literacies associated with remixing (i.e. mashing, modding, and memeing). They are meant to help students see academic writing as a form of "textual remix" which involves:

Mashing – locating relevant source materials and combining them together in effective and appropriate ways;

Modding – modifying, altering, or building upon the ideas that have been borrowed from others to create some kind of new idea or perspective;

Memeing – presenting the new idea or perspective in a way that makes it memorable, relevant, useful and/or emotionally compelling for readers.

These processes, whether they are associated with internet remixing or academic writing, require students to consider two kinds of questions:

(1) Questions about the *ethics* of borrowing (whether or not their borrowing is "fair use" based on things like the amount they have borrowed, the purpose of the borrowing, and whether or not they have given credit to the creators of the original source material);

(2) Questions about the *effectiveness* of borrowing (whether or not the borrower is able to create some kind of new or original product out of source materials).

Both students and teachers will undoubtedly find that, for many writing or remixing tasks, the answers to these questions are not cut and dried: there may be considerable room for debate as to whether a particular instance of borrowing is either ethical or effective. Such debates can be particularly instructive for both teachers and students, because they remind us that ethical borrowing and creative production are not a matter of "following rules," but a matter of *making decisions* based on the particular goals and circumstances of each new writing task and on the standards agreed upon within the particular community of writers or creators that one belongs to.

References

ABC News (2013, April 29) A cheating crisis in America's schools. Retrieved on 15 September 2013 from http://abcnews.go.com/Primetime/story?id=132376&page=1.

Arewa, Olufnmilaya B. (2006) From J. C. Bach to Hip Hop: Musical borrowing, copyright and cultural context. *The North Carolina Law Review* 84(2): 547–645. Retrieved on 15 September 2013 from http://www.cs.northwestern.edu/~pardo/courses/eecs352/papers/sampling%20and%20copyright.pdf.

Bakhtin, Mikhail M. (1981) *The Dialogic Imagination: Four Essays* (ed. Michael Holquist, trans. Caryl Emerson and Michael Holquist) Austin: University of Texas Press.

Barthes, Roland (1978) *Image-music-text* (trans. Stephen Heath) New York: Hill and Wang.

Berger, Jonah (2013) *Contagious: Why Things Catch on.* New York: Simon & Schuster.

Campbell, Don (2006) The plagiarism plague. *National Crosstalk* Winter. Retrieved on 15 September 2013 from http://www.highereducation.org/crosstalk/ct0106/news0106-plagiarism.shtml.

Dawkins, Richard (2006) *The Selfish Gene: 30th Anniversary Edition.* Oxford: Oxford University Press. http://dx.doi.org/10.1080/02602930500262452.

Duggan, Fiona (2006) Plagiarism: Prevention, practice and policy. *Assessment and Evaluation in Higher Education* 31(2): 151–154. http://dx.doi.org/10.1080/02602930500262452.

Jenkins, Henry (2013) *Spreadable Media: Creating Value and Meaning in a Networked Culture.* New York: New York University Press.

Jones, Rodney H., Bhatia, Vijay K., Bremner, Stephen and Peirson-Smith, Anne (2012) Creative collaboration in the public relations industry. In Rodney Jones (ed.) *Discourse and Creativity* 93–107. Harlow, U. K.: Pearson Education.

Jones, Rodney H. and Hafner, Christoph A. (2012) *Understanding Digital Literacies: A Practical Introduction.* London: Routledge.

Lankshear, Colin and Knobel, Michelle (2003) *New Literacies*: London: Open University Press.

Lessig, Lawrence (2004) *Free Culture: How Big Media Uses Technology and the Law to Lock Down Culture and Control Creativity.* New York: Penguin

McCabe, Donald, Butterfield, Kenneth D. and Trevino, Linda K. (2012) *Cheating in College: Why Students Do It and What Educators Can Do about It.* Baltimore: Johns Hopkins University Press.

Murray, David K. (2010) *Borrowing Brilliance: Six Steps to Business Innovation by Building on the Ideas of Others.* New York: Gotham.

Potter, John (2012) *Digital Media and Learner Identity: The New Curatorship.* New York: Palgrave Macmillan.

Rife, Martine C. and DeVoss, Nicole, D. (2012) Teaching plagiarism: Remix as composing. In Michael Donnelly, Rebecca Ingalls, Tracy A. Morse, Joanna C. Post and Anne M. Stockdell-Giesler (eds.), *Critical Conversations about Plagiarism* 78–100. Anderson, South Carolina: Parlor Press.

Schur, Richard (2012) Sampling is theft? Creativity and citation after hiphop. In Michael Donnelly, Rebecca Ingalls, Tracy A. Morse, Joanna C. Post and Anne M. Stockdell-Giesler (eds.), *Critical Conversations about Plagiarism* 69–77. Anderson, South Carolina: Parlor Press.

Spigelman, Candace (2000) *Across Property Lines: Textual Ownership in Writing Groups*. Carbondale: Southern Illinois University Press.

U. S. Copyright Office (2013). Copyright Law of the United States of America and Related Laws Contained in Title 17 of the *United States Code*. Retrieved on 15 September 2013 from http://www.copyright.gov/title17/92chap1.html.

Author Index

CPSIA information can be obtained at www.ICGtesting.com
Printed in the USA
BVOW05*0457241215

429702BV00003B/2/P